ALL ABOUT CRYSTALS
Connie Islin
ISBN 965-494-111-2

ALL ABOUT TAROT
Hali Morag
ISBN 965-494-062-0

**ALL ABOUT THE WICCA
OF LOVE**
Tabatha Jennings
ISBN 965-494-110-4

**ALL ABOUT THE SIXTH
SENSE**
Tom Pearson
ISBN 965-494-138-4

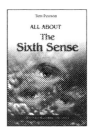

ALL ABOUT NUMEROLOGY
Lia Robin
ISBN 965-494-109-0

ALL ABOUT PALMISTRY
Batia Shorek
ISBN 965-494-094-9

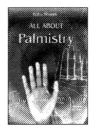

ALL ABOUT DREAMS
Eili Goldberg
ISBN 965-494-061-2

**ALL ABOUT PREDICTING
THE FUTURE**
Sarah Zehavi
ISBN 965-494-093-0

ALL ABOUT SYMBOLS
Andrew T. Cummings
ISBN 965-494-139-2

ALL ABOUT CHAKRAS
Lily Rooman
ISBN 965-494-149-X

ALL ABOUT

Symbols

Andrew T. Cummings

Astrolog Publishing House Ltd.

Cover design: Na'ama Yaffe

ISBN 965-494-139-2

All rights reserved to Astrolog Publishing House Ltd.

P. O. Box 1123, Hod Hasharon 45111, Israel

Tel: 972-9-7412044

Fax: 972-9-7442714

E-Mail: info@astrolog.co.il

Astrolog Web Site: www.astrolog.co.il

Published by Astrolog Publishing House 2003

10 9 8 7 6 5 4 3 2 1

contents

 Graphic and Geometrical Symbols   13-42

Symbols in the Animal Kingdom   43-114

contents

Mythological animals, Legendary Creatures and Monsters   115-138

contents

Symbolism in human images   139-149

Symbols in the plant kingdom   149-180

Acacia	Fleur-de-lis	Peach
Almond	Fruit	Pear
Aloe	Gardenia	Peony
Apple	Garlic	Persimmon
Apricot	Grapevine	Pine
Ash	Grass	Pineapple
Aspen	Hyacinth	Pinecone
Aster	Hyssop	Plane tree
Bamboo	Iris	Plants (general)
Barley	Ivy	Plum
Basil	Jasmine	Pomegranate
Bean	Juniper	Poplar
Beech	Laurel	Poppy
Buttercup	Lemon	Pumpkin
Camellia	Lily	Quince
Cedar	Lotus	Reed
Cherry	Magnolia	Rice
Chestnut	Malva	Rose
Chrysanthemum	Mangrove	Rosemary
Citron	Marigold	Sycamore
Clover	Mould	Straw
Convolvulus	Mulberry	Strawberry
Coral	Myrrh	Sunflower
Corn	Myrtle	Thorn
Cyclamen	Nut	Tulip
Cypress	Oak	Verbena/Vervain
Daisy	Olive	Wheat
Date	Onion	White mistletoe
Elm	Orange	Willow
Fennel	Palm tree	Wormwood
Fig	Pansy	Wormwood
Fir	Parsley	

Symbolism in objects 181-222

Alcohol	Drum	Room
Anchor	Ewer (jug)	Rope
Ark	Fan	Sail
Arrow	Flute	Scale
Ax	Furnace, kiln	Scalpel, chisel
Bag, pouch, sack	Gate	Scissors
Ball	Glass, goblet, cup	Scroll
Basket	Guitar	Scythe
Bell	Hammer	Seal
Belt	Harp	Shoe
Bonfire	Honey	Spoon
Book	Hourglass	Steering wheel
Bottle	House	Sword, saber
Bow	Ink	Torch
Box	Key	Tower
Bread	Knife	Treasure
Bridge	Labyrinth, maze	Vinegar
Brush	Ladder	
Bunch of flowers	Lamp	
Candle	Lance, spear	
Chain	Lock	
Chariot	Loom	
Chimney	Lyre, lute	
Comb	Mask	
Cradle	Milk	
Crossroads	Mirror	
Crown	Oar	
Dagger	Oil	
Dice	Oven	
Distaff, spindle	Peace pipe	
Doll	Pen	
Door	Roof	

Parts of the body 223-243

Arm
Beard
Blood
Bones
Breasts
Breathing
Ear
Eye
Face
Finger
Foot, leg
Hand
Hair
Head
Heart
Heel
Intestines, guts
Kidneys
Knees
Lingam (penis)
Liver
Marrow
Mouth
Nail
Saliva
Scalp
Skeleton
Skin

Skull
Spinal column
Spleen
Stomach, paunch
Teeth
Thigh
Thumb
Tongue
Uterus, womb
Yoni (vagina)

Symbols of landscape and nature 245-266

Abyss	*Soil, earth*
Air	*Spring*
Cave	*Star*
Cloud	*Storm*
Crescent moon	*Stream*
Dawn	*Thunder and lightning*
Day	*Twilight*
Desert	*Valley*
Dew	*Vegetation*
Ebb and flow	*Water*
Field	
Fire	
Forest	
Garden	
Ice	
Island	
Lake	
Mist	
Mountain	
Mud	
Night	
Ocean, sea	
Rain	
Rainbow	
River	
Rock	
Sand	
Seasons	
Shadow	
Sky	
Smoke	
Snow	

Graphic and Geometrical Symbols

Ankh

The ankh is an Egyptian life symbol. It symbolizes the universe and life, both celestial and human, and it is the symbol of immortality, the key to sublime and recondite knowledge, to secret wisdom. The ankh is combined of the male and female symbols of Osiris and Isis, the two forces of life, and therefore it symbolizes the union between heaven and earth, and the unification between the feminine and masculine principle. It is a symbol of power and domination, of eternal life and the after life.

Some interpret this symbol according to its two parts – the oval shape symbolizes infinity, and the cross that comes out of it is continuation, extension.

In Egyptian hieroglyphs, the sign of the ankh creates words such as "health" and "happiness". Its phonetic meaning is made of a combination of the signs for activity and passivity and creates a merger of the two. It also symbolizes fate.

As a macrocosmic symbol, some see it as a symbol of the sun – the round shape on upper part of the ankh, the sky in its vertical line and the earth in the horizontal line.

As a microcosmic symbol (i. e., analogous to the individual, the microcosm of the universe), the circle on top of the ankh symbolizes the head, the horizontal line symbolizes the arms and the vertical line symbolizes the upright body. Maat, the goddess of truth, is holding an ankh in her hand.

Ball

The ball symbolizes wholeness, the soul, the universe and all the possibilities that exist in this world. It is the primordial shape that contains all other shapes, the cosmic egg, eternity, the abolition of time and space, the dome of the sky, the spirit of the universe and the matter that makes up the soul, the cyclical motion of regeneration and the heavens. In Muslim symbolism the ball is the wind, the primordial light.

Black sun – sol niger

The symbol of the sol niger is a simple black circle. It symbolizes the spirit of the sun during its cyclical transitions through the underworld. In ancient cultures there was a widespread belief that the sun disappears and reappears again. According to Egyptian manuscripts, during this transition the sun becomes "the hidden one" or "master of death", "saker" that is hidden in a secret pyramid of "the greatest darkness". The darkness of the black sun is as dark as the light of the sun is bright. The black sun, that was mainly a masculine symbol, became the symbol of "the dark twin" of the god of the sun. As dualism developed, the dark twin became the rival of its fair brother, a struggle that divided the world between the forces of light and darkness – good and evil.

The black sun symbolizes many of the gods of the underworld such as Saturn, Pluto, Hades, Paiton, Apollo, Yamah and "fallen angels" – angels that fall sanctity into the material world such as Lucifer, Satan and Beelzebub who symbolize the devil in monotheistic religions.

Nevertheless, the sun continues to shine in the sky every day and therefore many people kept the original idea of the black sun as a secret and wiser version of the god of the sun who knew the underworld as well as he knew the heavens.

In Medieval alchemy, the meaning of the black sun is the "prima mater" – the initial material or the material in its initial and primordial state.

Caduceus – the snake staff

The caduceus that is known today mainly as the symbol of medicine is made of a staff with two snakes wrapped around it, usually with two small wings or a winged helmet. This is a very ancient symbol that existed in many totally different cultures all over the world. Some believe that its source is the legend about Mercury's bet in an argument with two snakes, and this is why they were wrapped around his staff, but the symbol is much older than the legend. In Roman culture, it symbolized a moral balance and good self-governance. The meaning of the symbol stems from its components – the staff itself symbolizes power and strength, the snakes symbolize wisdom and the wings perseverance and diligence. The helmet that sometimes appears in this symbol is symbolizing sublime thoughts and meditations. The caduceus represents the merger of the four elements: the staff symbolizes the element of the earth, the wings the element of air and the two snakes water and fire (because of their movement that reminds the motion of water and waves which is also the movement of the flame).

↔ SYMBOLS ↔

In India, this symbol which was found engraved on stone plates is called nagaklas and it is imprinted on temple doors as an offering for keeping up a vow. Some see a resemblance in sound between the Sanskrit nagasha and the biblical copper snake nehushtan. The origin of this ancient symbol is probably in Mesopotamia, and it was found on the cup of King Gudea Malgesh from 2600 B. C. but its source maybe even older. Like the copper snake that appears in the Bible, the Mesopotamians saw the caduceus is the symbol of the god that cures all illnesses. This meaning was passed on to the Greek culture and it still exists in this symbol today. The symbol of the caduceus is a basic symbol in homeopathy in which illnesses are cured by a highly diluted extract of the cause of the illness itself. The story that appears in the Bible clearly describes how the caduceus became a homeopathic symbol. When the Israelites wandered in the desert they complained "Wherefore have ye brought us up out of Egypt to die in the wilderness?" (Numbers, chapter 21, verse 5). God's response was to send against them the serpent snakes - poisonous snakes. After they repented, Moses prayed for them and received the following instruction: "make thyself a serpent and set it upon a pole: and it shall came to pass, that whoever is bitten shall look at it and he shall live" (Numbers, chapter 21, verse 8). And this is what Moses did: "And Moses made a copper snake and put it on a pole and every man who was bitten by the snake looked at the copper snake and lived". The snake on the pole was the caduceus and looking at it cured the illness that was caused by the poisonous snake. True, there is only one snake, but there is a duality in sound – nahash (snake in Hebrew) and nehoshet (copper). Nhash in Aramaic is copper. The name "nehushtan" was given to the cooper snake by Hiskiyah king of Judea probably as a sign of contempt, diminution and emphasis that it was only an object made of copper, after he had destroyed it since it became an object of idolatry among the people of Israel. The copper snake did not have wings like many caduceus symbols, but on the other hand, there is the element of air since it was necessary to look up because of the height of the pole on which the snake was placed.

The caduceus's symmetry strengthens its meaning as "cure", since symmetry represents perfect balance that is disrupted in times of illness. The symmetry also represents the active balance of the opposite forces that balance one another in order to create a higher static form. The snakes and wings in the symbol mean that balance can and should be reached on both levels – physical (physical-mental) – that is represented by the snake, and spiritual, that is represented by the wings. This balance, which is sometimes achieved through struggle between opposing forces, will create self-control and strength that bring health.

↔ SYMBOLS ↔

According to esoteric Buddhism, the caduceus staff symbolizes the axis of the world and the snakes symbolize the force that is called condlini. According to tantarian teaching this force rests in the area of the caudal bone at the end of the spine and it symbolizes the evolving power of pure energy. Today the caduceus is the symbol of the Catholic bishop of the Ukraine and the symbol of medicine in general and homeopathic in particular.

Circle

The circle is a universal sanctified symbol in most cultures as the most natural shape. It symbolizes wholeness, original completeness, eternity, infinity and timelessness since it has no beginning and no end, simultaneity, the unfulfilled, the self and equality – since it has no hierarchical features unlike other graphical shapes. It is a symbol of the solar cycle, all cycles and circular movements, infinite movement, fulfillment, a protected or sanctified space and a ritualistic space in which all participants are equal.

The circle is also a symbol of god, according to Hermes Trismagisto: "god is the circle whose center is everywhere and its circumference is nowhere". In the tenets of Hinduism the circle also symbolizes the power of the universe, the one, in almost the same words – the one is "a continuos circle, which no circumference since it is nowhere and everywhere". As a symbol of the sun, the circle is the symbol of masculine power. But as a symbol of the psyche or the soul it is feminine, and the circular, infinite movement is also part of the maternal principle, that is the opposite of the linear, definite and straight movement that represents the creative paternal force. As a feminine symbol the circle reminds the shape of a full moon.

Nevertheless, the circle is a familiar symbol in many cultures of the sky (which is considered a masculine symbol) and the heavens, while the square symbolizes the soil, the earth. As a result of this symbolism praying tents, temples, and many other sacred buildings had a circular base or other circular features unlike residential buildings and agricultural plots which where square or rectangular.

The sacred pagan dances were circular, like folk dances in many cultures today. The circles of prehistoric stones, like Stonehange, that is also known as "the dance of the giants", show how much ancient cultures revered the circle. The egalitarian concept of the circle was preserved in mediaeval tales as well. The knights of King Arthur sat around a round table in a circle in order to eliminate any sign of hierarchy between them. As a result of the concept of round "the sacred space", close circles continued to symbolize protection, mainly in the eyes of wizards and sorcerers.

The concept of the cosmos as a continuous circle that repeats itself in the Gnostic image of the snake of the universe that creates a circle with its tail in its mouth, the orobouros (see entry). The circle is connected to the number ten, since the one symbolizes the center and the nine is connected to the symbolism of the circumference.

Cross

Although the cross is known mainly as a Christian symbol, it is actually an ancient universal symbol that appears in many cultures in different variations. The swastika (see entry) is one of the variations of the cross and the Egyptian ankh (see entry) is also an ancient variation of the cross. The cross was widely used as a graphic symbol, mainly as a result of Christian influence, but also because of its basic features.

The cross is a symbol of the center of the world and the point of contact between the upper and lower worlds. It is a symbol of the axis of the world and therefore it shares the symbolism of the cosmic tree, mountain, pillar, ladder and other symbols of the axis mundi. Thus it symbolizes the "ladder" or "bridge" on which the soul climbs on its way to upper worlds or to god. It represents the tree of life. It is a symbol of the universal man, the archetype that is capable of infinite expansion both horizontally and vertically. The vertical line is considered to be positive, active, masculine, celestial, spiritual and intellectual. The horizontal line is considered to be negative, passive, feminine, earthly and rational. The whole cross creates the primordial, primeval androgynous (see entry). It symbolizes dualism and the union of opposites and the spiritual union and merger of the human spirit in the vertical-horizontal aspects that are necessary for a full life. It symbolizes the descent of the spirit to the material world, and it is also a symbol of a person in its full height with his arms outstretched to the sides and symbolizing the supreme identity. Since it can continue indefinitely both horizontally and vertically, it symbolizes immortality. The cross is also perceived as an image of the four rivers of paradise that begin from one joint source, from the roots of the tree of life. It also symbolizes the four united elements in the fifth point, the center and the Four Corners of the Earth. The cross is also a symbol of martyrdom, agony and torment, mainly because it is the symbol most identified with Jesus Christ. It is also a symbol of the connection between the principle of the superior world (represented by the vertical line) and the earthly world (horizontal line). This is the origin of the "fall" or "descent" to the world of matter (the earthly world), and the need to live in this world in a state of separation from the origin, or god. The T shaped cross emphasizes even more the almost perfect balance between opposing principles.

↔ SYMBOLS ↔

Jung claimed that in a number of cultures the cross is a symbol of fire and existential suffering. This view probably stems from the fact that the two arms of the cross are connected to the two pieces of wood that pre-historic men used for making fire by friction and Jung saw them as masculine and feminine.

In principle the cross can be perceived as a symbol of the combination between opposites – the positive (vertical) and the negative (horizontal), the upper and the lower, life and death. Therefore, it is a symbol of existence in this world that is made of opposites (like the Yin-Yang perception). It symbolizes the possible and impossible, construction and destruction. The cross is considered as the antithesis of the ouroboros (see entry), the snake or the dragon that symbolize the ancient, anarchic dynamism that existed before the creation of our organized, orderly universe. Unlike the endless cyclical movement of the world of the ouroboros, the shape of the cross sustains, stops and destroys all free movement simultaneously. There is a conceptual and figurative connection between the cross and the sward. The figurative connection is obvious from the similar shape of the two objects, and the perceptual connection is based the view that both are used for the banishment and destruction of evil or ancient monsters.

Among the Bushmen and Hottentots the cross symbolizes the celestial entity and is used as a symbol of protection during the birth of a baby. In Native-American culture the cross symbolizes the human form as well as the rain, stars, fire tree, the four directions and the Four Corners of the Earth. The northern arm of the cross symbolizes the northern wind, the omnipotent, the giant that conquers all, the cold, the head and wisdom. The eastern arm of the cross symbolizes the eastern wind, the heart and the source of love and life. The western arm of the cross symbolizes the gentle wind that comes from the spirit of the earth, the final breath and the journey into the unknown. The southern arm symbolizes the southern wind, the place of fire and passion, melting and burning. The center of the cross symbolizes the earth and mankind that is driven by the conflicting forces of the gods and spirits. The lodge cross (the pavilion or ceremonial tent) that is engraved at the center symbolizes the sacred space, the cosmic center. The four dimensions of space within the celestial circle symbolize the wholeness of the Great Spirit. The cross symbolizes the cosmic tree in this culture as well. In Buddhism the cross symbolizes the axis of the wheel of the law and the cycle of existence.

In Celtic culture the cross is a phallic symbol of life and fertility. In Christianity the cross symbolizes redemption through the sacrifice of Jesus, faith and agony and therefore the acceptance of agony or death. The X-shaped St. Andrew's cross symbolizes the union of the upper and lower worlds as well as humility, martyrdom and agony. In the Middle Ages there was a popular belief that the cross of Jesus was created from the tree of knowledge, the reason for the explosion of Adam and Eve from Paradise, and thus it became a means of atonement. The two arms of the cross represent mercy (charity) and judgement. And in Christian art sometimes the sun and moon appear on top of them on each side as a symbol of these qualities, as well as the two sides of Jesus (celestial and earthly) that are symbolized by the vertical (celestial) and horizontal (earthly) lines of the cross. In Hinduism too the vertical line represents the satvas, the celestial, supreme condition of existence and the horizontal line the tamas, the lower or earthly state of existence. The cross is also connected to the sacred river Ganges and Agny's crossed sticks of fire. In Islam the cross symbolizes the perfect unity of all states of existence and the sublime identity. In Australian aboriginal culture the cross symbolizes the goddess of the moon and goodness. In the Maya culture, the Tao cross symbolizes the tree of life. In Mexican culture the cross also symbolizes the tree of life, and god is sometimes depicted on the cross as a crucified martyr. The cross also symbolizes the Four Corners of the Earth and fertility. The cross is the symbol of Tlalok and Ketzelkuatl. In Scandinavian and Teutonic cultures the Tao cross is the hammer of Thor and represents the thunder, lightening, storm, rain and fertility and the power of the gods of thunder. In Sumerian and Semitic cultures, the cross appears in Babylon with the sickle of the moon by its side in connection with the deities of the moon. In Assyria, the cross symbolizes the four directions in which the sun shines, and the cross of the sun was worn as a sign of superior rank by the nobility. In Phoenician culture it symbolized life and health. In Chaldaia, the cross with six lines represented the six days of the week, the six phases of time and the universal time span. Some see the cross with six lines as a symbol in the Cabala with that exact meaning.

According to Platonic philosophy the cross symbolizes the creator that "divides the whole world lengthwise into two parts and connects them together again on their broad side". Among the alchemists the cross was a symbol of the natural order of the elements. In Gnostic tradition, the cross symbolizes the balance of perfection. The general symbolism of the cross is preserved even when it appears within other graphic shapes since the features of the graphic shape are combined with the symbolism of the cross. A cross within a circle symbolizes the movement of the sun, the wheel of change and the wheel of fortune. The cross within a square is the Chinese symbol of the earth and stability. The cross with the wheel at its center is the Indian symbol of Chakra, a solar symbol of power and royalty.

The graphic symbol of the cross comes in many variations. Some of them are used as symbols in a number of cultures and this shows that it is an ancient and universal symbol that had different meanings in many cultures even before the Christian era. The Maltese cross symbolizes the four great gods of Assyria: Ra, Anu, Balus and Hea. It is the symbols of the knights of Malta. The cross of the rose is a symbol of the heart, center and harmony.

The Tao cross symbolizes the tree of life, regeneration, recondite knowledge, celestial power and law and future life. It is also the symbol of the hammer of the gods of thunder and the battle-ax of Thor. The double cross is the symbol of Zeus as the god of the sky. A cross with a hand was used as an ancient talisman against the evil eye.

Cube

The cube is the symbol of stability since it is connected to the number four and the square. It represents the world of the four elements, our world, the earth and the material world.

Together with the ball, as a symbol of the primordial state, the beginning of cycles and movement, the cube symbolizes the final stage of a cycle that is characterized by immobility. The cube also symbolizes truth since it is always identical and equal in its shape no matter from which angle you look at it. It is the symbol of perfection and pure, faultless law.

In traditional architecture, the cube, as a symbol of stability, serves as the foundation of different structures. In alchemy, the cube represents salt, the product of the crystallization of sulfur and mercury. In Chinese symbolism, the cube symbolizes the deity of the earth, together with the ball that symbolizes the celestial deity.

Diameter

The diameter is a symbol that originated from the horizon of the sea or the desert that divides the world into two halves, lower and upper. Some believe that the source or the Latin word diameter is "the mother goddess" and may relate to ancient myths of creation in which the body of the mother goddess (Tihamat, Tetis, Temu, Mah) was split into a upper half and a lower half. Usually water is considered to be the primeval matter, the symbol of the Dia Mater – the mother goddess, that is connected to the dividing of the water above and below the face of the earth (upper and lower water). In alchemy diameter means "salt" that is connected to the sea.

Double wheel

In ancient eastern traditions the double wheel means infinity and eternity. It symbolizes the eternal cycle of life on earth, surrounded by the larger circle or cosmic universe. Therefore, this symbol is mainly used as a sign of universal deity or the spirits of the forces of nature and the elements. Ezekiel's vision of "a wheel within a wheel" includes the traditional personification of the elements – man, lion, ox and eagle – who look like winged angels.

Egg/Cosmic Egg

The egg as a symbol appears in many cultures and its symbolic source is ancient. In prehistoric graves and Russia and Sweden were found clay eggs that were placed there as a symbol of immortality. In Egyptian hieroglyphs, the sign of the egg represents potential, the seed and the mysteries of life. In "the Egyptian ceremony", the universe is called, "an egg which conceives at the hour of the one, the mighty, who has the dual strength". This meaning also appears in the writings of the alchemists, who added the idea that the egg was the vessel of matter and thought. This idea is connected to the idea of "the egg of the world" or "the cosmic egg", which is found in many symbolic traditions. The dome of the sky was known as an egg, wrapped in seven layers, which were connected with the idea of the seven heavens. The Chinese believed that the first man emerged from an egg that was laid by Tyan from the sky and floated over the ancient waters. This idea was popular in ancient times and was embodied in the perception that the primordial universe or the great mother who created it – were in the shape of an egg.

As a result of these myths, and due to its elliptic shape that contains invisible life, the egg became a symbol of the principle of life, completeness and wholeness. It is also a symbol of potential, of the inseparable, the seed of creation, of primordial motherhood of the world of chaos. It is the hidden source and the mysteries of cosmic existence, time and space, the beginning, the womb, the symbol of primordial parents, the perfect situation of unified oppositions, revival and hope.

A Babylonian seal which shows the worship to the cosmic egg.

↔ SYMBOLS ↔

There are myths such as the myth of Leto, who created/laid the sun and the moon (Apollo and Artemis) from an egg, and Hathor, the great mother of Egypt who created the "golden egg" from the sun at the beginning of the world.

The cosmic egg of the mystical iconography contained all the letters and numbers and the Arab letters were written in an ellipsis in order to show that everything is countable or readable when it is included in one shape of the beginning. Therefore, the cosmic egg became a substitute for the "logos" and an expression of the primum mobile – the first motive, the cause of causes, the God, in which deities are created by human symbols. The Easter egg is also a symbol of immortality that contains the ancient symbolism of the egg. In Hindu, Egyptian, Greek and Chinese symbolism, the cosmic egg, as a source of the universe, hatches suddenly, and all that exists was contained in it and emerged from it when it hatched. The symbol of the egg as the source of the world appears in Egypt, Phoenicia, India, China, Japan, Greece, Central America, Fiji, and Finland. The golden egg symbolizes the sun. The snake wrapped around the egg is the ouroboros. The ostrich egg, or the great porcelain egg which is hanging in temples, Coptic churches and mosques, symbolizes creation, life and revival. The alchemists used to say that from the egg grew the white flower (silver), the red flower (gold) and the blue flower (the flower of the wise). The egg was likened to a hermetic vase in which the great work was being carried out. "The philosophers' egg" is symbolic to creation. In Buddhism, the egg's shell is "the shell of ignorance" and the hatching from it is the second birth when one achieves enlightenment. In Chinese tradition the egg symbolizes wholeness. The egg yolk symbolizes the sky and the egg protein symbolizes the earth. During the creation of the world, the cosmic egg was split in two, and from the two halves the heaven and the earth were created. In Druid tradition, the cosmic egg is "the egg of the snake" symbolized by a fossil of the sea snail. In The Egyptian Book of the Dead, there is a description of the birth of the sun, Ra, from an egg that was laid by the goose of the Nile. Knef, the snake, produced a cosmic egg from its mouth, which symbolizes the logos. In Orphic tradition, the egg is sometimes described as containing the four elements, and it symbolizes the mysteries of life, creation and rebirth, and surrounded by the Ouroboros. In Hinduism, the cosmic egg was laid by the celestial bird on ancient water. Brahma emerged from a golden egg and the heaven and the earth were created from its two halves.

The goddess of the moon from Mesopotamia in the shape of an egg.

↔ SYMBOLS ↔

The cosmic egg is divided into three parts, the domain of the senses, the sky and the shapeless world (the immaterial). The egg also symbolizes the eon (see entry). The cosmic tree is sometimes described as growing from the cosmic egg that floats over the waters of chaos. In a number of oceanic cultures the first man emerged from an egg that was laid by a birth. In Sumerian and Semitic traditions, the world was created from the cosmic egg.

Ellipsis
The ellipsis is connected to the symbolism of the egg, the vasika Pisces (see entry), the zero, and serves sometimes as the feminine symbol of life. Due to its shape, the ellipsis is a symbol of the vagina. It also serves as a symbol of the halo of saints.

Feathered sun
This is a flat Native-American symbol with feathers facing inside and outside – inside to the center and outside to the circumference. The feathered sun combines the symbolism of the sun and the eagle and describes the universe. It symbolizes the center, solar power and the radiance of power and royalty.

Horseshoe
The shape of the horseshoe was one of the most sacred shapes in the ancient world. It represents entrances and exists in general, and therefore it is found on the doors of house and temples. Some believe that its origin is an eonian shape – the female genitalia, as a symbol of the source of life, entrance and exit. The shape of the horseshoe was found in Druid temples. It is the shape of the Hindi and Arab arches and is connected to the Greek Omega that resembles a horseshoe. The horseshoe was hanged over doors for good luck in both Christian and pagan eras. But there was always a difference of opinions whether the open side of the horseshoe should face down or up. The Orthodox Christians claimed that the horseshoe should hang facing upwards, so that "the luck will not run away", but according to pagan traditions the eonian like symbol should preserve its original form upside down (like the vagina). The two ways of hanging the horseshoe are reminiscent of the symbols of witchcraft called "the dragon's head" and "the dragon's tail". The knot going up and the knot coming down that are connected with the course of the moon above and below the course of the sun. They create a wave-like line that represents the lunar snake. When the open side of the horseshoe faces downwards it reminds the lunar sickle, and represents the moon and the goddess of the moon. It symbolizes the rays of power and

protection and it is a symbol of good luck. When the horseshoe hands upside down, some believe it is devoid of power and luck.

Mandala

The mandala is a symbolic illustration, usually circular or oval, with radial (focal) symmetry, but sometimes it is also a square, a rectangular, a diamond or a polygon. Eastern mandalas, mainly in India, are sometimes more complex. They are usually perceived as a mystical map of the universe or divine realms and intended for meditation as a religious ritual. Other mandalas can be simple personal expressions of feelings or consciousness. The graphic material in the mandala can be anything, identifiable humanoid figures, animals, plants or totally abstract designs. The circular mandala usually relates to a circular view of nature, fatality, time or a combination of the three.

May pole

The May pole is a pagan symbol of the king of May Palus. It was erected in the spring festivals in May that symbolized the beginning of a new era of regeneration and fertility. In the May pole dance men and women moved in circles around the pole while holding ribbons in their hands.

Medicine wheel

A very popular symbol in Indian tradition connected to the universal symbolism of the wheel. In the Rocky Mountains there are about fifty known examples of Indian medicine wheels, some of them created about 2500 years B. C. The usual number of spokes in the medicine wheel is twenty eight, the lunar number, with the twenty ninth spoke symbolizing the center piece.

Octagon

The octagon is something between the square and the circle and therefore it symbolizes spiritual regeneration. The number eight (see entry) symbolizes regeneration, rebirth, change and transition. After the seven steps of initiation, the eighth step is the return to paradise and in the eight day the new man was created. The octagon is widely used in sacred architecture and as a shape that repeats itself in baptism basins since the octagon symbolizes rebirth and regeneration. In many temples the rounded roof is supported by eight columns standing on square bases as through they turn the circle into a square. The eight sides of the octagon are likened to eight doors that enable the transformation from one state into another. In Hinduism they also symbolize the eight parts of the day.

Orb

The three-dimensional orb was considered to be the model of the earth in classical times (this information was obscured and lost in the Dark Ages). The holding of the orb in the left hand (the "feminine" hand) symbolizes the monarch's claim to dominate the entire earth. The orb's counterpart was the scepter (a phallic symbol) which was held in the right hand (the "masculine" one), so that the monarch himself represented the holy union between the king and the earth, who was a feminine entity. In the Christian period a cross was added to the orb which was like a "crown" on top of it that symbolized the dominance of the church over the earth, and reminded the king that he was a king in God's grace. Nowadays, almost every royal orb stands in the shadow of the sign of the cross that is added on top of it.

The orb symbolizes the ruler's total power, although its actual might is restricted by "territory".

There is a connection between the symbol of the orb and the symbol of the egg.

Ouroboros

The ouroboros is a snake or a dragon that bites its own tail. This symbol appears most among the Gnostics, but it is mainly a universal symbol that

appears in many cultures. It represents the saying "the end is the beginning". It symbolizes the inseparable, the wholeness, the primordial unity, time and life span. It reproduces itself, mates, impregnates and destroys itself. It is the cycle of separation and inclusion, a power that forever consumes and renews itself. It is a symbol of the eternal cycle. The cycle of time, truth and recognition of the "one", the primordial united parents, the androgynous (see entry), the ancient water, the darkness before creation, the universe in chaos before the creation of light, the power before it is executed.

A Greek Symbol of an egg with a snake belt.

Sometimes it comes with the inscription on top of it "Hen to Pan" which means "the one, the whole".

In art the ouroboros appears as the symbol of immortality, eternity and wisdom. In many myths it encompasses the entire world and it is the cyclical path of the water that surrounds the earth. It can support and preserve the world and bring death to life and life to death. It seems stationary, but it is actually in constant movement around itself. In Orphic cosmology it surrounds the cosmic egg. Macrobious connects between the ouroboros and the movement of the sun (as it was believed to move in ancient times). The letters alpha and omega were sometimes identified with the ouroboros.

In a number of variations of the ouroboros, its body is half light and half darkness, a symbol of the successful and complementary balance between opposite principles as symbolized by the yin-yang symbol. Some see it as a symbol of the disintegration of the body or the universal snake, which according to the Gnostic belief "passes through all things". It is the symbol of the inseparable, the "unchanging law" which applies to all things and connects between them. The snake that bites it tails is also a symbol of self-fertilization or self-sufficient nature, a nature that according to Nietzsche always returns to its initial source, it beginning. In the writings of alchemists the ouroboros as was described as half black – symbolizing earth and night – and half white – symbolizing sky and light. In alchemy it also symbolizes the unshaped matter, the hidden power of nature.

In Buddhism the ouroboros represents the samsara wheel (the world as changing and unreal, the cruel cycle of life and death). In Hinduism it also represents the samsara wheel and as hidden energy its symbolism is similar to the condlini. In ancient Egyptian culture it symbolizes the cyclical nature of the universe, its path to the sun. In ancient Greek culture the orobouros expresses the maxim "all is one". Epicures said "At the beginning everything was like an egg with a snake like a tight belt or a circle around it". In Orphic symbolism it is the circle around the cosmic egg and eon, the cycle of life of the universe. In Sumerian and Semitic traditions it symbolizes the "one and all", the one that is all.

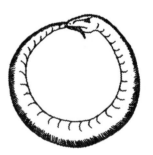

A drawing of the ouroboros.

Pentagram (fife-cornered star)/pentagon

The pentagram symbolizes the person with outstretched arms and legs that create five focal points – head, two arms and two legs. As such it symbolizes the integrated personality, the human microcosm. Since it is infinite, the pentagon contains the symbolism, power and completeness of the circle. Its five ends are the wind, air, fire, water and earth. It also symbolizes the five senses, and therefore some see it as a symbol of the world of the senses, the world of illusion and dreams. Like the circle, the pentagon has the power of containing the forces of evil and therefore it is a symbol of good luck. In Christianity, the pentagon symbolizes the five wounds of Jesus. In witchcraft, a five-cornered star upside down symbolizes the devil's goat and the leg of the witch. It is also the symbol of the opposite of the individual's true nature.

Pyramid

The pyramid is the symbol of the center of the world and the axis mundi (the axis of the world). It represents the ancient sacred mountain. The head of the pyramid symbolizes the most sublime spirituality, a hierarchic and spiritual feat. It also symbolizes the fire, the flame and the masculine power of the sun, and it is mainly a phallic symbol.

There is a clear contradiction in the symbolism of the pyramid. In megalithic cultures and European folklore that preserved the memory of the pyramid, it symbolizes the earth in its maternal sense and the idea of death and immortality that is connected to the great mother. The pyramid is a hollow mountain, the place of residence of the ancestors and a monument of the earth. The pyramid is made of stone. It has an accurate geometrical shape and relates to the element of fire, a typical masculine element, mainly in South East Asia.

Some see the pyramid as a synthesis of different forces, each with its own meaning. The base of the pyramid is a square, and therefore it represents the earth. The top is the point of beginning and end of all things, the mystical center. The head and base are connected by the triangle-shaped sides of the pyramid and symbolize fire, celestial revelation and the triangle principle of life. Therefore the pyramid symbolizes the complete work of creation in its three essential aspects.

The graded pyramid symbolizes the structure of the cosmos and the levels of consciousness and awareness, as well as the rise of the sun in the sky. Plato used the pyramid as a symbol of the element of the earth, with the cube as air and the octahedron as fire, the icosahedron (a polyhedron with nine sides) as water and the decahedron (a polyhedron with ten sides) as ether. In Aztec symbolism the pyramid is the fifth sun of Ketzelkuatel.

Rectangle

The rectangle is perceived as a square and as the most rational and mundane among all the geometrical shapes. This was the most preferable shape in all times and places for creating a space or an object for immediate use in everyday life – a home, a bed, a table etc. The rectangle creates tension and dominance through an abstract yearning for power, while the circle is disconnected from any earthly and material association due to its celestial symbolism. Less plain four-sided shapes than the rectangle such as a trapeze and a trapezoid are considered abnormal and express inner suffering and abnormality.

Ring

Like any other closed circle, the ring is a symbol of continuity and completeness. This is why the ring was a symbol both of marriage and the cycle of time that perpetually repeats itself. It shares the symbolism of the circle as a symbol of eternity, continuity, deities and life. It also symbolizes power, status, honor, rule, defense, and delegation of authority and noble power from a higher source, reaching perfection and cyclical time.

The ring is identified with personality and to give a ring means to delegate power and unite the personalities of the giver and receiver. It is also a powerful connecting symbol, like the wedding ring that connects between two entities and brings them to a new state of unity.

Sometimes the ring is in the shape of an animal such as a snake or eel that bites its tail (ouroboros), and sometimes as a pure geometrical shape. The head of the animal or monster holds the ring between its jaws symbolizes the guard of the roads. The open mouth is the gates of death and the ring is the path, or "the gate to the straits" or the door to liberation and insight. These shapes are usually placed on the door or gate to the house such as a doorknob or in other parts of the building that symbolize passage and entry.

In some legends the ring appears as a relic or the last connecting link. It is told that when Zeus permitted Hercules to save Prometheus, his condition was that Prometheus would wear an iron ring with a piece from the Caucasus Mountains as a sigh of his punishment.

Rings were the traditional symbol of the bond between the leader and his warriors in Anglo-Saxon Britain.

Among the Celts, a ring given by a woman to a man meant that she was sexually available. Inserting the finger into the ring symbolized sexual intercourse. Among Christian monks rings of this kind symbolized their "marriage" to the Virgin Mary and among the nuns – their "marriage" to Christ.

In pagan times there were similar stories about young men who "married" Venus and devoted themselves to the service of the goddess.

The idea that the wedding ring should be worn on the fourth finger of the woman's left hand comes from ancient Egypt, and it is based on the belief that from this finger "the vein of love" continues to the heart. The ring was like a "chain" that prevented "the feelings of the heart" from escaping.

In Chinese symbolism the ring symbolizes eternity, the source of all creation, authority and honor. A whole ring symbolizes acceptance and empathy. A broken ring symbolizes rejection and lack of empathy or both parts are kept as a contract or renewal of friendship. Half a ring symbolized excommunication or exile. A ring sent by the emperor was a sign to return to the royal court.

In Christianity the ring symbolizes eternity, union and spiritual marriage to the church. Different rings symbolized the position of the wearer. Cardinals wear sapphire rings and the ring of the bishop symbolizes the groom of the church.

In Ancient Egyptian culture the origin of the symbol of the ring and staff is unknown but it is assumed that it symbolizes the axis mundi (the axis of the world) or the universe that evolves and renewal itself, eternity and wholeness.

In Sumerian and Semitic cultures, the ring, usually made of three joint rings, is a divine symbol that was worn by all gods. Together with the crown, scepter and sickle is was a symbol of nobility.

In Judaism, the wedding ring is worn on the woman's index finger of the right hand since it is considered to be the "magic finger" that can cast spells by pointing.

In Hebrew tradition there are many references to magic rings. There is a legend that King Solomon had a ring for invoking the demon Asmodeus in order to make him help in the building of the temple. But the demon manipulated Solomon to lend him the ring and then used it to rule Jerusalem by impersonating as Solomon, while Solomon himself became a beggar (as described in the book of Ecclesiastes).

Another type of ring is the circle of flames that surrounds the dancing Shiva during the cosmic dance. The circle of flames can symbolize the wheel of fortune (zodiac) and like the Gnostic zodiac and ouroboros, it has an active half and a passive half (development and degeneration) and it symbolizes the life cycle of the universe and every individual entity. It is the circular dance of nature in the eternal process of creation and destruction. At the same time, the radiant light from the ring of flames symbolizes the eternal wisdom and sublime insight.

Spiral

The spiral is one of the oldest universal symbols. It exists as a symbol since the Paleolithic Age. It appears many times in ancient art and it is among the most common symbols in Pre-historic art. It appears in ancient Egypt, Crete, Mesopotamia, India, China, Japan, Pre-Colombian America, Europe, Scandinavia, Britain and Oceania, but not in Hawaii. The spiral is a schematic image of development in the universe. It is a symbol of growth and dynamism and it may stem from the circular movement of the earth. The spiral is also a classical shape that depicts the course of the moon, but it is as much a solar symbol as it is a lunar one, and it symbolizes the solar and lunar forces alike. It symbolizes the air (storm spiral), the water (vortex spiral), the rolling thunder and lightening. It symbolizes cosmic movement, upwards (clockwise) – opening and expansion, downwards (against the clock) – closing and decrease. It is connected to creation, movement and development. Since it grows bigger and smaller, the spiral can symbolize the increasing and decreasing radiance of the sun, the waxing and waning moon, growth and expansion as opposed to death and reduction, birth and death. Since it is essentially infinite, it also symbolizes continuity. It symbolizes the cycle of the seasons of the year and the dynamic aspects of nature. As the storm spiral it is connected to the Chinese rising dragon, and the vortex and storm spirals have identical meaning as the embodiment of energy in nature.

The spiral is also connected to the spinning of the thread of life and the scarf of the mother goddess, who rules destiny and spins the scarf of the illusion of life in the earthly world. The spiral is also connected to the symbolism of the labyrinth (see entry). In its metaphysical sense, the spiral symbolizes the different levels of existence and the wandering of the soul in its incarnation and final return to the center. Some connect the spiral to the Hebrew letter Vav. In the Egyptian hieroglyph system the spiral symbolizes cosmic shapes in motion or the relations between unity and multiplicity. The spiral is connected especially to ropes and snakes.

The spiral can be found in three main forms:

1. The expanding spiral, like the nebulous – in this case if is an active solar symbol

2. The shrinking spiral, like the sea or the storm vortex – this is a negative lunar symbol.

3. The fossilized spiral like the conch of the snail – also a negative lunar symbol.

The spiral is mainly macrocosmic, but it is connected to lunar animals and water. In ancient cultures we can find a distinction between two creative spirals – the one that is going up – the spiral that moves clockwise, and the one that is coming down, the spiral that moves against the clock. The spiral that is moving clockwise is attributed to Athena. The spiral that is moving against the clock is attributed to Poseidon. The spiral, like the snake and the condlini power in the Tantara), can also symbolize the potential center, like in the spider web. The Egyptian god Tut is presented with a big spiral on his head. Since it is connected to creation, development and movement, the spiral is a symbol of the power that con be found on the scepter of the Egyptian Pharaoh, and sometimes in contemporary waling sticks as well.

The spiral can also symbolize the relations between the circle and the center. It is connected to the idea of dance, mainly ancient dances and healing activities, in which the movement pattern develops in the shape of a spiral. In healing, the role of the spiral is most significant and the direction of its movement – clockwise or against the clock is used as a therapeutic tool for stimulating the patient's energy. It can "open" of blocked areas, or "close" areas in which there are "energy leaks" according to the needs of the patient who can be human, animal, vegetable, an open area or a building.

The conic shape of the pendulum is like a spiral and the pendulum's movement is spiral as well. In dance, the spiral movement can appear in dances that are supposed to bring the dancer to a state of ecstasy, and it can symbolize one's desire to "escape" the material world and enter another dimension through the "hole" that is symbolized by the mystical center.

Since the spiral is connected to thunders and lightening it symbolizes fertility. It can also be connected to the element of fire and represent flames. The spiral with this meaning often appears in Celtic symbolism. In Australian aboriginal culture the spiral symbolizes the masculine and phallic principle, although it is usually connected to the female genitalia like the sea conch spiral. In China, in Buddhism and Taoism, "the precious pearl" and "the dragon ball" are sometimes depicted as a spiral, and the double spiral has a yin-yang symbolism.

The spiral is symbolized by spiral shapes in nature – the ear lobe, the sea conch and the snail conch, the arms of the octopus, plants that grow in spiral shapes like the ivy, the cone of the fir tree as well as animal horns and crawled up animals such as sleeping dogs and cats and the crawled up snake. It is also connected to the ears of kings and gods and animals that bring the rain, to reptiles and to the Condlini sleeping crawled up snake. The gods of the storm, the elements and movement such as Rudra and Pushen have braided hair in the shape of a spiral or a conch. The spiral is also connected to the navel as the center of power and life.

The double spiral symbolizes the increase and decrease of solar or lunar forces, the changing rhythms of development and degeneration, life and death. It can also symbolize the two hemispheres, the two poles, day and night, all the rhythms of nature, the yin and yang, shakta and shakti, the material and immaterial and continuity between cycles. It symbolizes the androgynous and it is connected to the symbolism of the Caduceus and the solve et coagula in alchemy. This is the bilateral movement of decomposition and congealing (or solidification), division and union, the decomposition of the imperfect material and its restructuring in a new and more superior form.

Both single and double spirals were among the sacred symbols of Neolithic Europe. They appear on Megalithic monuments (large stones that were used for building sacred edifices in ancient times) and on temples all over Europe and the British Isles.

The spiral labyrinth penetrated by a cross was a popular symbol as well.

Spirals represent the keepers of the snake in Sumerian temples.

The spiral is connected to the idea of death and rebirth – the idea of entering the mysterious earth womb, penetrating its center, and exiting from the same path.

Many sacred dances imitated this movement.

Spiral labyrinths can be found in Cathedral ornaments that were taken from the ancient temples that existed earlier in their place.

The magical material called lituus was used by Roman fortunetellers for marking sacred places and their marking usually ended with the shape of a spiral.

Square

The square symbolizes the integration and merger of the four elements. It is related to the symbolism of the number four as a symbol of stability, foundation and permanence and all the existing divisions into four (four seasons of the year, Four Corners of the Earth etc.).

From a psychological point of view, since the shape of the cube symbolizes permanence and stability, it is a symbol of organization and construction that usually relates to the material level as a symbol of the earth. The circle, on the other hand, symbolizes the sky, the earthly existence and static wholeness (unlike the triangle that symbolizes dynamism). Some see it as symbol of the incarnation of god in creation. It also symbolizes honesty, sincerity and candor. It is also a symbol of mortality and death that is the opposite of the dynamic circle of life and movement. The four seasons, Four Corners of the earth, four stages in a person's life – all represent the organization and order that exist in the universe.

In Egyptian hieroglyphs the square symbolizes achievement and the square-shaped spiral symbolizes constructive energy, an energy that turns things into matter. In agricultural symbolism the square symbolizes the stability of farming communities and people who live in permanent settlements, unlike the dynamism and infinite circular dynamism of the nomads tents. It is a symbol of borders and therefore it symbolizes defined shape. In sanctified architecture the square symbolizes sublime knowledge, the archetype that dominates all works. The circled square or squared circle is a transformation of the ball-like shape, the sky, into the rectangular shape of the earth and vise versa in sanctified buildings such as temples and churches. It is the mystical union of the four elements. In Chinese symbolism the square represents the earth and all that is static. Together with the turning circle of the sky, the square and the circle together are a union of Yin and Yang, uppers and lowers, and a symbol of the perfectly balanced individual. In ancient Greek and Roman cultures the square was the symbol of Aphrodite/Venus as the feminine power of fertility. In Hermetic symbolism, a square standing on its base symbolizes stability, when it is on its top it symbolizes movement, and with the circle at its center it symbolizes the anima mundi – the soul of the world. In Hinduism the square symbolizes the pattern of the order of the universe, the perfect dimensions of the individual and the standard proportion. It serves as the basis for temples or any other sacred place and it is the symbol of the perfectly balanced shape. It symbolizes space, essence, the pairs of opposites, the Four Corners of the Earth, four castes etc. In the symbolism of Pitagoras the square symbolizes the soul.

↔ SYMBOLS ↔

Star

The star as a graphic shape is a very popular symbol. Its symbolism is determined by the number of its corners and its length, shape and color, if it has a color. "The burning star" is the symbol of the mystical center and the growing forces of the universe. The four-cornered star, also called "the Maltase cross", is connected to Shamash as the god of the sun and the god of love and justice. The five-cornered star is the most common one. In Egyptian hieroglyphs it symbolizes "rising upwards towards the point of origin" and it was used in words such as "bring", "educate", "teacher" and the like. When it points upwards it symbolizes ambition, light, the spiritual and education. A five-cornered star pointing downwards symbolizes the inferno in black magic. It is the symbol of witchcraft and evil. The six-cornered star symbolizes creation. It is called "King Solomon's seal" and is connected to the Star of David. It is a combination of the feminine and masculine triangles, of fire and water. The eight-cornered star surrounded by a circle is a symbol of Gula, Shamash's companion.

In Chinese symbolism star/stars are appear together with the sun and moon, and they are the symbol of the superior wisdom of the rulers. In Christianity the star symbolizes charity and divine guidance. Twelve stars symbolize the twelve tribes of Israel and the twelve apostles.

On the symbolism of the star as a celestial object see in "Landscape and nature symbols".

Star of David/ Hexagram/King Solomon's seal

The Star of David or the hexagram is also called "King Solomon's seal". It is comprised of two joined triangles, one with its top facing upwards and the other downwards. This is why the Star of David symbolizes the law that "all is the same upwards and downwards", and the joining between the upper and the lower. Some call it "the star of the microcosm", or the sign of the spiritual potential of the individual that may deny himself indefinitely. It is the symbol of the human soul as a combination of the conscious and the unconscious. In alchemy it represents the principal of the immaterial, that is symbolized by the middle point of the star of David, that is not actually seen but it must be perceived by the mind's eye, like in some of the Tibetan and Indian mandalas.

The Star of David or the hexagram symbolizes the union of opposites, male and female, positive and negative, particularly when the upper triangle is in white and the lower in black. It symbolizes increase and decrease, the hermaphrodite (see entry), the perfect balance that is created through the combination of complementary forces such as fire and water (upper triangle symbolizing fire, lower triangle symbolizing water). It also symbolizes the androgynous aspect of divinity, the individual looking into its own nature, the twin forces of creativity. It is the synthesis of all elements, with the upper triangle as the celestial nature and the lower triangle as the earthly nature, the whole that represents the universal individual who unifies the two as an intermediary. As King Solomon's seal it is also the symbol of the power of the mind over matter.

In Chinese symbolism, there are eight trigrams of the pakuas connected symbolically and each represents the Yin-Yang forces and the forces of nature. The eight trigrams are divided into to sixty-four hexagrams that symbolize the infinite interactions between these forces.

Swastika (twisted cross)

In The 20th century the swastika became a well-known Nazi and Neo-Nazi symbol, but it is actually one of the most ancient and complex symbols in the world. This graphic symbol can be found back in prehistoric times, and it existed in almost every ancient culture all over the world. It can be found on Christian catacombs, in Britain, Ireland, Gascony, among Etruscan, Hindu, Celtic and Germanic nations, in central Asia and Pre-Colombian America, and practically all over the world except parts of Sumer and Africa. It was widely used among Buddhists and the disciples of Vishnu and among the Hittites. It was found in poetry in Cyprus and Troy, and appeared in early periods in western and northern Europe, Iceland, Lapland, Finland and Scotland. It first appeared in Egypt only a several centuries after the birth of Christ, and it did not appear at all in central Africa and lower Mesopotamia, but some consider four-faced gods and the four-faced Horus as swastika symbols. The swastika appeared extensively on altars, vases, china and pottery, shields, weapons, dresses, and coins. It was a symbol of good luck, goodwill, blessings, longevity, fertility, health and life.

The uses and meanings of the swastika are many since it is a synthesis of two symbols of independent power – the Greek cross with the equal arms the cross with the four arms twisted at the same direction. Some say that during the Iron Age the swastika symbolized the supreme deity. Others see the swastika as connected to agriculture and the Four Corners of the Earth. The source of its current meaning, that is mainly negative, stems from the fact that the swastika is an ancient symbol of the Arian nations which symbolizes their superior deity – the sun and Deius, the god of the sky. The swastika usually appears as a solar symbol since it often appears with the solar disc that is a typical solar symbol.

Some see it as the specific symbols of the turning around an axis, or the symbol of the turning of the sun, the radiant wheel of the midday sun. It is also the symbol of the chariot of the sun, the Four Corners of the Earth and the four seasons. It is the movement of the storm, the symbol of the "center", a creative force in motion, the regeneration of cycles, the turning of the life cycle since the horizontal and vertical lines represent mind and matter and the four levels of existence.

Some see the swastika as a human figure turned into a graphic symbol, a person with two hands and two legs, or a symbol of the union between the masculine and feminine principles. It also symbolizes the dynamic and static, mobility and immobility, harmony and balance and the two complementary phases of movement – centrifugal and centripetal (strives for the center) inhaling and exhaling, going out of the center and returning to the center, beginning and end.

The swastika as a labyrinth shape can also be perceived as a symbol of water in motion, a combination of the two Z shapes of lightening and the two bent sticks carried by the Indian queen Arani in order to create fire. Some see the swastika as the cabalist letter aleph that symbolizes the primordial movement of the huge breath of the chaos that turns around the creative center. It can also represent the Scandinavian snake of the sun in double shape. It was also suggested that the swastika is a symbol of surrender and submission like hands crossed on the chest in a gesture of surrender.

The swastika appears with gods and goddesses alike. Since it is identified with the feminine principle it was suggested that it represents the four states of the moon, but it is mainly connected to solar symbols such as the lion, antelope, deer, horse, birds and the lotus. The shape of the swastika is interpreted as a solar wheel with horns and legs. In the Middle Ages, the most popular interpretation of this graphic symbol was that it symbolizes movement and the power of the sun. But at the same time it was also interpreted as a typical symbol of the symbolism of the number four, mainly in the sense of "the configuration of the movement that splits into four parts" and connected to the poles and the Four Corners of the Earth. In Native-American culture the swastika symbolizes good luck, fertility and rain. In Buddhism it symbolizes the seal of Buddha's heart, Buddha's esoteric wisdom and the cycle of existence, and it is one of the good signs that appear on Buddha's footprint. In Celtic culture the swastika is a symbol of good luck and it appears with the gods of thunder. In Chinese symbolism it symbolizes the "accumulation of the lucky signs of the ten thousand useful things". The swastika is an early shape of the letter Peng that symbolizes the four quarters of space and earth. It also symbolizes continuity, no beginning and no end and the eternal regeneration of life. It symbolizes completeness, lawful movement, longevity and blessing. In Christianity the swastika often appeared in catacombs as a symbol of Jesus as the power of the world. In the Middle Ages it symbolized the four Evangelists with Jesus at the center. In ancient Greek culture the swastika symbolized Zeus as the god of the sky and Helius as a solar symbol. It also appears with Hera, Ceres and Artemis. In Hinduism, the origin of the word swastika is "all that is good". It symbolizes life, movement, happiness and good luck. It is the symbol of the Indian god of fire Agni, and Diaus, the ancient Arian god of the sky that later became Indra. It is also connected to Brhama, Surya, Vishnu, Shiva and Ganesha as finder of the path and god of crossroads. The swastika was sometimes used as a seal on jars containing holly water from the Ganges. Among Asian Muslims, the swastika symbolizes the Four Corners of the Earth and the angels that dominate the four seasons, one in each corner. In Japanese symbolism it symbolizes the heart of Buddha and good luck. In the Teutonic and Scandinavian cultures, the swastika symbolizes Thor's battle-ax or hammer as god of the air, lightening and thunder and a symbol of good luck. In Lithuania the swastika is a talisman for good luck and appears in its Sanskrit name. In Semitic cultures the swastika is usually accompanied by other solar symbols, but it also appears as a symbol of the feminine generative force on Astarte's triangle.

There are two forms of the swastika and each can be interpreted separately: the right swastika – that moves clockwise and the left swavastika, which moves against the clock. The two swastikas symbolize the masculine and feminine, the sun and moon, movement clockwise and movement against the clock, the celestial forces and the earthly-negative forces, the spring sun growing stronger and the autumn sun growing weaker and maybe the two hemispheres. In China, two swastikas symbolize the yin and yang. Two intertwined swastikas are called "Solomon's knot" and symbolize the celestial depth and infinity.

Symbol of infinity

The symbol of infinity, which is known as the figure 8 lying horizontally,

came to the western world through the Arab digits, that some believe that their true origin was in India, not Arabia. In Hindu religion it symbolizes infinity or wholeness since is its made (in its traditional representation) of a circular shape that moves clockwise and another circular shape that moves against the clock. That is right side that symbolizes masculinity and solar imagery is connected to the left side, the feminine and lunar. The symbol is infinite in its shape. It has no beginning and no end. It is closed and continuos.

Like the figure 8 it represents, it is a karmic number. The symbol of infinity also described the sexual union and the sense of wholeness – two who become one.

Since in the figure eight none of the circles is on top of the other, the symbol implies the equality between the masculine and feminine forces, which leads to intimate knowledge of the infinity that contains these two poles

Triangle

The triangle is the geometric image of the number three and is identified with the symbolism of this number. In its most sublime sense it relates to the holy trinity.

The triangle symbolizes the nature of the universe that is connected to the number three – sky, earth and mankind, father, mother and child and the individual as body, mind and spirit.

The triangle symbolizes fire because it resembles the shape of the flame. When its vertex facing upwards it symbolizes striving to rise up towards the union of all things, while the base symbolizes horizontal expansion.

Two triangles, one facing up and the other facing down symbolize fire and water joined together and creating the six-cornered star that is called King Solomon's seal (also "Star of David" see entry). They symbolize the human soul. The triangle whose vertex points upward symbolizes life, fire, flame, heat, the masculine principle, the lingam, the shakta and the spiritual world. It is also the trinity of love, truth and wisdom. When its color is red it symbolizes royal grandeur.

The triangle with the vertex pointing downwards is lunar and symbolizes the feminine principle, water, the world of nature, the body, the eonian, the Shakti and the great mother. The horizontal line is the earth and the color of the triangle is white.

In the mountain and cave symbolism, the mountain is masculine - a triangle that points upwards, and the cave is feminine - a triangle that points downwards.

A triangle within a circle symbolizes the shapes that are held in the triangle of eternity. Three combined triangles symbolize the unity of the three figures of the trinity.

Two triangles placed next to one another horizontally with connected vertexes are a lunar symbol that describes the waxing and waning moon, eternal repetition, death and life, dying and resurrection. The point of contact is the darkness of the moon and death.

In alchemy two triangles are essence and content, forma and materia, mind and spirit, sulfur and mercury, the solid and the volatile, spiritual power and material existence. The triangle in various forms symbolizes in alchemy the elements. The ordinary triangle symbolizes fire, the triangle with the chopped vertex symbolizes air, the downward facing triangle symbolizes the element of water and a downward facing chopped vertex triangle symbolizes the element of the earth. Two combined triangles symbolize the union between two of opposites that becomes "liquid fire" or "burning water".

In Buddhism the triangle symbolizes the pure fire and the three jewels of Buddha, the dharma and the sangha. In Christianity the triangle made by three combined circles symbolizes the united trinity and the equality between the three entities. The triangle halo symbolizes god the father. In ancient Egypt the triangle symbolized trinity. In the right-angled triangular, the perpendicular is attributed to the male, the base to the female and the rest to the descendent of the two: Osiris as the beginning, Isis as the intermediary or vessel and Horus as the completion (according to Plutarch). The image of three double triangles surrounded by circles with a joint center symbolizes the obscure, the land of the spirits. In ancient Greek culture the triangle-shaped delta symbolized the door of life, the feminine principle and fertility. In Hinduism the triangle pointing upwards and the triangle pointing downwards are shakta and shakti, lingam and the eonian or Shiva and his shakti. In the philosophy of Pitagoras, the equilateral triangle symbolized Athena as the goddess of wisdom. In Cartage, a triangle with horns was the Carthaginian symbol of Tanit.

Vasika Pisces

Vasika Pisces, the basin of the fish, is an oval, almond-like shape, standing vertically. This shape usually surrounds holy figures, like the halo of saints. This shape is comprised of an ellipsis within an ellipsis with a very narrow space between them, and it is a basic shape in sanctified geometry.

Wheel

The symbol of the wheel was very popular in ancient cultures. The entire universe was perceived as a huge wheel whose revolving could be predicted by the cycles of the celestial bodies and the seasons of the year. Most of the mother goddesses are described as spinning on the wheel of fortune the thread of life of the universe and the people in it. In different cultures, symbols of small wheels, as a model of the cosmos accompanied the dead to their graves. The wheels served also as a magical symbol that protected helmets, shields, weapons and homes. In Celtic culture, the Celtic gods held wheels in their hands or were decorated with wheels beside them. In India, the goddess Kali dominated the wheel of time (Kala-Kakra). The Etruscans had a goddess of the wheel by the name of Wortumna – "she who turns the wheel of the year". The Romans turned this name into "Fortune", the goddess who incessantly turns the celestial wheel in which the seasons of the year and human destinies are engraved, and dominate the wheel of birth, regeneration and transformation.

The ancient belief in reincarnation created many cyclical rather than linear images of the universe in which the wheel was the model of the individual's life cycle. The wheel is also likened to the cosmic process that is beyond the single life cycle the individual experiences, that is the life of a soul that reincarnates again and again. The wheel is also connected to the idea of karmic retribution. The idea "life that repeats itself", in which every entity pays for past mistakes in the possibilities to make amends it experiences in the present, and in the cosmic turns of fate of "rags to riches and to rags again" in the individual's life.

In Jewish and Christian symbolism the wheel has a deep meaning as well. In Hebrew manuscripts one of the types of angels is called "ofanim" (wheels), whose turning means revelation. This perception is similar to the Hindu perception of the universe as a giant carriage, which carries all the gods and creatures on it wheels trough the eternal cycle.

Fortune's huge wheel gradually became the Medieval "wheel of fortune", and its goddess became "the lady of fortune". The wheel of fortune, which is a popular symbol even today, sometimes has six spokes and sometimes eight, and reminds in its shape the Hindu Dharma wheel. In Germany, a wheel with eight spokes was the Achtwan that was used for magic and witchcraft. At the time of Dante, the wheel of fortune was described as having eight spokes of eight opposite situations in human life: richness-poverty, war-peace, humility-glory and tolerance-passion. The strong and universal symbolic meaning of the wheel led to its inclusion in the tarot cards, the tenth card in the Major Archana. The card number ten has a symbolic meaning of completeness, of ending a cycle and beginning a new one (see "symbolism in numbers"). This card represents the balance between opposing forces of restriction and expansion, activity and passivity that move the universe. The wheel is also connected to the symbolism of the zodiac (see entry).

Yin-Yang

The Yin-Yang symbol called ta-ki (ta-chi) is a popular Chinese symbol that has deep meaning. It symbolizes the dual nature of the universe, the existence of two opposing forces whose merger creates perfection, who are inseparable and indivisible and characterize all that exists. It symbolizes the balance between them, a balance that is dynamic, continuous and changing. The two forces are the feminine principle – the yin, the passive one, and the masculine principle – the yang, the active one. The yin-yang symbol is a circle divided by a sigmoid line (like the letter S horizontally) that creates two parts which seem to move - dynamism that flows from one to the other, that would not have appeared if the symbol was divided by a straight line. The half that represents the yang is fair and the dark part represents the yin. But in each of the parts there is a dot of the opposite color because every situation must include the seeds of its opposite, since the yin can not exist without the yang and vise versa, and there is no force that is entirely feminine or masculine. Therefore, this symbol creates the wholeness, the androgynous (see entry), the primordial, the perfect balance and perfect harmony, the pure essence that is neither yin nor yang, but still contains them both. The two forces are in a state of permanent tension, but not antagonism. They are dependent on one another and influence each other. They are one in essence but two in reality. They symbol represents the constantly evolving union-conflict between the two opposites, the continuity and transformation that exist in opposite situations. The entrance to and the exit from this movement are outside the movement itself, just like birth and death are outside the life of the individual with regard to conscious knowledge and choice. The invisible vertical axis of the symbol contains the "unchanging intent", i. e. the mystical "center", in which there is no circular movement, no impulse, no existential suffering of any kind. The yin-yang symbol also expresses the balancing tendency of development and degeneration. In Chinese trigrams the yin is symbolized by the broken line and the yang by the continuos line. The dual traits of the yin-yang are attributed in Chinese tradition to existential forces,  qualities, human life and traits, animals, plants and even objects. The yin and yang can be seen in everything. Sometimes the yang qualities are more prominent and sometimes the qualities of the yin play a more dominant part. The yin is supposed to come always before the yang since it represents the primordial darkness before the yang – the light of creation. The yin also symbolizes the primordial water, the passive, female and feminine, the negative, the instinctive and intuitive nature, the psyche, depth, concentration, and the soft, flexible and easy to shape. It is symbolized by everything that is dark in color or nature and associated to the wet principle such as the earth, the moon, the valley, trees, nocturnal animals, wet or aquatic creatures and by most of the flowers. It represents circularity, support, lightness and broadness.

The yang is the active, male and masculine principle. It represents the positive, the rational nature, the wind, height, expansion, the hard and firm. It is symbolized by light and everything that is fair, dry and high such as mountains, the sky, all the solar animals and most of the birds.

The magical animals, the dragon, phoenix and ki-lin (chi-lin) are both yang and yin. They are endowed with both types of qualities and symbolize the perfect combination between the two forces or essences of the universe. Among the flowers, the Lotus has yin and yang qualities.

In the pakua (bagua) trigrams, the yin and yang lines create the four pairs of opposites, who together symbolize all the forces that exist in the universe. The first pair is the universal opposites – heaven and earth. It is called the "pure" couple since the earth is all yin and represented by three yin lines (broken lines), and the sky is all yang and represented by three yang lines (straight lines). The second pair is the organic opposites – fire and water. The sign of fire that is part of the masculine principle is made of two yang lines – upper and lower and a yin line between them. The sign of water that is part of the feminine principle is made of two yin lines - upper and lower and a yang line between them. The third couple is the elementary/natural opposites – the mountain and the lake. The mountain is made of an upper yang line and two lower yin lines and the lake is made of an upper yin line and two yang lines underneath. The fourth and last couple is the impulsive opposites – wind and thunder. The wind is symbolized by two upper yang lines and a lower yin line, and the thunder is symbolized by two upper yin lines and a lower yang line.

Symbols in the Animal Kingdom

Conch

The conch usually symbolizes the rising and setting sun, the lunar spiral and the water and its symbolism is similar to that of the shell. In Buddhism, the conch symbolizes the voice of the preaching Buddha. It is connected to speech, sound, learning and overcoming the samsara. The white conch symbolizes earthly power. In Hinduism, the conch is consecrated to Vishnu as the god of water. From the conch emerged the ancient word "Om". In Chinese symbolism, the conch symbolizes royalty and a prosperous journey. In the cultures of ancient Greece and Rome, the conch was the symbol of Poseidon/Neptune and Triton. The Tritons used to blow a conch when they carried Poseidon's chariot. In Islam the conch symbolizes the ear that hears the Divine

Word. In Mayan culture the conch frequently appears in symbols connected to water.

Feather

The feather symbolizes truth, lightness, flying, dryness, the sky, speed, space, flight to other realms, the soul, faith, observation, a message from superior worlds, the element of the spirit as opposed to the element of humidity. Whether it appears alone or as part of a group, the feather is connected to the element of air.

Feathers symbolized the gods of creation in the Egyptian pantheon: Ptah, Hathor, Osiris and Amon and the goddess Maat as the goddess of truth. As a hieroglyphic symbol, the sign of the feather is used in words such as "emptiness", "dryness", "lightness", "height" and "flight".

Since the feather is such a quintessential symbol of the element of air, culture in which aerial myths had an important role used feathers for ritualistic costumes on many occasions.

The Native-American chief's crown of feathers brings him closer to the demiurgic (creator of the world) bird. Wearing feathers on the head or body means taking on the force or mana of the bird, and thus connecting between the wearer of the feathers and the knowledge and magical powers of the birds.

A white feather symbolizes clouds, the foam of the sea and even cowardice, since the white feather or feathers in the tail of a fighting cock were considered a sign of a birth defect and therefore a sign that the it has no inclination to fight bravely.

Two feathers together represent light and air, the two poles and resurrection.

Three feathers are connected to the fleur de lis (see entry) and are also the symbol of the Prince of Wales.

The crown of feathers symbolizes the beams of the sun in Native-American culture. The feathers of the eagle symbolize the thunderbird, the Great Spirit, the universal spirit and the beams of light. In Celtic culture the feather robes the priests wore represent the journey to the other world. The fairies in Celtic culture also wore dresses made of feathers. In Scandinavian mythology, Frigg had a magic robe made of fathers that enabled its wearer to fly in the air. In Christianity the feather symbolizes faith and observation. In Shamanistic symbolism feathers had an important role. The feather robes of the Shaman's give them the power to fly to other realms and go on learning expeditions. In Taoism, the feather is attributed to the priest, to the "feathered wise man" or the "feathered visitor", and symbolize communication with the other world. Among the Toltecs, feathered sticks symbolized prayer and observation.

Animals

Albatross
The albatross symbolizes a long and exhausting flight and faraway oceans, patience and endurance, resilience and the understanding of the importance of long-term parental commitment, the ability to sustain emotional relationships for a long time and inconvenient and bizarre beginnings and endings, that nevertheless are effective. It is also considered an omen of storms and strong winds at sea, and there is a widespread belief that the soul of a drowned sailor can reincarnate in an albatross, and therefore
Killing an albatross brings bad luck.

Ant
The most popular symbolism of the ant is that of endless diligence in the service of society. This symbolism stems directly from the activities of the ant in the ant society, the long train of ants that gathers food for winter. The ant carries huge loads in proportion to its size and continues to carry them regardless of the obstacles it may encounter on its way. It is one of the most popular symbols of

work and service to society, as a result of its constant search for food, not for itself but for the entire society of ants. It symbolizes patience, endurance, planning, energy and dedication needed to complete a task or work, community life and saving for the future – all these are attributes that stem directly from the ant's life in nature.

In the Indian myth the ants symbolize the smallness of living beings – the fragile nature of life human and helplessness in human existence. But at the same time ants also symbolize a life superior to human life. Ants were attributed with foresight in the direct sense of saving for a time of need, but also of fortune telling skills. In Chinese traditions the ant symbolizes the "righteous insect" as a symbol of organization, honesty, values and patriotism. In Jewish tradition the ant is a symbol of diligence.

Antelope

In Bushman tradition, divinity can appear as an antelope. In Asia Minor and Europe, the antelope is considered a lunar animal connected to the great mother. In Egypt the antelope was sacrificed to the god Set but could also represent Osiris and Horus. In the Heraldic tradition it symbolizes courage, strength and danger. It is depicted as having a heraldic head, a body of a deer, a tail of a unicorn and an elephant's tooth on its nose. In Indian tradition, the antelope is a sign and a symbol of Shiva. Suma and Handra have chariots pulled by antelopes and Pavana, god of the winds, rides on an antelope. In the Sumerian-Semite tradition, it is a form of Eaa and Marduch. Eaa-Oanes is "the antelope of the underground ocean", "the antelope of Apsu", and "the antelope of creation". The dragon aspect of the antelope can also replace of the ox, buffalo and cow. The lunar antelope is consecrated to Astarte. In Native-American tradition the antelope symbolizes taking a stand, the ability to leap over obstacles, survival skills, speed, gentleness and a bond with the earth.

Baboon

In ancient Egypt the baboon was called the "caller of dawn". With its arms raised it is the symbol of wisdom, saluting to the rising sun and symbolizing the god Thoth (God of wisdom) and consecrated to the god Hepi (god of the Nile). In Native-American tradition it symbolizes protection of the family.

Badger

The badger symbolizes playfulness, mischief and love of play. In Chinese tradition the badger is a lunar yin animal who symbolizes super-natural powers.

In Japan the badger also symbolizes super-natural forces, Fata Morgana and the creator of ignes fatui – strings of illusion that tempt and lure. In Europe the badger symbolizes worthlessness and weather forecasting, and is sometimes called the "horse of greed". In Native-American traditions, the badger symbolizes the keeper of stories, passion, cunning and deceit. Due to its tendency to hold on and not let go from anyone who upsets it or trespass its territory, it also symbolizes aggression, blunt and courageous self-expression, vindictiveness and vengeance, stubbornness and perseverance and control. It is also an antidote to passivity or victimhood and a symbol of perseverance in the service of some cause and defense of rights and spiritual ideas. Since it is an animal with a deep connection to the earth it symbolizes settling, knowing the land, magic connected to the land and knowing the wisdom of the land.

Bat

In African tradition the bat was an ambivalent symbol. It symbolizes acute perception and understanding but also darkness and ambiguity. In Alchemy, due to its dual nature as both bird and rat it symbolizes sometimes the androgynous and sometimes treated like a dragon. Among the Native-Americans it symbolizes the deliverer of rain. In Native-American tradition in general is symbolizes shamanistic death and rebirth, initiation, transition and change, the beginning of new ideas, perception of previous life, understanding sorrow, camouflage, the ability to see the unseen and use of sound vibrations. In Buddhism it symbolizes obscured understanding. In Chinese tradition the bat is a yin animal since it is nocturnal, but as a homophone (a word identical in its articulation to another word but written differently) to happiness, "pu" became the symbol of happiness and good fortune, wealth, longevity and peace. A pair of bats symbolizes positive wishes and is the symbol of Shu-sing, god of longevity. A group of five bats represents the five blessings: health, happiness, longevity, peace and joy.

In Christianity the bat symbolized the "bird of the devil", and incarnation of the "prince of darkness", and the devil is sometimes depicted has having wings of a bat. As a hybrid of bird and rat it symbolizes duality, deceit and hypocrisy. As an animal that lives in desolate places and ruins it symbolizes melancholy. In Europe the bat was associated with black magic and witchcraft and symbolized intelligence, cleverness and shrewdness and revenge. In Jewish traditions the bat symbolized impurity and idolatry. In Japan it symbolizes upsetting restlessness and a chaotic state.

Bear

The bear symbolizes revival since it comes out from his hibernation cave with a new cub born in the spring. It is the symbol of new life and initiation that is connected with rites of passage. In heroic myths the bear is the sun. In Indonesian myths the bear is depicted as lunar, and when it is connected with goddesses such as Artemis and Diana, it has lunar meanings as well. In alchemy the bear symbolizes the nigrado, the prima materia, and therefore it is connected to all the primary stages of life and instincts. The bear was attributed to the dangerous aspect of the subconscious, as the symbol of a cruel and brutal person. In Native-American tradition the bear symbolizes super-natural powers, inner reflection, healing, death and rebirth, connection with the spirit, transformation, change, wisdom, courage and bravery, loneliness/isolation, the air vortex, the storm and star voyages, and is depicted as the creature of dreams, shamans and mystics. Its image sometimes symbolizes the man of vision. In shamanistic traditions it symbolizes the messenger of the spirits of the forest. In Celtic traditions it symbolizes lunar power and the symbol of the goddess of Bern. In Chinese tradition the bear symbolizes heroism and strength. In Christianity the bear symbolizes evil, the devil, cruelty, greed and physical appetite. The bear cubs were believed to be born amorphously and therefore they represented transformation and the regenerating forces of Christianity over paganism. The bear was the symbol of St. Blendina. David's struggle with the bear symbolized the conflict between Jesus and Satan. In Greek tradition, the bear was consecrated to the lunar goddesses Diana and Artemis, and as the symbol of Atlanta and Euphemia. Girls who participated in the rituals of the goddess Artemis were called the "she-bears". They wore yellow robes and imitated bears. Diana turned Calisto into a bear. In Japanese tradition the bear symbolizes generosity, wisdom and strength. In Scandinavian and Teutonic traditions the bear was consecrated to Thor. The female bear Atla is the feminine principle and the male bear Atli is the masculine principle. The bear was the symbol of the Kingdoms of Persia and Russia.

Bee

The symbolism of the bee is divided between metaphysical symbolism that connects it with superior worlds and spiritual activities, and practical symbolism that stem from its physical activities and life cycle. The metaphysical symbolism of the bee also stems from some of its traits that were revered in ancient times and even today. The bee symbolizes prosperity, concentration, understanding the energy of the warrior woman, reincarnation, communication with the dead, helping the spirits that are still connected to the earth to move on to their proper resting place, immortality, rebirth, industrialism, productivity, diligence, purity, organization and the soul.

In various places in the world there was a widespread belief of the bees asexual reproduction, and therefore they symbolized virginity, chastity and purity. They carried a heavenly product, honey (see entry) that was considered the gift of sublime deities. Sometimes the bees symbolize the stars or winged messengers who bring tidings and massages from the world of the spirits. "To tell the bees" about death or an important occasion is to send the message to the other world or to the spirits. The bees were considered to be the messengers of the god of the spirits and the god of the oak tree. Since they are engraved on tombstones they symbolize immortality. In Celtic tradition, the bees were considered the bearers of the secrets of the wisdom of the other world. In Chinese traditions, the bees symbolize productiveness and thriftiness. In Christianity, they are a symbol of perseverance and diligence, clever organization, purity, chaste virgins, courage, thriftiness and economic wisdom, prudence, cooperation, sweetness, religious eloquence, a righteous and organized society that "produces offsprings, rejoices in birth but cherishes virginity". The Virgin Mary, who "produced" Jesus, is the bee and Jesus is represented by the honey. As a result of the belief that the bee never sleeps it is a symbol of vigilance, alertness and enthusiasm. The bee's flight in the air symbolizes the soul going up to paradise.

In ancient Egypt the bee was called the "giver of life", and symbolized birth, death and resurrection, productiveness, chastity, harmonious life and royalty. It symbolized the Pharaoh of Lower Egypt. The tears of Ra, which fall to the earth, become diligent bees. The symbols of the bee were engraved on the tombs of kings.

In ancient Greece the bee symbolized productiveness, prosperity, immortality (the souls of the dead may be reincarnated as bees) and purity. Demeter was the "pure mother of bees". The great mother was also known as the queen of the bees and its priestesses were the bees. She was always represented by the lion and bees in Greek art. The appearance of the bee foretold the coming of a guest or a stranger. As a symbol of Demeter, Diana and Sybil, the bee was considered a lunar and virginal animal. The gods Pan and Priapus were the defenders of the bees. Bees fly around Cupid who stabs loves with a bee sting. In Hindu tradition a bee on a lotus is the symbol of Vishnu, and blue bees on the forehead symbolize Krishna and the element of ether. The bee sting causes a sweet pain that is connected to the string of the arch of Kama, god of love, and a train of bees follows him. The bee is depicted together with the lion. Suma, the moon, is called "bee". In Islam, the bee symbolizes complete faith, wisdom and harmlessness. The Islamic scholar Iben El-Atir described the bees as: "instrumental to the blooming of flowers, practical, working during day light, do not eat food that was gathered by others, stay away from filth and foul smells and obey their ruler. They do not like the ambiguity of indecision, the clouds of doubt, the turbulence of revolt, the bad smoke, the water of luxury, the fire of passion". In Mithridatic culture, the bees symbolize the soul, the vital principal that is connected to the triad of ox-bull-cow. Bees and oxen, who are sexless (an ox is a castrated bull) were considered androgynous. The bee with the staff and snake (caduceus – symbol of medicine) represented Mercury, shepherd of the souls, when the bee symbolizes the soul. In Roman tradition, swarms of bees symbolized bad luck. The headless bee, together with the headless frog, was used to "extract" the evil eye. According to Virgil, the bee is the "breath of life" and Seneca connects it to royalty. In Jewish tradition, in the proverb on Samson (Judges 14, 8) the bee means royalty.

Boar

The boar as a symbol has an ambivalent meaning. On one hand, its is a model of fearlessness and symbol of tremendous courage, protection, use of an angry mask, the ability to sense danger and find the truth. On the other hand, it symbolizes the irrational impulse to suicide and represents promiscuity, lawlessness, lust and gluttony.

The boar is sometimes defined as a solar animal and sometimes as a lunar one. As solar, it represents the masculine principle, but a white boar is lunar, feminine and symbolizes the principle of water and the dweller of the swamps. In Celtic tradition it is a sanctified animal, and symbolizes the super-natural, prophecy, magic, warfare, and protection of warriors and hospitality. It is connected to the gods and forces of witchcraft, and with the tree, raven, wheel and man's head. It was sacrificed to the Celtic god Dagda. The boar's head symbolized health and avoiding danger, the power of the force of life and vitality that can be found in the head, and therefore it also symbolized plentifulness and good fortune for the next year. The boar and bear together represented spiritual rule and spiritual power. In China, the boar represents the richness of the forests and the white boar is a lunar animal. The druids called themselves "boars", probably because they were recluses attracted to the forests. In Christianity, the pig is a symbol of brutality, rage, evil, carnal sins and cruel rulers and princes. In Egypt the boar symbolized evil, as a representation of Set in its evil aspect, when he swallows the eye of the god of day. In ancient Greece and Rome the boar was consecrated to Ares/Mars, god of war, and symbolized struggle and destruction. It also symbolized the winter as the killer of Adonis and Atis who represented the solar force. The boar that killed Adonis was sacrificed to Aphrodite. The boar symbolizes Demeter and Atlanta. Hercules captured the wild boar of Arimentus. In Jewish tradition, the boar symbolizes the enemy of Israel, who destroys its vineyards. In Heraldic tradition, the boar is one of the four heraldic animals of hunting. In Hindu tradition, Varahi, the third incarnation of Vishnu, or Pargepati, saved the land from the waters of chaos in the shape of a boar and was the first farmer. The boar also represents Vageravarhi, the goddess of dawn and queen of heaven, as a boar and a source connected to life and fertility. In Iranian tradition, the "shining boar" is connected to the sun. In Japanese tradition, the white boar is the moon. The boar symbolizes courage, conquest and all the virtues of the warrior. In Teutonic and Scandinavian tradition, it symbolizes the harvest and fertility. It is a storm animal, an animal of funerals and burials and consecrated to the gods Odin/Wodin, Free and Frigg, who rode on boars. Masks and helmets of board gave the warriors the protection of Freyia and Frigg. In Siberian traditions the boar is a symbol of courage, conquest, stability and permanence and all the virtues of the warrior. In Sumerian-Semitic traditions the winged boar murdered Tamus. The boar can also be the messenger of the gods and bring tidings from them. In Babylon, the boar was a sanctified animal. In Celtic and Gaelic traditions it is always described positively.

Buffalo

In Indian tradition the buffalo is a symbol of plenty and prayer. It also symbolizes super-sensual forces, power, courage and feminine courage, heroism, endurance and bravery, creativity that is connected to the earth, knowledge, generosity, hospitality, cooperative work, challenge, survival, giving to help others and developing useful plans for the individual and community. In Buddhism, Yama, the god of the dead, is sometimes depicted as a buffalo or with the head of an ox. In Taoism, Lao Tsu rides on a buffalo or bull and he rode on a green buffalo when he disappeared in the east. Riding on a buffalo symbolizes controlling and directing the animal-like nature of man. Sometimes the buffalo takes the place of the ox in "ten pictures of driving an ox", in which the buffalo, as nature unyielding to spiritual awareness, "sinning" nature begins as totally black, and by domestication and taming, it begins to whiten, until in the tenth picture it completely disappears..

↔ SYMBOLS ↔

Butterfly

The butterfly symbolizes the soul, immortality, the power of the storm and air vortex, transformation, reincarnation, magic/witchcraft and change. Since the butterfly changes its shape from a caterpillar, through a state of "death" and isolation from the world as a chrysalis, that look as though it is wrapped in shrouds, and eventually it transforms into a celestial winged creature, it symbolizes rebirth, redemption and resurrection. The butterfly is also a symbol of the great goddess. In ancient times, the butterfly, together with the recurrent symbol in many cultures of the soul, represents the unconscious attraction to light.

In Gnostic traditions, the angel of death was depicted as a winged leg trampling a butterfly and this indicates that the butterfly symbol was connected more to life than to the soul, that does not stop living when the angel of death comes. In psychoanalysis the butterfly symbolizes rebirth.

In Celtic traditions the butterfly symbolizes the soul and the fire. Among the Australian Aborigines the butterfly also symbolizes the soul. In Chinese symbolism the butterfly symbolizes immortality, freedom as a result of plentifulness, joy and happiness. The butterfly with the chrysanthemum represents beauty in old age. In Christianity the butterfly symbolizes resurrection. Its stages of development represent life, death and rebirth. Sometimes it is painted on the hand of baby Jesus. In ancient Greek tradition too the butterfly symbolizes the soul and immortality, but it also symbolizes the psyche, and in Greek art it is frequently used to depict the soul. In Japan, the butterfly symbolizes a vain, useless woman, a geisha or frivolous lovers. A couple of butterflies symbolize marital bliss. A white butterfly symbolizes the soul of a dead person.

The chrysalis symbolizes the potential power of the spirit, forces of witchcraft and magic, the place of birth of the soul as a butterfly and the soul, wrapped and protected.

Camel

The camel is a desert ship that can carry heavy loads, eat sufficiently when food is available and live on the small quantities of food and water that can be found in the desert. It symbolizes the transformation of loads that man carries and the ability to save for the future, knowledge of open spaces and learning to walk through moving sands of time. In Christianity the camel symbolizes moderation, majesty, honor and endurance, and is connected to St. John the Baptist who wore a loincloth from camel hair. Since the camel kneels to accept its burden, it is a symbol of humility and obedience. In Iranian traditions, the camel is connected with the snake-dragon, and in Chinese tradition too the camel is one of the aspects of the dragon since its head resembles the head of a camel. In Roman tradition the came was used as a personification of Arabia on coins.

Cat

The cat symbolizes independence, seeing the invisible, protection, love, brave warrior that can even be cruel when cornered. The cat enables people to dream and helps in meditation and reflection. The cat's secondary symbolism is connected to the color of the cat. In certain traditions a black cat symbolizes darkness and death.

The cat's eyes change according to the intensity of the light, and therefore it symbolized the changing power of the sun during solar eclipse, when it enters the realms of the goddess of the moon. It also symbolizes the process of the waning of the moon and the secrets of the night. It symbolizes silence, passion and freedom. A black cat is considered lunar and symbolizes evil and death. Only in modern times various cultures started to attribute to the cat symbolism of good fortune. In Celtic traditions, the cat appears in contexts of funerals. In Chinese tradition it is a yin animal, since it is nocturnal, and it symbolizes the forces of evil and transformation. A strange cat symbolizes unwanted change and a black cat symbolizes bad luck and disease. In Japanese tradition the cat symbolizes forces of transformation, calmness, tranquility and peaceful sleep. In Christianity the cat symbolized the devil, darkness, lust and sloth. In Egypt the cat was considered a lunar animal, consecrated to Set as darkness, and symbolizing Bast, the goddess of the moon, the moon and Isis the mother goddess and was consecrated to her. It symbolizes the pregnant woman, when the moon helps the seed to grow in the womb. In Greek and Roman mythologies, the cat symbolizes the lunar Diana, goddess of liberty, who is depicted with a cat lying at her feet. In Scandinavian traditions it symbolizes Frigg, whose chariot is pulled by cats.

The cat was also considered to be the friend of witches who sometimes wore the shape of a cat. The black cat, as the companion of the witch symbolizes evil and bad luck. Dogs and cats in the witch's retinue were believed to cause rain (and this is the source of the expression "it's raining cats and dogs").

Chameleon

As a psychological symbol the chameleon symbolizes the ability to change faces, shapes, opinions and appearances. Since it is lying on a branch in the sun for a long time, the chameleon became a symbol of the use of the sun as a source of energy. While its ability to lay motionless until the "prey" gets closer and then send a long tongue and catch it made it symbol of patience and attracting things as a means of survival. Furthermore, the chameleon symbolizes the ability to climb up in order to achieve goals and the use of color for camouflage. It represents the element of air since in ancient times there was a widespread belief that the chameleon was nourished by the wind (the wind brings the chameleon its food). In Christianity it is depicted as Satan wearing different masks in order to fool mankind. In a number of African tribes it is considered the deliverer of rain.

Cicada

The cicada is sometimes called the "demon of light and darkness". It symbolizes the cycles of light and darkness.

In Chinese tradition the cicada symbolizes redemption, immortality, eternal youth, happiness, and restraining vice and greed. Cicadas made of jade were placed in the mouths of the dead in order to secure them an eternal life. In Greek tradition too the cicada symbolizes immortality (there was s belief that the cicada has no blood and lives on dew) and it was consecrated to Apollo. But contrary to Chinese symbolism, the legend on the cicada is a story about immortality without eternal youth. According to the legend, Titonius, who is symbolized by the cicada, was a young man that Eos, the Greek goddess of dawn, fell in love with. Titonious was a mortal and he lavished many gifts on his divine love and used to sing to her songs of praise and glory. Eos loved Titonious so much that she succeeded in getting her human lover eternal life, but not eternal youth. As time went by, Titonious became old, weak and frail and so did his voice in which he continued to praised Eos and sing to her songs of glory. His voice became higher and higher until he became a cicada. Eos locked her lover in her room where he would greet her every morning in his cicada voice. Some believe that this legend explains why the cicadas can be heard at dawn every morning. The cicada also symbolizes the rejected and abandoned lover.

Cobra

The cobra is considered the guide of the soul. It symbolizes the memory of the world of the soul and memories from previous life, the wisdom of superior feminine energy, transformation of the soul and freedom from religious persecutions. The cobra also symbolizes the great mother in her negative and destructive aspect. But when the cobra appears together with the lotus, it is a symbol of the great mother that gives both life and death, a symbol of the duality of existence and the tension between two opposites in the process of transformation toward the perfect unity. In ancient Egyptian culture the cobra was a celestial and superior being that symbolized royal wisdom and power, knowledge and gold.

Cock

As a bird that heralds the dawn, the cock is a solar animal, a symbol of the gods of the sun, except in Scandinavian and Celtic symbolism, and a symbol of activity and alertness. It symbolizes the masculine principle, as can be seen in its Hebrew name "gever" (man), and can symbolize protection of the family and community. As a result of its strong voice and proud walk the cock is called the "bird of glory". It symbolizes superiority, courage, alertness, dawn and forces waking up at sunrise. Its strong and "fearless" voice make it a symbol in many cultures, mainly in Native-American culture as well as New Age symbolism, of the power of the voice, of hearing the inner voice and listening to the inner voice, as well as to the understanding of language. In various traditions, two cocks fighting symbolized the struggle of life. The black cock was considered an "agent" of the devil.

In Buddhism, the cock, together with the snake and the pig, are the center of the "circle of existence" in which the cock represents sensuality and materialism, lust and pride. In Celtic traditions, the cock is considered a symbol of the gods of the underworld. In Chinese tradition, the cock symbolizes the yang principle, generosity, courage and heroism, loyalty and credibility. The red cock is considered an original form of the sun and a protector against fire. The white cock is a protector against ghosts. Th cock is the tenth symbolic animal of the twelve animals of the earthly branches. A cock with a crown on its head it symbolizes the literary spirit. A cock with spurs is a warlike image. A cock with a hen in a garden symbolize the pleasures of rustic life. In a number of Chinese initiation ceremonies a white cock is killed as a symbol of the death of the pervious life and the purity of the new life after initiation. The word cock is homophonic to "lucky", and therefore it serves in funerals as a means of expelling and weakening the forces of evil spirits. In China, the cock symbolizes sunset. When it is aggressive or depicted as such it is a symbol of war. In Chinese astrology the cock is October, and in the past this was the month of the beginning of the preparations for war. In the Middle Ages, the cock became an important Christian symbol that appears on the towers of cathedrals as a symbol of resurrection. The cock was also believed to greet the sun of Jesus in the East.

It symbolizes Jesus who lights the dark and evil forces. It also represents alertness and vigilance and therefore it was used as a weather vane on houses, that moves in different directions in order to watch and warn against the forces of evil. A cockfight symbolized the passion of the Christians to Jesus. In ancient Egypt the cock symbolized alertness and vigilance and seeing the future. In Gnostic traditions the cock with a cob of corn in its beak symbolizes alertness that creates plentifulness. In Greek and Roman traditions it symbolizes vigilance and alertness, quarrelsomeness and belligerency. It was consecrated to Apollo, Asclepius, Ares, Mercury, Priapus and Athena. It is connected to Persephone in the spring as the regeneration of life and was sacrificed to Lares. Since it was connected to Priapus and Asclepius, it was considered a healer of the sick. In Jewish tradition, the cock symbolizes fertility, masculinity and male potency. The cock and hen are connected to the newly wed couple. In Heraldic tradition the cock symbolizes the courage of the warrior and religious aspiration. In Iranian traditions the cock was considered a royal bird and was sometimes added to the royal scepter. In Japan it is a Shinto symbol that represents the drum that calls people to prayer in the temple. In Mithridatic culture, the cock is consecrated to Mithras as the god of the sun. In Scandinavian cultures it is considered a bird of the underworld and its calling wakes the heroes of Valehala to the last mighty battle. In Sumerian tradition, Nirgal is sometimes depicted with the head of a cock.

Cow

The cow symbolizes love, nurture, vigilance in the face of danger, content, connection to green pastures and the ability to share that is expressed in community life. It is connected to the earth and the great mother goddesses and lunar goddesses. Many of the lunar goddesses wear cow horns on their heads in their nurturing aspect. The cow is called the "great mother" and it symbolizes the productive power of the earth, the humid principle, plentifulness, reproduction, motherhood and maternal instincts. The cow's horns symbolize the crescent of the moon. Since it symbolizes both the earth and the moon the cow is both celestial and earthly. In Celtic tradition the earthly cow is depicted as a red cow with white ears. In Chinese tradition the cow represents the yin, the earth principle, and is sometimes depicted together with a horse that represents the yang and heavens. In ancient Egypt the cow was connected to the notion of "reviving warmth". It symbolized Hathor, the great mother of Egypt. The double-headed cow represents Lower and Upper Egypt. The legs of the celestial cow-goddess, Nut, mistress of the sky, are the Four Corners of the Earth, and the stars of the sky ornament the lower part of her body. Hathor, Isis and Nut are all depicted sometimes as cows or as having cow horns. In ancient Greek tradition the cow symbolizes a shape of Hera and Iou, a young girl Zeus fell I love with, and the jealous Hera turned her into a heifer, but she did not lose her speech. In Hindu tradition the cow is a sacred animal. It symbolizes fertility, plentifulness and the earth. Nandini, the cow that makes all wishes come true, gives milk and magic potion. When the cow represents the earth it appears together with the ox of the sky. The four legs of the sacred cow are the four castes. A black barren cow is consecrated to Niriti, goddess of misfortune and disease. Vak, the feminine aspect of Brahma, known as the "melodic cow" and the "cow of plenty" appears in the first description of the idea of the creation of the world from sound, and depicts the feeding of the world with milk, the gentle dust of the Milky Way. In Hindu faith, the cow and the ox represent the feminine and masculine aspects of the force that moves the universe. In Scandinavian tradition, the ancient cow, the "nurturer" emerged from the ice and started licking it in order to create the first man.

Coyote
In the Native-American tradition the coyote has an important symbolic meaning. It is the symbol of wisdom, intelligence and the ability to laugh at one's own mistakes. It is also a symbol of transformation, learning the balance between risk and safety and understanding that all things are sacred, and yet nothing is sacred. The symbol of the coyote also means learning that only when all the masks are removed it is possible to find the way to the source. It also symbolizes a song of glory to creation and a naive belief in the truth. The coyote is attributed with the ability to teach people how to raise the young (children, the inner child), enlightenment and the ability to sneak. It also brings about the rain and the flood. It symbolizes the transformer, the savior of heroes, the way out of danger. It is a lunar animal that symbolizes the spirit of the night, the "trickster" or deceiver of the Native-Americans in the western mountains. In Aztec tradition, one of the shapes of Ketzelkuatel – the double-headed coyote is its earthly aspect.

Crab
The crab symbolizes the understanding of the power of dance, the ability to escape by moving aside, the ability to pass through water (emotions), finding new uses for what seems unusable, the masculine aspects of the community and protecting the domestic sphere. Its strange walk, the crab walk, made it in certain

cultures a symbol of people that can not be trusted, dishonesty, unreliability, deception and the symbol of moneylenders.

In Buddhism the crab symbolizes the sleep of death, the time between reincarnations and rebirth between successful reincarnation. In Inca culture it symbolizes the horrifying aspect of the great mother, the waning moon, the devourer of the secular world. In Sumerian culture, crabs, shrimps and scorpions are connected with Nina, mistress of the lakes.

Crane

The crane is a symbol of light and spring, a symbol of star voyages in shamanism, as well as a symbol of longevity, new knowledge and elegance. It is also a symbol of helping others, wisdom, ability to see all the things connected to secrets and unique use of voice. In a vide range of cultures from China to the Mediterranean, the crane is an allegory of justice and longevity and a symbol of the good, persistent and diligent soul. It symbolizes the messenger of the gods, communication with the gods and the ability to enter into higher states of consciousness. In Celtic tradition, it is a shape of Pwyll, king of the underworld, a messenger that foretells war or death. It also symbolizes thriftiness and stinginess and a wicked woman. In Chinese tradition it is called the "patriarch of the tribe of the feathered creatures". The crane is the messenger of the gods, connector between heaven and earth, bearer of the souls to the western paradise, immortality, longevity, protective motherhood, vigilance and alertness, prosperity, high political position and happiness. The crane is usually connected with the sun and pine tree. Completely white cranes are sacred birds that live in the sacred islands. In Japan the "honorable lord crane" has an absolutely identical meaning to its symbolism in China. In Christian tradition the crane symbolizes vigilance, loyalty, kindness and good order in monastic life. In Greek and Roman tradition the crane was consecrated to Apollo as the messenger of spring and light.

Cricket

The cricket symbolizes finding the way out of the darkness by following the personal song and it is considered to be the one who teaches the power of the song in times of darkness. It is a symbol of good luck, of understanding the right timing and jumping out of dangerous situations and of communication and connection with the world of plants. In western culture the cricket is a symbol of family life and domesticity. In China it symbolizes the summer and courage. In Aesope's Fable that gave the cricket its symbolic meaning, the idle cricket enjoys the life of the moment and does not care about the future. Unlike the ant that works hard to gather food for the hard winter days. But than he suffers from cold, hunger and hardship when the winter comes because he did not work hard during the summer. Some see this fable as symbolic not just to wisdom versus sloth or lack of foresight, but also to "accumulating" good deeds instead of indulging in the pleasures of the material world.

Crocodile (alligator)

There are several different aspects in the symbolism of the crocodile. Due to its awesome look and strength it posed a real danger to people the areas in which it lived, and thus it symbolizes in the hieroglyph system of ancient Egypt evil and rage. In various traditions, being swallowed by a crocodile was considered going to hell. This leads to another meaning that was attributed to this animal – going through the dark in order to reach the light. The crocodile with the open mouth symbolizes going against the current and therefore it symbolizes liberation from the bonds of the world. Sometimes the crocodile is depicted as the "doorkeeper". In various traditions it described the dual nature of man, since the crocodile lives both in water and on the land. Like the lizard the crocodile also symbolizes silence – both were believed in to have no tongue. Its ability to lie quietly for a long time and wait for its prey while being almost invisible made it a symbol of patient revenge and a symbol of the ability to detect deceit and cunning. The crocodile is identified with the fertility of water, and at the same time it symbolizes a connection to mother earth. It symbolizes Set in its negative aspect as cruelty and evil. The Egyptian god Sobek has the head of a crocodile and symbolizes evil lusts, cunning, trickery, pretence and hypocrisy. After the crocodile swallowed the moon it cried with "crocodile tears" – tears of hypocrisy. It is consecrated to Apep, Serapis and Sobek, and sometimes depicted at the feet of Ptah. In Native-American culture, on the other hand, it symbolizes protection against manipulations, maternal protection, connection to mother earth, understanding the weather, ability, initiation and discovering ancient knowledge. Since it lives between the water and the earth and connected to mud and flora, it symbolizes fertility and strength.

Another aspect of the crocodile stems from its resemblance to the snake and the dragon as a symbol of knowledge. In ancient Egypt the dead were often described as turning into crocodiles of knowledge, an idea connected to the zodiac sign of the Capricorn (whose tail is a tail of a dragon). It is also a symbol of subverting the usual order and rebirth.

↔ SYMBOLS ↔

Cuckoo

The cuckoo symbolizes resilience, meeting one's personal fate and new and effective beginnings. The cuckoo's symbolism varies from love and marriage to betrayal and breaking the marriage vows or unacceptable/inappropriate behavior in marriage. In southern Europe the cuckoo symbolizes the spring and it was the sacred bird of the month of May, springtime in pagan rituals. In northern Europe it symbolizes the summer. The name of the cuckoo stems from the sound it makes that sounds to the human ear like "coo-coo". The English term for a betrayed husband "cuckold" stems from the cuckoo. Some say it has to do with the pagan spring festivals to which the cuckoo was consecrated and in which marriage vows were temporarily dissolved. Another explanation for "cuckoldry" – betrayal of spouse, also stems from the name of this bird, since it lays its eggs in the nests of other birds. This habit also made it a symbol of an unfaithful mother, of opportunism and irresponsibility. In ancient Greek culture the cuckoo symbolizes wedding, marriage, one of the transformations of Zeus in order to win Hera, and sometimes it appears in Hera's lap. In India the cuckoo is consecrated to Kama, god of love. In Japanese tradition, the cuckoo symbolizes love that is not rewarded or returned. In Phoenician tradition, the cuckoo symbolizes a royal bird that is carried on the royal scepters.

Deer

The deer is sometimes depicted together with the tree of life. It symbolizes beauty and gracefulness, listening skills, gentleness in touch, speech and thought and understanding what is necessary for survival. It also symbolizes gratitude and giving, self-sacrifice for noble causes, finding alternative ways to reach a goal, agility and light feet. In Native-American and Jewish cultures the deer is a symbol of light feet. In the Bible it appears as a symbol of masculine beauty. In the Song of Songs the beloved is described as a gazelle or a young hart. The same word (zvi) in the bible that is pronounced differently describes beauty and grace. This word was found in expressions describing beauty and grace that do not relate to the deer. Therefore, some see expressions such as "land of the deer" which appear in the bible as descriptions of the beauty of the Land of Israel. Others see the deer as a symbol of the Land of Israel as the deer is a common wild animal in Israel since ancient times (and still is if it is preserved), and there is even the species of this animal that is called the Israeli deer. In Buddhism, one deer on each side of the "wheel of law" represents Buddha preaching in the deer park in Sarneta, which made the wheel move. The deer represents meditation, humility and gentleness, but it is also one of the "three senseless creatures" of

Chinese Buddhism. It symbolizes love sickness together with the tiger as anger and the monkey as greed. In Celtic culture the deer are super-natural creatures of the world of animals and they are the cattle fairies and heavenly messengers. The deer's hide and horns were used as ritualistic cloths. In Chinese tradition the deer symbolizes longevity, high rank, success in a political position, wealth – since it is homophonic to the word "lu" which means reward, payment. In ancient Egyptian culture the deer was consecrated to Isis. In ancient Greek culture the deer was sanctified to Artemis, Athena, Aphrodite and Diana as lunar goddesses and to Apollo in Delphi. In Japanese tradition it symbolizes the gift of the gods of longevity but it also isolation and melancholy, when it is connected to the maple tree. As a symbol of self-sacrifice, the deer appears in mythology in the same context as its kinsman the hart appears in the story of the binding of Isaac. Agamemnon, king of Mycenae and the great Greek warrior and father figure was forced to sacrifice his daughter, the princess Iphigeneia, who was still a child, in order to appease Artemis, goddess of war. According to the legend, after the fire was lit and the girl was tied to the altar she "disappeared" or was abducted by the goddess or one of her heralds and in her place appeared a deer with a sliced throat. It should be mentioned that idea of replacing the human sacrifice with a deer is a rather late one, and some see it as a "transformation" of the legend since in later times the Greeks wholeheartedly rejected the custom of human sacrifices to the gods. Since the deer is a symbol of beauty, gentleness and even innocence and shyness, it became the appropriate symbolic "substitute" for the young princess.

Dog

Today the main meaning of the symbolism of the dog is of "man's best friend". The dog symbolizes absolute loyalty, camaraderie and friendship, unconditional love and protection of the home and friends. The dog was engraved at women's feet in mediaeval tombs bearing this meaning. Like the lion, it symbolizes the masculine trait of courage and heroism. The dog also symbolizes vigilance and alertness to danger, the ability to "smell" troubles from a distance, knowledge of all the sensual things and everything that is connected with the senses and healing emotional wounds in people. Like the falcon, it symbolizes nobility, and Plutarch said that it symbolizes "the conservative, vigilant, philosophical principle of life". "The dog with its coarse neck and black or golden face, symbolizes the messenger that travels between the high and low forces" (Apolious). At a somewhat similar meaning the dog symbolizes the understanding of the duality of faith and doubt and the keeper of the boundaries between this world and the other world. The gatekeeper to the underworld (the dog Cerberus in Greek mythology), the servant of the dead and Psychopomp (who escorts the dead to the other world). When the dog represents a lunar animal, together with the rabbit and lizard, it is the intermediary between the deities of the moon. In South East Asian cultures it is a solar animal, a yang animal during the day but a yin animal during the night. In ancient Egypt and Sumer, it was considered a solar animal. The dog is connected to all messenger gods and gods of destruction, and it is an attribute of Anubis and Hermes/Mercury. In Zoroastrianism, the dog and the seal are considered special among the "clean animals" and killing them is a sin. Hecate has her war dogs. The northern Garmer the "devourer" is usually depicted as a dog, and Brimo as the destroyer is accompanied by a dog.

The dog sometimes accompanies the "good shepherd" and is usually depicted as the companion of healers such as Asclepius, and of all the hunters of the mother goddess. The mother goddess is sometimes called the "bitch" and is depicted as a bitch giving birth. A black dog symbolized witchcraft, satanic forces, the dammed and death. Dogs and cats, as the witch's retinue, sometimes represent the witches' power to bringing rain and this is the source of the expression "it's raining cats and dogs". Since it is such a loyal friend of man, there was a widespread belief that as the dog accompanies its owner in life it can also accompany him after death and serve as an intermediary between him and the gods of the underworld. The dog is attributed with the qualities of the "deliverer of fire" and an expert of fire, as the inventor of fire by creating friction, or in certain cultures, as the one who saw the masculine secret of the making of fire and told it to the woman. When the dog is connected to fire, it has sexual symbolism as a result of the symbolic connection between sexuality and fire. In African culture, the dog is usually a folk hero, the inventor and deliverer of fire. In Alchemy, the dog, together with the wolf, is the dual nature of the philosophical mercury, and some say that it represents, together with the wolf, the refining of gold in antimony (a chemical element). In Native-American tradition the dog sometimes replaces the coyote. It is a thunder animal, deliverer of rain and the inventor of fire, and like the coyote a folk hero, ancient ancestor and messenger. At the beginning of the New Year the Araucanians used to sacrifice a white dog that would take their prayers to the other world. In Aztec culture, Kesoltel, god of death and the setting sun, had the head of a dog and was the patron of dogs. The dog was sacrificed many times in order to accompany the dead in their journey to the other world. The dog is the last sign in the Mexican zodiac, and it represents the time of "no-time" or chaos. It is a symbol of the end of the year and death, but also of rebirth and resurrection. In Buddhism, the lion dog, as a protective animal and keeper of the law, represents obedience and submission and repression of desires by the law. The dog is also an attribute of Yama, god of the dead. In Celtic tradition, the dog is connected with the healing water and accompanies the gods of hunting, gods of war and warriors and symbolizes the god of healing Noden. In Chinese tradition the dog symbolizes loyalty and devotion. The coming of a dog is an omen of future prosperity. The celestial red dog Tian Quo, is yang and helps to chase away the evil spirits. But as the watchman of the hours of the night, the dog becomes yin and symbolizes destruction and catastrophe. The dog is connected to meteors and solar and lunar eclipse when it gets "mad" and bites the sun or the moon. Buddha's lion dog is often depicted in Chinese art. In Christian tradition the dog represents loyalty, vigilance and alertness in the face of danger and even loyalty in marriage. As a shepherd dog it represents the "good shepherd" – a bishop or a priest. The dog is considered to have an extra sense because the shepherd dogs have very acute senses of hearing and smell. In ancient Egyptian culture, the dog was the guide of the solar god with the head of the hawk that kept the sun in its right course. It was consecrated to Anubis, the god with the head of the jackal or dog and to Hermes as the messenger god. The dog is an attribute of the great mother, Amenti. In the cultures of ancient Greece and Rome, the Greek term "cynic" (the origin of the word canine) that means "like a dog", represents boldness and flattery. According to Homer, the dog is shameless, but it is also an attribute of Hermes/Mercury, who are both messengers and as good shepherds are accompanied by the dog Serius "the alert one who sees all", that also accompanies the hunter Orion. The dog is connected to Asclepius, the god that heals by rebirth into a new life. Its loyalty lasts even after death. The dogs of Hades represent the gloom of dawn and sunset, that have hostile forces and are considered dangerous and demonic times. The monstrous dog Cerberus is the gatekeeper to the underworld. Hecate has dogs of war and dogs were sacrificed to her at crossroads. The dog was consecrated to Hercules and Diana/Artemis.

In Jewish tradition the dog represents impurity. In Hinduism, the hound is an attribute or companion of Indra. Yama, god of the dead, is depicted as a dog with four eyes, and it has a similar meaning to Hades in Greek mythology. In Islam the dog symbolizes impurity and it can be kept only as a watchdog. Devout Muslims avoid toughing it. In Scandinavian tradition, Odin/Wodin has two dogs and two ravens for counselors. The monstrous dog Garmer is the gatekeeper of the underworld. In shamanism, the dog represents the messenger of the spirits of the forest. In Semitic symbolism, the dog is connected with the scorpion, snake and all reptiles as hateful, evil and demonic. But in Phoenician iconography, the dog accompanies the sun and symbolizes Gala, the great healer, as an aspect of the great mother and the Accadian Blit-Eili whose crown is supported by dogs is depicted with a dog by her side. The dog is also an attribute of Astarte.

Dolphin

The dolphin is an animal with a strong mystical meaning. It lives in water, but it is a mammal, and it has amazing communication abilities, an attractive shape and face which seem to smile, that made it a positive, friendly and mainly spiritual symbol. The dolphin symbolizes divine gift and knowledge of the sea. It is the patron of mariners and sunken ships, king of fishermen and the power of the sea. It also symbolizes spells connected to the element of water, security and confidence, agility, balance and harmony, change, freedom, superior communication abilities, understanding the force of rhythm in personal life and the use of breath to release repressed or stressful feelings.

Two dolphins facing opposite directions represent the duality of nature, the dual cosmic stream of degeneration and development. The dolphin with an anchor symbolizes speeding and slowing down – "restrained" speed, i.e. prudence and cleverness, the intermediary stage between the two extremes of speed and slowness. Like the anchor, that symbolizes salvation, the dolphin is also an allegory of salvation and redemption. This image stems from ancient tales in which it is depicted as the friend of mankind. In Celtic tradition the dolphin is connected with the correct and proper cult of the gods and the forces of water. In Christianity it represents Jesus as redeemer of the souls and carrier of the souls over the water of death. A dolphin with a ship or anchor describes the church guided by Jesus. A dolphin pierced by a lance or anchor, is Jesus on the cross. When it replaces the whale, the dolphin symbolizes resurrection. In the culture of ancient Egypt, the dolphin is an attribute of Isis. In ancient Greek culture the dolphin escorts the souls to the islands of the blessed. It has both lunar and solar associations. Since it is connected to Apollo it is the light of the sun, but it also represents the feminine principle and the womb due to the resemblance between "delphis" (dolphin) and "delphys" (womb). It is a symbol of yearning when it appears with Aphrodite, the "woman of the sea" and with Eros. The dolphin is also an attribute of Poseidon, as the power of the sea and of Dionysos. Tetis rides naked on a dolphin. In Minoan culture, the dolphin symbolizes the power of the sea and is connected to Apollo Delphonis. In Mithridatic culture it is connected to Mithras, as light. In Roman culture, the dolphin represents the voyage of the soul beyond the sea of death the islands of the blessed. In Sumerian and Semitic traditions it replaced the fish in representing Eaa-Oanes. The dolphin is also an attribute of Ishtar and consecrated to Atargatis since it is connected to water.

Donkey

Like many other animals, the donkey has an ambivalent symbolism as well. It is highly valued because of its abilities and contribution to man, but the very "negative" traits that were attributed to it, such as stubbornness, usually stem from wisdom and knowledge of its limitations. On one hand, due to its simplicity and dreariness, it symbolizes humility, humbleness, patience, peace and fertility. On the other hand, it is also a symbol of stupidity, stubbornness, stiffneckedness, lechery, rudeness and profanity. The head of the donkey was attributed with fertility powers. As a beast of burden, it was used mainly by the poor and was popular symbol of hard work. This symbolism stems directly from the function of the donkey as a beast of burden that can carry very heavy loads on its back.

In ancient Egypt the donkey was a symbol of Set in its negative aspect. It symbolized the power of inertia and evil and was hated by Isis. In ancient Greek culture it is a symbol of laziness, blind love and senseless infatuation. As we can see in "A Midsummer Night's Dream", that uses this symbolism. In this play the queen of the fairies falls in love with a vagabond whose head is turned into a donkey's head as a symbol of blind love. It is consecrated to Dionysos and Tiphon as his coarse and ignorant aspect. It is consecrated to Priapus as the protective principle and to Chronos/Saturn. Silenus is sometimes depicted as riding on a donkey. King Midas was punished by Apollo who gave him donkey ears as a sign of stupidity and lack of musical hearing, when in a competition between Apollo who played the harp and Pan who played the flute, he judged in favor of Pan, although Apollo's playing was magnificent. In Jewish tradition the donkey represents stubbornness. In the prophecy of Zechariah a king would come to Jerusalem poor and riding on a donkey. This prophecy is connected in Christianity to Jesus, that in the New Testament entered Jerusalem riding on a donkey. In Christianity the donkey has a clearly ambivalent symbolism. It is a positive symbol in the context of the birth of Jesus, the escape to Egypt and his entrance to Jerusalem, and a negative symbol that was used to depict the Jews in the synagogues and as an animal with satanic connotation.

In Hinduism donkeys pulled the celestial chariot of Roana when he educated Sita. In Chinese culture the donkey represents stupidity. The expression "in year of the donkey and month of the horse" in response to the question "when?"

means – never. In Native-American traditions the donkey symbolizes stubbornness, the ability to carry out decisions, the ability to say no to others, resistance to do things that one knows that are wrong and ignoring the opinions of others. Bechaldia, goddess of death, is depicted beside a donkey in a boat around the river of hell. In dreams, the donkey, mainly when it appears decorated with symbols and in a ritualistic context, is usually the messenger of death or appears in connection with death, as destroyer of the continuation of life.

Dove

The Slavic tribes belief that at the time of death, the soul turns into a dove. The dove participates in the general symbolism of all birds – spirituality and transcendental power and sublimation. The dove itself symbolizes the spirit of life, the soul and the messenger of the soul, the transformation from one world or state to another. Therefore it symbolizes communication between two worlds, the spirit of light, purity and chastity (but in a number of cultures it is a symbol of passion and lust), gentleness and pleasantness, and it depicted as bringing peace and love. The doves were consecrated to all great mothers and queens of heaven and as such they represent maternity and femininity. Usually two doves accompany the mother goddess. The dove with the olive branch is a universal and familiar symbol of peace, but it also means regeneration of life and a symbol of Athena, the Greek goddess of wisdom. Doves drinking from a bowl symbolize the spirit drinking the water of the fountain of life. Consecrated doves are connected to funeral rituals. In Chinese tradition the dove symbolizes longevity, loyalty, order and organization and tradition transferred to future generations. It also symbolizes the spring, lust and is connected with mother earth. In Christianity the dove is a familiar and meaningful symbol. It symbolizes the Holy Ghost, purity, inspiring thought, peace, baptism, the annunciation if the birth of Jesus and the water of creation. Seven doves represent the seven gifts of the spirit. A flock of doves symbolizes the congregation of believers. A dove with an olive branch symbolizes peace, forgiveness and liberation, as Noah's dove brought an olive leaf as a sign of peace between god and mankind, and a symbol of forgiveness and the end of the flood (punishment). Christianity elaborates on the symbolism that stems from the biblical story – just as the dove could not find a resting place for its feet except the branches of the olive tree, so the Christian believer can find no other place but the church. A dove with a palm tree leaf symbolizes triumph over death. A white dove is the salvaged, purified soul, unlike the sinning soul that is represented by the raven. Doves on vine are the congregation of believers who seeks refuge in Christ. A pair of doves symbolizes love and harmony in marriage. A dove on the staff of Joseph (father of Jesus) symbolizes the husband of the pure virgin. The dove is the symbol of the knights of the Holy Grail and of the saints Benedict and Gregory. In ancient Egypt the dove symbolized innocence. The dove perching between the branches of the tree of life appears with the fruit of the tree and the fountains of the water of life. In Greek and Roman culture the dove symbolizes love and regeneration of life and a symbol of Zeus who was fed by the doves. The dove with the olive branch is a symbol of Athena as regeneration of life. The dove is consecrated to Adonis and Bacchus as bringing about first love and to Venus as the symbol of sensuality and love of pleasures. A dove with a star is the symbol of Venus Milite. In Jewish tradition, white doves, as a symbol of purity, were sacrificed in the temple for purification. The dove is also a symbol of the people of Israel. In the Bible it symbolizes simplicity, innocence, something unblemished, humility, humbleness, wholesomeness (from whole = complete), honesty and brooding. It physically personifies the soul of the dead.

In Hinduism, Yama, god of the dead, has owls and doves that serve as messengers. In Islam, the three holy virgins are represented by stones or pillars surrounded by doves. In Japanese tradition, the dove symbolizes longevity and respect and is consecrated to Hachimn, god of war. But a dove bearing a sword symbolizes the end of the war. In Minoan culture the dove is connected to the great mother. Doves and snakes symbolize the air and the earth and are attributed to her. In Semitic and Sumerian cultures the dove symbolized divine power. It was consecrated to Astarte and attributed to Ishtar as the great mother. A dove was sent from the ark in the Babylonian myth of the creation of the world on the seventh day of the flood.

Dragonfly
The dragonfly symbolizes both illusion and disillusion and seeing things as they are. It is a symbol of the mysteries of life in flight, the power of flight and the power of the storm. It symbolizes the ability to make a swiftly escape, activity, agility and speed. In various traditions it is connected to change and to the ability to understand dreams. It is also connected to the dragon (and this is why it is called the fly of the dragon – dragonfly). Sometimes its symbolism is similar to that of the butterfly, as a symbol of immortality and regeneration.

In Chinese symbolism the dragonfly symbolizes summer, instability and weakness. In Japanese tradition, the dragonfly symbolizes imperial and spiritual power. The dragon with the three seams symbolizes the Mikado (the emperor of

Japan). In Sumerian and Semitic traditions, the dragonfly symbolizes the "enemy" – the force of evil.

Duck

Since it floats on the surface of the water, the duck symbolizes the energy of water, mainly as emotional energy and the ability to clearly see through emotions on one hand, and the superficiality on the other. The smooth and natural movement of the duck in the water made it a symbol of grace in water. Since it is mostly on top of the water surface, it symbolizes cleanness and purity on one hand and the clear path through the water of emotion and life on the other. The duck is considered the spiritual helper of mystics and clairvoyants. In some cultures it was depicted as the symbol of chatter and deceit. In Native-American culture, the duck was considered to be an intermediary between the water and the sky. In Chinese and Japanese tradition it symbolizes marital bliss and loyalty, happiness and beauty. The male and female duck together symbolize the union of lovers, consideration and mutual understanding and loyalty. The duck is a yin animal. In ancient Egyptian culture, the duck was connected to Isis.

Eagle

The eagle is a solar animal. It symbolizes the heights, the spirit as the sun and the spiritual principle in general. It is a symbol of transcending the material in order to see the spiritual. It also symbolizes the ability to recognize spiritual truths, connection to higher truths and the ability to see the whole picture. The eagle represents the creative and intuitive spirit and connection to teachers, mentors and guides of the soul. It symbolizes all the gods of the sun, inspiration, elation, freedom from bondage, triumph, pride, power, tremendous strength and balance, observation, idolization, exemplary behavior, royalty, rule, height and the element of air. There was a belief that the eagle can fly to the sun, look into the sun's eye and identify with it, and therefore it symbolizes the spiritual principle of the person that can look straight to the heavens. Double-headed eagles are attributed to twin gods and may represent omniscience or double power. The conflict between the eagle and the ox, or between the eagle and the lion, in which the eagle always wins, symbolizes the triumph of the spirit or intellect over the physical. The conflict between the eagle and the snake, or the eagle with the snake between its claws symbolizes spiritual triumph. The eagle symbolizes the celestial powers of good and the snake symbolizes dark and evil forces. The eagle symbolizes the hidden light and the snake the hidden darkness. Both of them together are totality, cosmic unity and the union of mind and matter. An eagle that surrounds a pole is a symbol of the god of the sun as the "invincible sun" (sol invictus), and the triumph of light over darkness. As a bird that faces the full light of the sun, it symbolizes both the element of air and the element of fire. The opposite of the eagle is the owl, the bird of darkness and death. Since it is identified with the sun and with the idea of masculine activity that fertilizes the feminine nature, it symbolizes the father. Due to the eagle's amazing flight ability, speed and connection to the thunder and fire, it symbolizes heroic nobility.

In alchemy the eagle the flies high in the sky is the spiritual, liberated part of the primary matter, the "prima materia". The double eagle symbolizes the masculine-feminine mercury, the crowned eagle and the lion are the spirit and the earth, mercury and sulfur, representing the changing (volatile) principle and stationary principle, the changing of the stationary and solid by the volatile. Therefore, according to alchemist thinking, the lion surrounded by the eagle is wings = wind, flight = imagination, or the triumph of the spiritual, transcendence and sublimation (both refinement and the turning of solid matter into gas) over mater and the tendency to materialize.

In Native-American tradition, the eagle's feathers in the chief's crown represent the thunderbird, the universal spirit. The eagle is the reincarnation of the intermediary between heaven and earth and it also symbolizes the day. In certain cases the white eagle symbolizes the man and the brown eagle symbolizes the woman. Among the Australian Aborigines the eagle or hawk are identified with the deity. In Aztec culture, the eagle symbolizes celestial force, the lighted skies, the rising sun and the one that swallows the snake of darkness. In Buddhism, the eagle is the vehicle of Buddha. In Celtic tradition the eagle is connected to the healing water. In Chinese tradition the eagle symbolizes the sun, the yang principle, rule, warriors, courage, clutching ability and refusing to let go, acute sight and fearlessness. The eagle and the raven are connected to the gods of war. In Christianity the eagle symbolizes the spirit, transcendence, ambition, spiritual efforts, the day of judgement in which the sinners are thrown out of the nest. It also symbolizes the regeneration of youth. As a symbol of the ability to look into the sun without blinking, it symbolizes Jesus who sees god's splendor. Like the eagle that carries its young to the sun, so Jesus carries the souls to god. When the eagle goes down to draw out a fish from the sea it symbolizes Jesus who draws out the souls from the sea of sin. The eagle also symbolizes the inspiration of the apostles. When the eagle is depicted holding a snake in its claws, it symbolizes triumph over sin. When it tears its prey, it is the devil. The eagle is one of the four animals of the apocalypse. It is identified with the spirit of prophecy. The flight of the eagle, more than the bird itself, symbolizes the prayer that goes up to god and god's grace descending upon the individual. In ancient Egyptian culture the eagle is a solar symbol and it represents the sons of Horus. The letter A is represented by the shape of the eagle symbolizes the warmth of life, the source and the day. In Pre-Colombian America the eagle symbolized the struggle between the spiritual, celestial principle and the lowly world. In ancient Syria, in rites of identification, an eagle with human arms symbolized the cult of the sun. It also guided the souls towards immortality. In the culture of ancient Greece the eagle is solar and symbolizes spiritual strength, royalty, victory and the favor of the gods. It was attributed to Zeus and considered to be the carrier of his light and sometimes carry lightening in is claws. Originally, the eagle was the symbol of Pan, who gave it to Zeus. As a funerary symbol it symbolizes Ganimed, the handsome Trojan prince who was abducted by Zeus's eagle and brought to the Olympus, to serve as chief of butlers of the gods. Ganimed depicted as watering an eagle symbolizes the triumph over death. According to Homer, an eagle with a snake between its claws is a symbol of victory. The eagle is considered to be the bird that flies higher than all other birds, and therefore it was a sign of divine splendor in its highest sense. In Jewish tradition the eagle symbolizes regeneration, the east and parental compassion.

In Hindu tradition the eagle is the solar bird Garuda that Vishnu rides upon. It symbolizes Indra and is depicted as an important messenger who carries the Suma from Indra. In Mithridatic culture both the eagle and the hawk are attributed to Mithra as the god of the sun. In Roman culture the eagle is the bird of the solar storm, bearer of Jupiter's lightening and representing the emperor, honor, victory, grace and acute perception. Its image was engraved on coins as a symbol of the imperial power and of the Roman legions. In Scandinavian tradition the eagle symbolizes wisdom. It appears between the branches of the Yggdrasil tree as light struggling with the snake of darkness. It symbolizes Odin/Wodin. In Sumerian and Semitic traditions the eagle is the noon sun and attributed to Ninuirta or Ningvisu, the benevolent sun and the god of war of Canaan and Babylon. The eagle is consecrated to the Assyrian Ashur as the god of storm, lightening and fertility. The double-headed eagle symbolizes Nirgal, the scorching heat of the summer and noon sun. It also symbolizes Hitit and is the solar power and omniscience. Usually it holds between its claws a lunar rabbit or snake. Marduch is usually depicted as an eagle.

Jung, who ignored the multiple meanings attached to the eagle, simply defines it as "height" with all the implication that result from this specific location in space.

↔ **SYMBOLS** ↔

The star cluster of the eagle is located just above the person carrying the bucket of the Aquarius, that follows the movements of the bird so closely that it seems that he is pulled after it by invisible strings. Thus, Aquarius is identified with Ganimed, the handsome Trojan prince who was abducted by Zeus's eagle to serve as chief of butlers in the Olympus and with the notion that "even the gods themselves need the water of the forces of life".

Elephant

The symbolism of the elephant is somewhat complex since it contains a number of secondary mythical meanings. In the broad sense, the elephant is a symbol of the power and force of the libido (sexual drive), and of marital bliss. It symbolizes royalty, security, excellent memory, patience, loyalty, wisdom and the ability to take advantage of opportunities for learning and enrichment. Furthermore, in the more mystical sense – the elephant is connected to ancient wisdom. The elephant's tremendous power and its service to mankind as a beast of burden made it a symbol of the ability to overcome every obstacle, border or barrier. The elephant is also believed to have an excellent memory and it may be true in reality. The white elephant is considered a solar animal and it is a symbol of rarity, pedigree and uniqueness. In Buddhism the elephant is consecrated to Buddha. The white elephant appeared before the queen Maya to announce the birth of the ruler of the royal world. The elephant symbolizes compassion, love and kindness. Akshovia rides on an elephant. Although the elephant is the symbol of wisdom its skin symbolizes ignorance due to its thickness and coarseness. In Chinese symbolism the elephant symbolizes power, cleverness, intelligence and prudence and sovereignty. In Christianity the elephant is the symbol of Christ as the enemy of the snake when it tramples the snake under its foot. It also symbolizes purity, chastity and kindness. In Greek and Roman traditions it is attributed to Mercury as wisdom. It was said to be a religious animal that worships the sun and the starts and purifies itself when the new moon appears. It bathes in the river and awakens the heavens. In Roman art the elephant symbolizes longevity, immortality and triumph over death. In Hinduism the elephant is the vehicle of the god Ganesha, the power of sacred wisdom, cleverness, royal status, invincible power, longevity and intelligence. Indra, protector of the east, rides on the elephant Iravata. There was also a widespread belief that the world is supported by elephants. Due to their gray color and rounded shape, the elephants symbolize the clouds. As a result of a certain distortion of this symbolism there was a belief that the elephant can create clouds, and from that belief came the notion of the winged elephant.

↔ SYMBOLS ↔

Falcon

The falcon participates in a large part of the lunar symbolism of the eagle that it sometimes replaces. The falcon is the symbol of victory, ambition, flying over all plains, learning of swiftness and agility, controlling speed and movement, learning the tricks of life and understanding magic. The falcon helps to cure the soul and escorts the soul back to the world of the souls. It is a symbol of liberty and freedom and therefore symbolizes hope to all those who are in bondage whether moral, emotional or spiritual.

In Celtic tradition the falcon, like the eagle, is one of the first, primordial incarnations. It is the opposite of the lecherous rabbit and therefore symbolizes victory over lust. In Chinese tradition the symbolism of the falcon is ambivalent since it is both a solar force and a force of destruction and war. In ancient Egyptian tradition the falcon was the king of the birds. It represented the celestial principle and was used as an important and valuable hunting bird and as a representation of the omniscient Horus, who appears as a flacon or with a falcon head. In the burial ceremony of the Pharaoh, who was considered the physical incarnation of the god Horus, falcons were released to symbolize the king's soul flying to its heavenly home. Ra, the god of the rising sun, when identified with the Horus of the horizon, was also depicted sometimes with a falcon head. In Inca culture the falcon is a solar symbol and protecting spirit. In Scandinavian tradition Odin may travel to the earth in the shape of a falcon. The falcon is attributed to Frigg and symbolizes an aspect of Loki that is connected to fire. In ancient Greece the falcon was connected to Apollo and therefore, like the eagle, it was considered a solar bird.

Fish

The fish has many different symbolic meanings. Generally, it is considered a "spiritual" creature or a "penetrating movement", that is blessed with an "elevating" or "intensifying" force, that is connected to basic objects – i. e. the sub-consciousness. As a result of the close symbolic connection between the sea and the primary matter and the beginning of life, the fish became in some cultures a sanctified animal. In certain Asian rituals the cult of the fish was encouraged and its eating was prohibited for priests. Some see the fish as a symbol of the mystical ship of life, the spinning wheel that turns the cycle of life according to the lunar zodiac, i. e. the fish has multiple meanings that reflect the different aspects of its nature. In certain cultures, it has a phallic meaning, while in others it is a symbol with a purely spiritual meaning. Essentially, the symbolism of the fish has a double meaning. On one hand, it symbolizes the relations between heaven and earth, and on the other hand, due to the enormous number of the fish eggs, it became a symbol of fertility and reproduction, with a somewhat spiritual connection – fertility as a result of a heavenly blessing. In the later meaning, the fish can be found in the Babylonian, Phoenician, Assyrian, Chinese and Jewish symbolism. The fish is a common phallic symbol, a symbol of plenty, fertility and many offsprings, regeneration and rebirth, as well as renewed or reclaimed life, harmony, love and balance between intellect and emotion. Since it lives in water, it symbolizes the element of water and the power of water as giver and preserver of life, and as purifier and symbol of the world of emotions. The fish is connected with all the aspects of the mother goddess and all the lunar deities. Fish meals and the sacrifice of fish were part of the rituals of the gods of the lower world and the lunar goddesses of water, fertility and love such as Atargatis, whose son, Ichtis, was a sanctified fish, as well as Ishtar, Nina, Isis and Venus. Their day was Friday in which fish were eaten in their honor and the eating of fish was considered to be a remedy for infertility.

The fish were also a symbol of the followers and disciples of the various cults who swim in the water of life. Fish depicted together with birds are death and funeral symbols who symbolize hope for rebirth. The gods of fish and gods of the see ride on fish or dolphins who symbolizes freedom as the free movement in water – omnipotence.

A fish that swims downwards is a symbol of the "degeneration" of the mind in matter, and a fish swimming upwards symbolizes the development of mind-matter that returns to the primary principle. Two fish symbolize spiritual and physical force. Three fish with one head symbolize the Holy Trinity. This symbolism can be found in Celtic, Egyptian, Indian, Mesopotamian, Burmese, Persian and French tradition and it is almost universal, even today. Three joint fish symbolize the Trinity as well.

In alchemist symbolism, the fish symbolizes the mysterious matter. In Buddhism, the fish on the footprint of Buddha symbolizes freedom from passions, desires and attachments. Buddha was also called the "fisher of men". In Celtic tradition, the salmon and trout were connected to the sacred fountains as a symbol of profound knowledge of the gods. Noden was the fisher god. In Chinese tradition the fish symbolizes plentifulness, happiness, harmony, regeneration and the Emperor's effects. A lonely fish is a symbol of a lonely or solitary person – an orphan, widow or single man or woman. Two fish symbolize the joy of union, marriage and pregnancy. The fish is a symbol of Quan-Yin and the Teng dynasty. In Christian tradition the fish symbolizes baptism, immortality and resurrection (as the symbol of Jonah). In Christian art the sacrament fish with the wine and bread symbolize the Last Supper. The apostles are called "fisher of men". The fish symbolized Jesus in the Latin church but not in the Greek-Orthodox church. Three fish with one head symbolize the unity of the Holy Trinity and a combination of three fish symbolizes the baptism under the Holy Trinity. In ancient Egyptian culture the fish symbolized the phallus of Osiris. Two fish are the creative principle and a symbol of the bountiful Nile. The fish symbolizes fertility and it is the symbol of Isis and Hathor. In ancient Greek culture the fish is attributed to Aphrodite as the symbol of love and fertility, and to Poseidon as the symbol of the power of water. In the cult of Adonis, the fish were a gift to the dead. Orpheus was called "fisher of men". In Jewish tradition the meat of the whale is the food of the righteous in paradise. The fish is the symbol of the month of Adar (6th month of Jewish year), and in Passover fish is eaten so that "we will be the head and not the tail". The fish is an important fertility symbol in Judaism as well. In Hinduism the fish is the vehicle of Vishnu as the savior in his first incarnation when he saved the mankind from the flood and founded a new race at the beginning of the current cycle. The fish symbolizes richness, fertility and love. Two fish painted so that the head of one of them touches the tail of the other are an eonic symbol (see entry). In Hinduism a golden fish symbolizes Varuna as the power of water and as Manu, the savior from the flood. In Japanese tradition, the homophone of carp is love, and therefore fish (mainly the carp) symbolize love. In Rome the fish was a funerary symbol, a symbol of a new life in the other world, a symbol of Venus as the goddess of love and fertility and of Neptune as the power of water. In Scandinavian tradition the fish is attributed to Frigg as love and fertility. In Sumerian and Semitic cultures, the skin of the fish was used as a ritualistic costume for the priestesses of Eaa-Oanus, lord of the depths, who is depicted as a fish-goat or fish-ram. The fish is a symbol of Eaa and Tamuz as phallic and masculine, but it also symbolizes the feminine, love and fertility since it is connected with Ishtar. Adapa, "the wise", son of Eaa, is depicted as a fisherman. In Assyria, the fish appears with an axe, probably as a symbol of lunar and solar power and the power of the gods of water and the sky. In Crete we can find symbols of a fish with an axe. In Phoenicia and Syria fish were the consecrated food of the priests of Atargatis, who had sacred fishponds. The fish symbolized deities of love and was a sign of good fortune. In the zodiac, the mysterious matter is symbolized by two fish facing opposite directions, and the fish-goat is the symbol of the sign of Pisces. The sward fish is connected to the unicorn. The golden fish symbolizes harmony, peace, beauty, balance between intellect and emotion and prophecy.

↔ SYMBOLS ↔

Fly

The symbolism of the fly has a double meaning. The impressive traits of the fly have turned this insect into a symbol of transformation, sight and multi-dimensional vision, the ability to undergo necessary mutation, connection to colors and a symbol of courtship games. As such it is known in the more modern symbolism that is based on scientific research of the insect and its life. In ancient symbolism it symbolizes less positive traits since swarms of flies are attracted to things considered foul and defiled such as corpses, and tend to be a nuisance and a health hazard since they spreading diseases. Therefore, the fly is mostly connected with the gods of evil and corruption. Nevertheless, even in the ancient world some saw the fly as a symbol of super-natural forces, which created an ambivalent symbolism in itself, and sometimes the image of the fly was used to depict demons. In Christianity, the fly is a symbol of evil, deadly plague and sin. In Christian art there are paintings with the thorn bird symbolizing the savior while the fly symbolizes the disease. In Phoenician culture, Beelzebub, the lord of flies is the agent of the forces of destruction and decay. But some see it as the Psychopomp god who escorts the soul to its final resting-place and is considered to have prophetic powers. As we can see in the Old Testament in the story of king Ochozias (Akhaziah) (Kings 2, 1:2), that sent messengers to Accaron (Ekron) to ask Beelzebub whether he would recover from his illness. Like the bee, the fly appears in a number of ancient pagan cultures as a symbol of the soul that tries to enter into a woman's womb in order to reincarnate in the flesh.

Fox

The fox is a popular symbol of shrewdness, camouflage, sneaking and cleverness. Other widespread meanings of this animal (mainly in Native-American culture) are agility, perseverance, gentleness, the ability to move secretly and be invisible, observation and watchfulness, transformation, feminine courage, the ability to see the invisible and hypocrisy. In Chinese tradition, the fox symbolizes longevity, cleverness, powers of transformation and the spirits of dead souls. In Japanese tradition too the fox also symbolizes longevity as well as forces of magic and witchcraft, both good and evil, a messenger and the messenger of the god of rice, Inari. A black fox symbolizes good luck and a white fox – disaster. Three foxes together also symbolize disaster or destruction. In Christianity the fox was in the Middle Ages a common symbol for the devil, the deceiver. It symbolizes deception and trickery, shrewdness, cunning, falsehood and fraud. A fox that destroys the vineyard was symbolic of the infidels and enemies of the church. In Scandinavian culture, "light of the fox" is the shining light of the North Pole.

↔ **SYMBOLS** ↔

Frog

The frog symbolizes the transition from the element of earth to the element of fire and vice versa, since it is an amphibious creature. It is a lunar animal and there are many legends about the "frog on the moon". The frog also plays a major part in rain ceremonies. It is a rain-delivering animal that symbolizes purification and cleanliness, fertility and eroticism. Since it comes up from the water it symbolizes transformation, rebirth and revival. The "great frog" that supports the universe symbolizes the primary matter, prima materia, when it is black and unprocessed or separated. It represents the element of water and the primary mud, the basic material of creation.

In Celtic tradition the frog symbolizes the lord of the earth and the power of healing water. In Chinese culture it symbolizes the yin, lunar principle. A frog in the well symbolizes a person with limited understanding and vision. In Christianity the frog has an ambivalent symbolism. It symbolizes rebirth but also the repulsive aspect of sin, earthly pleasures, heresy, greed, evil and envy. In ancient Egyptian culture the green frog of the Nile symbolizes new life, plentifulness, fertility and yield. It is a symbol of the regenerating and reviving forces of nature, longevity and power that comes out of weakness. The frog symbolizes Heket as the embryonic forces in water, and the defender of mothers and newborn babies. It is also a symbol of Isis and Herit, the goddess who helped Isis in the revival of Osiris. In the cultures of ancient Greece and Rome the frog is a symbol of Aphrodite/Venus and a symbol of fertility, carnal lust and harmony between lovers. In Hindu tradition the "great frog" that supports the universe, symbolized the primary, black matter before its separation. In Native-American tradition the frog symbolizes the animal that reminds people the connection with all forms of life in the universe, the understanding of emotions and the songs that celebrate the beginning of the ancient sources of water.

According to Madam Belawsky, the frog is one of the main creatures that are connected with the notion of creation and rebirth, not just because it is amphibious but because of its changing periods of appearance and disappearance.

Goat, he-goat, mountain goat

The he-goat symbolizes manhood, independence, plentifulness, vitality and creative energy. As a symbol it sometimes replaces the deer and the antelope. Since it lives in high places it symbolizes superiority, search for new heights, security, stable foothold and light movement. Some also see it as a symbol of relieving feelings of guilt and the ability to understand the creatures and energies

75

of nature. The goat symbolizes the reproductive and creative feminine forces, fertility and plentifulness. In Chinese culture the he-goat is a homophone of Yang and thus it represents the masculine principle. It also symbolizes peace and goodness. In Christian tradition the he-goat became a totally negative symbol and was often used in art to describe the devil. It symbolizes the dammed, sinners, lust and lechery. In the cultures of ancient Greece and Rome it symbolizes male potency, creative energy and passion. The he-goat was consecrated to Zeus Dictinus. The mountain goat was consecrated to Artemis. The symbol and shape of Dionysos sometimes resemble the mountain goat as well. The satires are creatures that are half he-goat and half man, with he-goat horns. The god Pan had the legs, horns and beard of a he-goat. In Hinduism the he-goat symbolizes the fire, creative warmth and together with the ram it is a symbol of the Indian god of fire Agni who rides on a he-goat. In Scandinavian and Teutonic the he-goat was consecrated to Thor, god of thunder and fertility and his chariot was pulled by he-goats. In Sumerian-Semitic tradition the he and she goat usually appear with Marduch and the hunter gods. It is a symbol of the Babylonian god Ningirsu. The he-goat or fish-goat symbolizes Eaa-Oanes, lord of the depths of the sea. In ancient Egyptian culture the mountain goat was consecrated to Set and its symbolism was similar to that of the deer.

Goose

The goose is considered to be a benevolent animal that is connected with the great mother. We can find it mainly in folktales (The Grimm Brothers' fairytales and Beatrix Potter's Mother Goose Stories). It is connected to fate and symbolizes the dangers and fortune in human existence. It is a solar animal that symbolizes breath, the spirit, vigilance and alertness, love, the housewife and the capable wife. Sometimes it replaces the swan in the world of symbolism. In Celtic tradition, the goose symbolizes war and the gods of war. In China, the wild goose is considered to be a bird of paradise. It symbolizes the Yang, masculinity, light, inspiration, agility, the messenger bird, a messenger bearing good tidings, marital bliss, seasonal changes and the autumn. Although it is a solar bird, it is connected in Chinese art with the autumn moon. In Japan the goose symbolizes the goose the autumn, agility and the messenger bird and it is connected in art with the autumn moon. In Christianity the goose symbolizes vigilance and alertness, watchfulness, care and thriftiness. In Ancient Egyptian culture the goose of the Nile that is called the "great chatterer" is the creator of the world who laid the cosmic egg, from which the sun, Amon-Ra, emerged. The goose is also attributed to Set or Geb, god of the earth who symbolizes life. It is the symbol of Isis, Osiris and Horus. In ancient Greek culture the goose symbolizes vigilance and the good housewife. It is attributed to Hera and also symbolizes the solar Apollo, Hermes – the messenger, Mars, the god of war and Eros the god of love and the eloquent Paitho who masters the art of rhetoric. In Roman culture it symbolizes vigilance and standing on guard. Sacred geese were kept in Rome and were connected to Mars, the god of war, to Juno, the queen of the sky and to Priapus as a symbol of fertility. In Hinduism, the wild goose is the vehicle of Brahma, the creative principle. It symbolizes freedom from bondage, spiritualism, dedication, learning and eloquence. In Sumerian culture the goose was consecrated to Bao, goddess of the farmyard. In Native-American culture it symbolizes happiness, going along the path of the soul, understanding the power of community and helping others in times of need.

Grasshopper
The grasshopper symbolizes star voyage, leap of faith, a leap beyond space and time, a leap without knowing where the landing will be, leaping over obstacles, new leaps forward and the ability to change trades quickly. In Chinese tradition the grasshopper symbolizes plentifulness, many sons, good virtues and good fortune. In European symbolism the grasshopper symbolizes irresponsibility, wastefulness, no concern for the future and summer pleasures. In ancient Greece the golden grasshopper symbolized nobility, a born aristocrat. In Jewish tradition it symbolizes the insignificance of mankind, mainly in relation to god, but the spies who came to scout the Land of Israel also described themselves as grasshoppers in face of the mighty natives of the land.

Hawk
The hawk is a solar bird and a messenger bird in many traditions and shares some of the symbolism of the eagle. It symbolizes power, royalty, nobility, a messenger delivering spiritual messages, the ability to observe what is going on, acute perception, seeing the whole picture, long term memory and recalling previous life, wisdom, courage, guardianship, experience and experimenting, overcoming problems, creativity, truth, enlightenment and the ability to use opportunities wisely. In ancient Egypt the hawk symbolized the soul. On the other hand, in Mediaeval Christianity it was compared to the wicked mind of the sinner. It is attributed to all the gods of the sun and gods with the shape or head of a hawk are solar gods. Usually it symbolizes the sky. Like the eagle, the hawk is believed to be able to fly to the sky and look directly into its eye. In ancient Egyptian culture is symbolized the soul or the spirit and was considered a royal

bird, a symbol of inspiration and of the god Ra – the sun. Other gods depicted with a hawk or a hawk head are Ptah, Horus, Mentu, Rekhu, Soker and Kebensuf. Sobek-Ra is the alligator with the head of the hawk, and the sphinx sometimes has a head of a hawk as well. The hawk is also the symbol of Amenti, the great mother and goddess of the west and the underworld. In Aztec culture the hawk symbolizes a messenger of the gods. In the cultures of ancient Greece and Rome, the hawk is called "the speedy messenger of Apollo". In Hinduism, Gaiatri, the hawk, brought Suma from the sky. It is also the vehicle of Indra. In ancient Iranian tradition it is attributed to Aura-Mazde or Ormuzd, as light. In Mithridatic culture the hawk is attributed to Mithra as god of the sun.

Hedgehog
In must traditions the hedgehog symbolizes mainly innocence, the renewal of the sense of wonder and miracle in life and confidence in the spirit. Some see it as a symbol of creating one's personal path, the ability to allow others to go in their personal paths without disruption, and in general non-disruption and non-interference. Since it turns into a ball of thorns it became a symbol of guarding borders and the ability to defend one's self against threats. Contrary to the typical symbolism of innocence and shyness, that stem from the animal's life in nature, in Christianity the hedgehog was attributed with negative symbolism that is connected to the relations between the hedgehog and the farmer, i. e. the symbol of the hedgehog in the eyes of humans. Since it was claimed that the hedgehog damages the vineyards, it symbolizes the "wicked" evildoer, the robber of grapes as the devil is the robber of souls. In Sumerian culture it was attributed to Ishtar, and in general it can be seen as a symbol of the great mother.

Hen
The hen symbolizes caring and maternal concern, procreation, watchfulness and worry. Since it collects grains it symbolizes the ability to collect the answers others can not grasp. In Mediaeval Christianity, the black hen became a symbol of the diabolic agent, or an aspect of the devil. A hen that quacks loudly sometimes symbolizes a domineering wife, matriarchy or a courageous woman. In Christianity, a hen with chicks symbolizes Jesus with his flock.

Heron
The Heron symbolizes self-confidence, self-reliance, boarders, self-esteem, balancing multiple tasks, vigilance and alertness, variety, dignity and nobility. The heron is considered to be solar bird but it is also connected to water since it

is a water bird. In Buddhism and Taoism the heron has a symbolism identical to that of the stork. In Chinese and Japanese symbolism the white heron is connected to the black raven as yang and yin, sun and moon, light and darkness. The heron is considered to be quiet and serious. It is the "pensive" one while the raven is lively and chatty. In ancient Egyptian culture, the heron was considered the first incarnation of the soul after death. The Benu bird (a bird that is sometimes connected with the Phoenix and believed to be the incarnation of the soul of Osiris) is considered an aspect of the heron as well. The heron in ancient Egyptian culture symbolizes the rising sun, renewal, the return of Osiris as the bird of the tide of the Nile and the regeneration of life, as it leaves the river and flies over the fields at the tide of the Nile.

Hippopotamus
The hippopotamus symbolizes power, correct use of aggressions, protection of the family, the wrath of the mother defending her children, the birth of new ideas and the ability to move gracefully through emotions (as the hippopotamus moves in water that symbolizes the world of emotions) and the North Pole. Sometimes it is identified with the "behemoth" that appears in the bible. The source of the word "hippopotamus" is Greek and means "river horse". The Greeks did not encounter hippopotamuses in the rivers of their country and learned about them from stories of travelers and visitors. In ancient Egyptian culture the hippopotamus represents the great mother, Amenti. Taweret, the hippopotamus goddess symbolizes generosity and protection and is connected with the Egyptian ankh. The red hippopotamus is Set in its negative aspect and the hippopotamus hip is the "phallic leg of Set" as the symbol of power, masculinity and male potency. In the Hieroglyph system, the hippopotamus represents power and strength and is connected with water and fertility.

Horse
The horse symbolizes power, strength, endurance and stamina, dedication, awareness of the power that can be achieved by true cooperation, expending one's potential abilities, dominance and environmental control, freedom, trips and voyages. It also symbolizes communication between different species, warning against possible danger, a guide to overcoming obstacles and patron of travelers. When it is white or gold it is a solar animal and appears with the gods of the sun and pulls their chariots. But it is also lunar like the element of humidity, the sea and chaos and the horses of the gods of the oceans. It is a symbol of both life and death, solar and lunar. It symbolizes wisdom and

intelligence, knowledge, nobility, light, dynamic power, speed, quick thinking, the rapid passage through life, forces of witchcraft and knowledge of the future and the wind and the waves of the sea. A white horse galloping symbolizes sometimes star voyages. It also appears beside the gods of fertility. The winged horse symbolizes the sun or the cosmic horse, that is white as well, and symbolizes pure intellect, cleanness and purity, light and life and it is the horse of heroes. The black horse is a funerary symbol that symbolizes the death of heroes or heroic death and chaos. In Buddhism it symbolizes the invincible, the hidden nature of things. Buddha left his home on a white horse. In Chinese Buddhism, the winged horse carried the book of laws on its back. In Celtic tradition the horse was attributed to protecting gods of the horses, forces of darkness and forces of the dead. The horse is sometimes a solar symbol, a symbol of male potency and fertility. It also serves as a psychopomp (escorting the dead to the other world) and messenger of the gods. In Chinese culture the horse symbolizes the heavens, fire, yang, the south, speed and preserving the status quo. It is a benevolent symbol. The horse is the seventh among the symbolic animal of the twelve earthly branches. The horseshoe symbolizes good luck. When the cosmic horse is lunar it is parallel to the earth cow, but when it appears with the dragon, that symbolizes the heaven, the horse itself symbolizes the earth. The winged horse, carrying the book of the laws on its back represents good luck and wealth. It also symbolizes fertility and the power of the ruler. In Christian symbolism the horse symbolizes the sun, courage and generosity. During the Renaissance it became a symbol of sexual passion. The four horses of the apocalypse symbolize war and death. In ancient Greek culture white horses pulled Apollo's chariot of the sun and were also connected as the principle of humidity with Poseidon as god of the sea and earthquakes, who may appear as a horse. Pegasus, (winged horse, see entry) symbolizes the passage from one plane to another. It carries the lightening of Zeus. In Hinduism the horse is the physical vehicle that also drives the spirit. Kalki, the white horse, will be the last incarnation or the vehicle of Vishnu when it appears for the tenth time, bringing peace and salvation to the entire world. Varuna, the cosmic horse, was born from the water. The Gandahvas, the horsemen, symbolize the combination of natural fertility and abstract thought, wisdom and music. The horse is the protector of the south. In Iranian tradition, the chariot of Ardvisura Anhita is pulled by the four white horses of the wind, rain, cloud and rain mixed with snow. In Islamic tradition the white horse symbolizes happiness and wealth. In Japanese culture the white horse is the vehicle or shape of Bao Quwanon, goddess of grace and great mother. She may appear as a white horse, with a horse's head or with the shape of a horse in her crown. The black horse is attributed to the god of rain. In Mithridatic culture white horses pulled the chariot of Mithra as god of the sun. In Roman culture, white horses pulled the chariots of Apollo and Mithra. The horse was attributed to Diana, the huntress. In Scandinavian and Teutonic tradition the horse is consecrated to Odin/Wodin, who had an eight-legged horse Sleipnir. In shamanistic tradition the horse is a psychopomp (escorts the soul to the other world). The horse is also connected to sacrifice and it is a sacrificial animal of the shamans in Siberia. Its head and skin has ritualistic meaning. In Sumerian and Semitic cultures the chariot of the god of the sun Marduch was pulled by four horses. A horse's head was the symbol of Carthage. The winged horse appears on Carthaginian coins. In Taoist tradition the horse is the symbol of Chang Quo, one of the eight immortals in Taoism.

Hyena

The hyena has a somewhat ambivalent symbolism. In Native-American culture it symbolizing the knowledge of secrets of the wilderness. It is also a symbol of resilience, power, understanding how to control plagues, understanding the value of cooperation, patience, singing the personal song of the soul, perseverance in hunting, defense of borders, connection to the eagle, communication in dark areas and understanding the importance of life in a community. On the other hand, in a broader context, the hyena became the symbol of the greatest vice, impurity, instability and double-faced person. In Christianity it symbolizes the devil that feeds on the dammed.

Ibis

The ibis symbolizes ancient wisdom, intelligence, enlightenment and the ability to cast spells. In ancient Egypt the ibis symbolizes the soul, ambition, preservation of the status quo and the morning and it is consecrated to Thoth, the god of wisdom, magic, sorcery, writing and keeping records. There was a belief in ancient Egypt that Thoth was hovering over the Egyptian people like an ibis and thought them recondite knowledge, art and science. As the enemy of reptilians in their lunar aspect, the ibis is a solar bird, but since it lives near water, it is lunar and sometimes depicted with the crescent of the moon on its head. The Greeks connected the ibis with the messenger god, Hermes.

Jackal

The jackal that can see both in daylight and in the darkness of the night became a symbol of the ability to see in the darkness – both physical and spiritual. It is the symbol of the Egyptian god Anubis "finder of the path", "opener of the way" that is depicted as a black jackal or as having a jackal head. The jackal serves as a psychopomp who leads and guides the souls from this world to the other world and is also connected with cemeteries. Another symbolism is the depiction of the jackal as a symbol of understanding how to use of opportunities and some see it as a symbol of access to previous life, star voyages and a symbol of the connection to the Egyptian pyramids and to the Orion star cluster. In Buddhism the jackal is a symbol of a person that is deeply rooted in evil and can not understand the Dharma. In Hinduism, Jackals and ravens follow the goddess Kali as a representation of destructive force.

Jaguar
The jaguar is a symbol of super-natural sight, movement without fear in the dark and unfamiliar places, seeing the way through chaos, understanding the patterns of chaos, promoting the work of the soul, empowering the self and transformation. In Aztec culture it symbolizes the forces of darkness that struggle with the solar eagle. In Mexican culture it is considered the messenger of the spirits of the forest. In Shamanistic symbolism it is sometimes a spirit the shaman is familiar with or who cooperates with the shaman, and sometimes an animal that the shaman wears its shape.

Jellyfish
The jellyfish symbolizes sensitivity to the water's fundamental energy – emotions, understanding the value of floating rather than swimming in emotionally hard times and during emotional trials, correct use of softness and the ability to rescue one's self from life's dangers, both physical and emotional.

Kangaroo
The kangaroo, as an animal that carries its young in a pouch in its belly, became a symbol of protection of the young and creating a safe domestic environment. The special jumping power of this animal made it a symbol of leaping far away from problematic and negative situations. The kangaroo also symbolizes the ability to adjust to new situations.

Kingfisher
The kingfisher symbolizes peace, happiness, love and peace of mind and is connected to tranquil seas and oceans/ It also symbolizes clear vision through emotional water, complacency toward the environment and the ability to dive

into emotional water in order to draw out from them the personal dreams. In Christian tradition the kingfisher is connected to the legend of the Holy Grail and the fishermen at the Sea of Galilee who became the apostles of Jesus. The kingfisher is a master fisher and fishing according to Christian symbolism of the kingfisher is not just the "fishing of people" (as Jesus said to the fishermen at the Sea of Galilee, that from now on they would be fisher of men instead of fisher of fish). But it also symbolizes the ability to throw the bait into the most inner depths and pull out from them the hidden knowledge. In Chinese symbolism the kingfisher symbolizes days of tranquility, calmness, beauty, honor, speed, well made feminine costume and reclusive or shy nature.

Kiwi
The kiwi, a bird that lives on the face of the earth in Australia and New Zealand symbolizes connection to ancient aboriginal wisdom. It also symbolizes the understanding of transformations of the earth and the ability to "scrape" the truth out, like in the biblical phrase "the truth shell flourish from the land". The kiwi symbolizes finding the roots of the cosmic and sublime truth through observation and digging and scraping the earthly element, the land and the material world.

Lion
The lion, although it is a typical solar symbol, is somewhat ambivalent since it has lunar meanings in certain cultures and it symbolizes both good and evil. As a solar symbol it symbolizes the warmth of the sun, the heat and strong light of midday hours, royalty, strength, courage, justice, law, military power and the king of the animal. But it also symbolizes cruelty, rage and the animalistic side of mankind. It is a symbol of war and the symbol of the gods of war. As a lunar symbol, the lioness accompanied the great mother and pulls her chariot and symbolizes maternal instincts. It is usually depicted with the virgin warrior goddesses. The goddesses of Crete, Syria and Sparta, are all symbolized by the lioness. The lioness also appears with the winged Artemis, Sybil, Fortune and the Gorgons. In India and Tibet the lioness is the symbol of Tara, as the symbol of earth and motherhood.

The lion and unicorn symbolize the solar-lunar, masculine-feminine power struggle. The lion killing the boar symbolizes the power of the sun that kills the winter boar. The lion and dragon devouring each other symbolize a union without losing one's identity. The lion together with the lamb symbolize the primordial unity and return to paradise, the end of the material world and freedom from its struggles. A pair of lions is the "master of the double power". The lions are the keepers of gates, doors, entries and treasures and the guards of the tree of life. They usually support the symbols of the sun and symbolize courage, vigilance and alertness. The winged lion or Griffin may symbolize the union of the double nature of the androgynous. The green lion is the young god of grain before it matures and becomes the golden god of grain.

In alchemist symbolism, the red lion, sulfur, is the masculine principle, together with the unicorn, mercury as the feminine principle. The green lion is the beginning of alchemist work. Two lions symbolize the dual nature of Mercurios, the philosophical mercury – intellect, knowledge.

In Buddhism the lion symbolizes spiritual zeal, defender of the law, the wisdom of Buddha, progress, awareness and consciousness, enlightenment and courage. Buddha is sometimes depicted as sitting on the lion throne. The lioness is the symbol of Tara.

Ratnasambhva rides on a lion. A lion with a lion cub under its paws symbolizes Buddha who rules the world and a symbol of compassion. The lion's roar represents Buddha who bravely teaches the Dharma. In Chinese symbolism the lion symbolizes courage, energy and power. The lion with the ball symbolizes the sun or the cosmic egg and dualism in nature. The lion as power together with the horse as speed represent the man in marriage, while the flowers represent the woman.

In Christianity the lion has an ambivalent symbolism as the power and strength of Jesus and his royal nature as the lion of Judah on one hand, but on the other hand it also symbolizes the devil as the "roaring lion". There is a belief that the lion sleeps with its eyes open and therefore it symbolizes spiritual vigilance and alertness. There was a belief that the lion cubs are born dead and their father breaths into them the breath of life, and therefore the lion also symbolizes resurrection. As a solitary animal it symbolizes individualism, loneliness and the monk. In ancient Egyptian culture the lion symbolized defense and the watchman. It is a solar animal when depicted beside the disc of the sun and a lunar one when depicted beside the crescent. The double-headed lion represents the sun gods of sunrise and sunset. Two lions back-to-back with the sun disc are past and future or yesterday and tomorrow. The lioness is attributed to Sekmet and the mother goddess and symbolizes motherhood. But as Sekmet it can also symbolize vindictiveness. The lion with the disc of the sun symbolizes Ra, the god of the sun, and with the crescent it symbolizes Osiris, judge of the dead. Tafnut has a lion's head. In ancient Greek culture the lion accompanies Pheobus, Artemis, Sybil, Thiche and the Gorgons and often

Dionysos as well. The lion pulled the chariots of Sybil and Juno. The lion's hide symbolizes Hercules, who in this struggle with the lion symbolizes the solar hero who defeats death. In Jewish tradition the lion is connected to the tribe of Judah: "a cub of the lion of Judah". In Hinduism it symbolizes the fourth incarnation of Vishnu. Agni's lion is sometimes half-human half lion. The lion and lioness together depict the Shakta-Shakti; the lion is the superior master of rhythm and the lioness is the power of the spoken word. The lion is the defender of the north and attributed to the goddess Devi and Durga as destroyers of the demons. In Iranian symbolism the lion symbolizes royalty, solar power and light. In Islam it symbolizes protection against evil. In Japanese symbolism the lion is the king of the animals and appears together with the peony as the queen of flowers. The lion ball symbolizes emptiness. In Taoism, the lion ball symbolizes the sun and the fourth stage of initiation. The lion and ox together are the symbol of death. Th lion and the deer together symbolize the moment of death. In Roman culture the lion symbolizes solar power and royalty and is attributed to Apollo, Hercules and Fortune and symbolizes man's triumph over death. In Sumerian and Semitic cultures the lion symbolizes the fire of the sun, wisdom, power, courage and the symbol of the Sumerian god of the sun Marduch. Inanna/Ishtar as the great mother is accompanied by two lions. A lion with a branch between its paws or a double headed lion represents Ninib, a solar god and a god or war. The Chaldean Nirgal, the god of death and war, is depicted as a lion and symbolizes the hostile aspect of the sun. A lion accompanies Atargatis as the great mother.

In New Age symbolism the lion appears mainly in meanings of fraternity, courage, energy, power and strength, freedom from stresses and anxieties, strong family connections and self-fulfillment.

According to Jung, the lion, in its savage state, symbolizes repressed desires and is sometimes a symbol of being "devoured" by the subconscious.

Lizard

The lizard is considered a lunar animal. It symbolizes the principle of humidity. In ancient times it was believed that the lizard has no tongue and lives on dew, and therefore it symbolized silence. In Egyptian and Greek symbolism the lizard represents divine wisdom and good fortune and symbolizes Seraphis and Hermes. In Zoroastrian tradition it was the symbol of Ahriman and evil. In Christianity it also symbolizes evil and the devil. The lizard is a symbol of Sebazius, and it often appears in the hand of Sebazius. In Roman mythology the lizard is described as sleeping during winter and therefore it symbolizes death and redemption. The tarotaro lizard is a folk hero among the Aborigines in

Australia. In New Age symbolism and in Native-American culture the lizard symbolizes separation from the ego, coping with fears, controlling dreams, movement in other worlds and the ability to revive and renew all that has withered or lost.

Locust

The locust symbolizes the forces of destruction, disaster and calamity. The locust destroys everything it finds in its way. Mainly in Jewish and Christian symbolism the locust appears as a plague and divine retribution in Exodus and the Revelation of St. John in the New Testament. In the Revelation of St. John, the locust is described as a plague, divine retribution to those who do not bear the sign of God on their foreheads, that would torment these people for five months until they would seek death to escape their plight.

Mole

The mole symbolizes connection to the energies of the earth, knowing the plants, roots, minerals, seeds, rivers and hidden resources of the earth. It also symbolizes seclusion, inner reflection, blindness to the material world while seeing light and darkness only, sensitivity to touch and vibrations, understanding the energies and their flow and natural love. Sometimes it is called the "protector of low regions". Since it dwells in the depth of the earth it also symbolizes earthly-material powers and the powers of darkness. Some see it as symbolizing the misanthrope, the hater of mankind, due to its solitary existence deep in the earth.

Monkey

The monkey generally symbolizes unconscious or dark activity, but this symbolism has two sides – the unconscious activity can become dangerous when it make a person spiritually or mentally inferior. But on the other hand it can become an advantage – like all the subconscious forces – in the most unpredictable moment. Therefore, in China the monkey is a symbol of good health, success and protection when it is connected to spirits, sorcerers and fairies. Another symbolism of the monkey in Chinese tradition is of ugliness, trickery, power of transformation, playfulness, causing damages, arrogance and imitation. It is the ninth animal of the twelve animals of the earthly branches. In Christianity the monkey symbolizes malice, deception, lust, sin, something improper, frivolity, contempt, life of luxuries and pleasures, the devil and those who lead the world astray. It is also a symbol of idolatry. On the other hand, in

Chinese tradition the monkey symbolizes overcoming sin, and a monkey with an apple in its mouth symbolizes autumn. In Hindu tradition the monkey symbolizes generosity, a symbol of the monkey god Hanoman. The Native-Americans saw the monkey as a symbol of good health, movement through the ego, understanding success, the ability to change the environment, protection of the family and understanding states of exaggeration and excess. In the Maya culture, the god of the northern star had a monkey's head.

The three mystical monkeys, one covering its eyes, the other covering its ears and the third covering its mouth symbolize "see no evil, hear no evil and say no evil". In Buddhism it is considered one of the tasteless animals, always greedy and wants to take more and more.

Nightingale

The nightingale's symbolism stems mainly from its singing ability. It is also connected with the night and the moon. In Native-American tradition, the nightingale symbolizes correct use of song for healing, use of song to overcome fears, connection with the moon and using frequency energy in order to see between the shades.

Octopus

The octopus symbolizes wisdom, destruction of negative barriers and swift movement to escape danger when necessary. It is connected to the dragon, spider and spider web and the spiral. The last two usually symbolize the mysterious center and the revelation of creation. Sometimes it serves as a symbol of thunder or signifying lunar periods. It is connected to the sign of cancer in the zodiac, to the depths of the sea and to the longest day of the year. It is sometimes accompanied by the symbol of the swastika.

Ostrich

The ostrich symbolizes spiritual truth, understanding all aspects of denial, evasion, avoiding behavior, community life, the ability to run faster than the rival and is considered helpful in chasing away evil spirits. An ostrich feather symbolizes truth and justice since all the feathers are equal in length. In ancient Egypt, it appears on the heads of the gods, "lords of the truth" and in depictions of the day of judgement of the dead. The ostrich symbolizes the goddess of truth, justice and law, Amaunet, goddess of the west and the dead and Shu, as air and space. In Semitic mythologies the ostrich is a demon and may represent the dragon. In Zoroastrianism the ostrich is the bird of the celestial storm. The ostrich egg was kept in temples, Coptic churches and mosques and sometimes on tombs as well. It symbolized creation, life, resurrection and alertness. In Africa the ostrich symbolizes water and light.

Owl

The owl is an ambivalent symbol. On one hand, it is a common symbol for profound wisdom, and on the other hand it symbolizes darkness and death. It is a symbol of secrecy, swift and quiet movement and sneaking ability, acute eyesight and the ability to see beyond the facade. The owl is considered to be the messenger of signs and secrets. It symbolizes transformation, connection between the darkness and the invisible world to the world of light, the ability to accept shadows in one's personality, magic and witchcraft connected to the moon and freedom. In Native-American tradition the owl symbolizes wisdom and knowledge of the future. In Celtic tradition, it symbolizes negative-earthly forces, the "night witch" and the "bird of corpses". In Chinese symbolism the owl is a symbol of evil, crime, death, panic and ungrateful children. An owl on an urn of ashes symbolizes death. In Japanese tradition it is considered a bad omen and a symbol of death. In Mexican culture the owl also symbolizes the night and death. In Hinduism the owl is a symbol of Yama, god of the dead. In Christian symbolism the owl symbolizes the devil, the forces of darkness, loneliness, lamentation, mourning and bad news. The call of the owl symbolized the Jews who preferred the "darkness" rather than "the light of the New Testament". In ancient Egyptian culture the owl symbolizes death, night and cold. In the hieroglyph system the shape of the owl symbolizes all these and passivity as well. It also symbolizes the "dead sun" – the sun that set beyond the horizon into the water of the river or sea of darkness. In the cultures of ancient Greece and Rome the call of the owl symbolized wisdom and the owl was consecrated to the goddess of wisdom Athena/Minerva. The owl was attributed to the Etruscan god of darkness and night. In Jewish tradition the owl symbolizes blindness.

Ox

The ox is a complex symbol, both psychologically and historically. In esoteric tradition it symbolizes the Hyperburans – a people that lives in the land of eternal sunlight, as a totem against the "dark" Negros. It is identified with the god Thor, son of heaven. In principle, the ox symbolizes the superiority of the mammals over the reptiles. The main conflict in this symbol is its interpretation as on one hand representing the earth, soil, great mother and the "humid" principle and on the other hand representing the sky, the sun and therefore the father too. It is depicted as a lunar animal almost as much as it is depicted as a solar one. Various commentators believe that it should be perceived first and foremost as a lunar animal, and originally it was indeed lunar and its horns symbolized the crescent of the moon. On the other hand, as a solar animal it takes second place after the lion.

Usually the ox symbolizes the masculine force in nature, the reviving solar power that is consecrated to all the gods of the sky. It symbolizes fertility and reproduction, the protective masculine force, the royalty of the king, but also the earth and the humid power of nature. When it is lunar and the goddesses of the moon such as Artemis and Europa ride on it, then it also symbolizes the taming of the masculine and animalistic power. Riding on an ox or an ox pulling a chariot is a symbol of a solar warrior and it is connected to the sky, storm and gods of the sun. The roar of the ox symbolizes thunder, rain and fertility.

Since the ox symbolizes the protective force, it is connected to the fertilizing forces of the sun, rain, storm, thunder and lightening and therefore it is connected to both the dry and humid principles. The gods of the sky and weather appear in the earliest paintings as oxen and the goddess usually appears with them as their consort.

The symbol of the ox was very common in Sumerian and Semitic cultures. The man-ox is usually the protector who guards the center, treasure or doors, and keeps away all evil. The ox's head symbolizes sacrifice and death. The butchering of an ox in the New Year feast symbolizes the death of winter and the birth of the creative force. According to Assyrian traditions, the ox was born from the sun. The sacrifice of the ox appears in the cults of Atis and Mithra and the ancient New Year feasts.

In Buddhism the bull is the moral self, the ego, and it symbolizes Yamah, god of death, who is sometimes depicted as having a head of an ox. In Celtic traditions, the ox gods are divine power and strength. For the druids the ox is the sun and the cow is the earth. In Chinese tradition, the ox is one of the twelve animals of the "twelve earthly branches".

In Christianity the ox symbolizes brutal force. In ancient Egypt the ox Apis was the incarnation of Osiris, and "the second life and the servant of Ptah". It was worshiped also under the shape of Mnves or Merver, and it was consecrated to the solar Ra, that like the ox of the sky fertilized daily the goddess of the sky Nut. Neb, the god of the earth, was also the ox of the goddess of the sky. The thigh of the ox was the phallic leg of Set, as a representation of fertility, power and the North Pole (on the axis).

In Greek mythology, the ox symbolizes Zeus as god of the sky and Dionysos that was horned and sometimes had the head of an ox when representing the masculine principle. The ox was consecrated to Poseidon, whose wine bearers in Aphesus were "oxen". As a "humid" power the ox symbolized Aphrodite. In Hindu traditions, the ox symbolizes power, speed, fertility and the reproductive power of nature. The ox Nandin was the vehicle of Shiva, protector of the west who rode on an ox. It symbolizes Agni the "mighty ox" and it is a shape of Indra in his fertilizing aspect. The ox is also the reviving soul of Aditi, who embraces all. The power given by Suma is sometimes described as the power of the ox. Rudra unites with the cow goddess. In Iranian traditions – the ox symbolizes the soul of the world. Its reviving forces are connected to the moon and the clouds of rain as a symbol of fertility. It is considered to be the animal that was created first and killed by Ahriman. From the soul of the ox came all that was created later. In Minoan culture, the ox represents the great god. It was sacrificed to the earth and the god of earthquakes. In certain cultures the ox was considered to be the creator of earthquakes by turning the earth with its horns and its roar is the sound that is heard during earthquakes.

In Crete the ox appears as a fertilizing force of nature. In Mithridatic culture the ox symbolized the god of the sun and the sacrifice of the ox was the primary cult in Mithriadatic faith, and represented the penetration into the feminine principle by the masculine principle. It also represented triumph over the animalistic nature of man. The lion and ox together symbolized death. In Roman tradition the ox symbolizes Jupiter as god of the sky. It was sacrificed to Mars and symbolized Venus and Europa as lunar goddesses. Europa is carried at dawn along the sky by a solar ox. In Scandinavian traditions the ox symbolizes Thor and is consecrated to Frigg. In Sumerian and Semitic cultures the celestial sky plows the great furrow in the sky. Raman, Ashur and Adad who ride on bulls are the "oxen of the sky". Marduch is identified with Gudibir, the "ox of light". The sun, Enil or Enki is "a wild ox of heaven and earth". Sin, a lunar god, has the shape of an ox. Teshub, the Hittite god of the sun has the shape of an ox as well. It is an aspect of Eaa as lord of witchcraft and is usually depicted in Sumerian culture has holding the frames of the door. Baal, the Syrian or Phoenician god is the solar god of fertility and earth and is also symbolized by the ox. The Accadian "led" ox starts the year's wheel of fortune. Winged oxen are protective spirits.

In the zodiac, the ox – Taurus is a solar symbol that symbolizes the creativity of the spring.

↔ **SYMBOLS** ↔

Oyster

The oyster symbolizes the womb, the creative power of the feminine principle, birth and rebirth, initiation, cosmic law and cosmic justice. In modern symbolism it symbolizes the closing of the doors in order to prevent loss of energy, the ability to filter out the static elements in life, maintaining a strong and durable external defense and sensitivity to environmental changes. In Chinese symbolism the oyster represents cosmic life, the yin power, fertility, the power of water and the sanctity of the moon.

Parrot

The symbolism of the parrot is based mainly on its ability to utter words. It is a symbol of imitation, use of language, wisdom that helps a person to think before he or she speaks and the connection between a man and a woman. The parrot is also a rain-delivering bird. In various traditions the parrot was a symbol of lack of intelligence or silly repetition of words that are not really understood. In Chinese tradition it symbolizes glamour and glitter and a warning to unfaithful wives. In Hinduism the parrot is unique to Kama, god of love, and a rain-delivering bird. The parrot had the same symbolism in Pre-Colombian America.

Partridge

The partridge symbolizes fertility, mobility, connecting to feminine energies and solitary work. In Christianity the partridge has an ambivalent symbolism – on one hand it symbolizes the truth of Jesus, and on the other hand it symbolizes deceit, robbery and fraud. St. Jerome expressed in his worlds the opinion of many of the authors and philosophers of ancient times and the Middle Ages about the partridge. "As the partridge lays eggs and raises young birds that will never follow it, so an unrighteous man accumulates wealth he does not deserve that he has to leave behind". Additional symbolism stems from the bird's ability to deceive and camouflage itself. When Medieval writes referred to the birds Hebrew name "kore" (caller) they saw it as the devil deceiving and seducing the masses with his voice. In ancient Greek culture the partridge is attributed to Aphrodite and the god of the sun Telus and in Crete it is consecrated to the Cretan Zeus.

Panther

In Christian tradition the panther is considered the savior of people from the claws of evil or the dragon. In the heraldic tradition it is usually depicted as full of rage and symbolizing wrath, mercilessness and cruelty, recklessness and impatience.

In Shamanism the Black Panther symbolizes star voyages and protective energy. It is also the symbol of femininity, understanding of death and rebirth and the ability to recognize in the dark. It is an important symbol in Native-American tradition of regaining personal powers that were taken away or returning parts of the soul.

Peacock

The peacock is a solar symbol that is connected with the cult of the tree and sun. It symbolizes all aspects of beauty, immortality, honor, the ability to see into the past, present and future, self-confidence, ability to recover after a strong blow, love and longevity. It is considered a natural symbol of the stars in the sky. Since it becomes restless before the rain, it is connected to storms. In folk symbolism, the peacock was attributed with meanings of arrogance, pride, boastfulness (since it walks with a spread tail) and earthiness. In Buddhism it symbolizes compassion, vigilance and prudence. In Chinese tradition it symbolizes status, dignity and beauty. A peacock's feather was given to public officials as a token of good service and symbolized the favor of the emperor. It is also the symbol of the Ming dynasty. In Christianity the peacock symbolizes eternal life and resurrection, and there was a widespread belief that a peacock's feather can not be corrupted. The "thousand eyes" of the peacock's feathers symbolize the church that sees everything. In ancient Greek culture the peacock is a solar bird that represents the bird god Paon. It was originally attributed to Pan, who gave it to Hera. In Rome it was considered to be Juno's bird and a symbol of an empress and princess. In Hinduism it is the vehicle of Lakshmi and Skanda-Kartikia, god of war. When Kama, god of love, rides on a peacock, it symbolizes impatient love. It symbolizes Sarasvati, goddess of wisdom, music and poetry. In Iranian tradition, the peacock that stands on each side of the tree of live represents duality and the dual nature of man. It is also a symbol of royalty. In Islam it symbolizes light "that saw the self as a peacock with a spread tail". The peacock's eye is connected to the eye of the heart. The peacock's tail sometimes appears as a symbol of the merger of all colors and the idea of totality.

Pheasant

In Modern symbolism that is based on Native-American culture and shamanism, the pheasant symbolizes movement beyond the ego, using color for healing, developing and expanding self-awareness and understanding the use of rituals. In Chinese tradition it is a yang bird that symbolizes the light and the day, morality and virtues, beauty, good fortune and prosperity. In Japanese symbolism the pheasant symbolizes protection and maternal love.

Pig

The pig symbolizes fertility and plentifulness, cleverness and shrewdness, but also gluttony, greed, selfishness, carnal lust and rage. In various cultures the pig is a symbol of impure desires, of turning the good into evil, the high into low and of immoral decay and corruption and something profane and unclean. In New Age symbolism that is based on Native American tradition and certain aspects of paganism the pig symbolizes knowledge from pervious life, strong earthly magic/witchcraft and turning invisible in times of danger. The pig is connected with the great mother, and has celestial, lunar and fertile symbolism. In Native-American culture the pig is the deliverer of rain, a thunder animal and a lunar animal. In Buddhism, at the center of the wheel of existence, the pig symbolizes ignorance and greed, and it is one of the three creatures identified with the sins that bind the individual to the world of illusion, senses and rebirth. In Tibetan Buddhism, the diamond sow – Vageravarhi, is the great mother and the queen of heaven. In Hinduism, the sow Vageravarhi, queen of heaven, is the feminine aspect of the third incarnation of Vishnu as a boar and a source of life and fertility. In Celtic culture, the sow goddess, the "white old woman" – Cerridwen, is the great mother, and so is Pwyll, the "shining", goddess of the moon and fertility. The pig is also attributed to Manannan, who supplies supernatural food with the help of his pigs who were butchered and eaten and came back every day.

In Chinese symbolism the pig symbolizes undomesticated nature, greedy and filthy in nature, but useful and fertilizing when tamed. In Christianity the pig symbolizes the devil, gluttony and sensuality. In ancient Egyptian culture, the pig was consecrated to Isis as the great mother and to Bes, but it can also symbolize Set in his negative aspect. In ancient Greek culture the pigs were the symbol of Aleusis and sacrificed to Ceres and Demeter as goddesses of fertility. In Roman culture the pig was sacrificed to Mars as the god of agriculture and to Telus and Ceres as well during the harvest. In Sumerian and Semitic cultures the pig is attributed to Rimon and Tihamat and the great mother goddess. In Jewish tradition the pig is considered a profane animal and forbidden food. In Islam the pig also symbolizes the profane and its eating is prohibited.

Praying mantis

The praying mantis symbolizes maneuvering, the ability to maneuver time, understanding the cyclical nature of time, the ability to move between moments, the ability to remain still and silent and offensive strategies. Since the female praying mantis is bigger and stronger than the male and since it decapitates the head of the male during mating, the praying mantis symbolizes feminine fighting energies. Among the Bushmen in Africa it symbolizes the trickster, the deceiver. In Chinese culture it represents greed and stubbornness. In ancient Greek culture it symbolizes fortune telling and prophecy. In Christianity the praying mantis symbolizes worship and prayer.

Quail

The quail symbolizes living close to the earth, the ability to fade in the background, courage to cope with hard work and finding peaceful solutions to dangerous situations. The quail is connected to the night, but also to good luck and the spring and it has a connection to the Phallic and symbolizes the display of love. In Chinese symbolism it symbolizes courage, military zeal, the summer and poverty as well. In ancient Greek culture the quail symbolized the spring, the regeneration of life, and is connected to Zeus and Letona, Apollo and Diana. In Jewish tradition it symbolizes miraculous feeding in the desert but also the food of rage and desire. In Phoenician culture the quail was sacrificed to Melkarth after defeating Tiphon/Siphun who represents darkness. In Roman culture the quail represents courage and victory in battle. In Russian folklore the quail and the rabbit are the sun and the moon that were found by the virgin of dawn. It symbolizes the sun, the spring and the Czars. In connection with witchcraft the quail is considered the bird of the devil, witchcraft and satanic forces.

Rabbit

The rabbit is a typical lunar animal and the symbol of all lunar deities. It is almost universally connected to the moon. Since it is so strongly connected to the moon it symbolizes rebirth, regeneration of youth, revival and intuition – a beacon of light shining in the darkness. It is often connected with the ritualistic fire and "life through death". It is a universal symbol of fertility and a folk symbol of shyness, introversion, shrewdness, quick escape and cowardice. Like the dog and the lizard, the rabbit is considered a connector between the deities of the moon and mankind. In the western world the white rabbit symbolizes snow. A rabbit's head or leg is used as protection against witchcraft, but the rabbit itself is sometimes considered a servant or friend of the witches. In Scotland, this connection between the rabbit and witch is expressed in a name used for both – malkin or maukin.

In African tradition too, mainly among the Hottentots the rabbit is connected to the moon. In Indian and Buddhist art, the rabbit appears with a crescent. In Indian tradition, the great rabbit, Manabuzu, father and protector, is the creator and transformer – transforms the animal-like nature of man. He is the redeeming hero, the judge and hero of dawn, the personification of light, the great manitu (universal spirit, supreme super-natural force). The rabbit lives on the moon with its grandmother and is considered the "provider of all water, master of the spirits and brother of the snow". In Chinese symbolism the rabbit symbolizes the moon. As a yin animal the rabbit symbolizes the feminine, the power of the yin, the imperial consort. It is also a symbol of longevity. The rabbit is the fourth of the animals of the twelve earthly branches. The rabbit on the moon, with the pestle and crater, prepares the elixir of immortality. The rabbit is the defender of the wild animals. The white rabbit symbolizes deities and the red rabbit symbolizes good luck, peace, prosperity and benevolent rulers. The black rabbit symbolizes good luck and successful rule. For the moon festival images of rabbits and white rabbits were prepared.

In ancient Egyptian culture the rabbit symbolized the dawn, the beginning, opening, periods and seasons. The rabbit was the symbol of Thoth and even in this culture it was connected with the moon. In Egyptian hieroglyphs the rabbit is a sign that defines the concept of the universe. In Europe too the Easter Bunny symbolizes dawn and new life. It is attributed to the goddesses of the moon, probably to Ostara (Teutonic) or Eostra (Anglo-Saxon) who gave her name to the feast of Easter. Therefore, the rabbit symbolizes rebirth and regeneration like the regeneration of the moon after its disappearance.

In Christianity the rabbit has an additional symbolism of fertility and lust, that turned the rabbit into a popular symbol of carnal lust and active sexual life. On the other hand, the white rabbit at the feet of the Virgin Mary symbolizes the victory over lust. In Greek and Roman cultures too the rabbit symbolizes fertility and lechery and is attributed to Aphrodite and Eros. Cupid is sometimes painted with a rabbit by his side. Additional symbolism of the rabbit is that of a messenger animal and therefore it is attributed to Hermes/Mercury.

In Celtic culture the rabbit is attributed to the lunar goods, like in many other cultures, but it also represents the hunter, and since was often hunted it is attributed to the hunting gods and usually depicted in the hands of one of the hunting gods. In Scandinavian tradition Frigg is accompanied by rabbits. In

Teutonic culture, the goddess of the moon Holda is accompanied by a train of rabbits holding torches.

In Buddhism the rabbit symbolizes total self sacrifice because when Buddha was angry the rabbit offered itself as sacrifice and jumped into the fire.

The rabbit also became a symbol of clear thought, of receiving intuitive and hidden massages, strong intuition, humility, life according to one's personal intelligence and the ability to overcome fear (contrary to the rabbit as symbol of cowardice). It is also a symbol of paradoxes and contradictions, deceit and cunning.

Ram (hart)

The ram symbolizes male potency, masculinity, creative male force, creative energy and protective force. It is connected to the gods of the sun and the sky as and aspect of the regeneration of the power of the sun. The spiral of the ram's horns is a symbol of thunder and can be connected with both the gods of the sun and the goddesses of the moon.

In Celtic symbolism the ram symbolizes fertility. It is attributed to the gods of war and also appears as a snake with a ram's head that is connected to the horned god Sernunos. In Christian symbolism the ram symbolizes Jesus as the leader of the flock. In ancient Egyptian culture it symbolizes solar energy, protection, creative heat, the regeneration of solar energy, and the personification of Amon-Ra. The god with the ram's head, Khnum, later turned into Khnum-Ra. In ancient Greek culture the ram was consecrated to Zeus as god of thunder. It symbolizes fertility and creative power. It is consecrated to Dionysos as the creator. The Mendes ram was consecrated to Pan. In Cyprus the ram was connected to Aphrodite. It symbolized the month of March in the zodiac. In Hinduism the ram was consecrated to Agni, the Indian god of fire and symbolized the sacred fire. In Islam it is considered a sacrificial animal, and in Jewish tradition as well since this is the ram that replaced Isaac as the sacrifice in the story of the binding of Isaac. In Scandinavian symbolism rams pull the chariot of Thor. In Sumerian-Semitic symbolism the ram symbolized Eaa, lord of the sea and fate. The Phoenician Baal, Hamon, as god of the sky and fertility, is usually depicted with ram's horns on his head. Rashap is depicted with ram's horns and his crown is supported by a ram.

Rat

The rat has an ambivalent symbolism that stems both from its size and nature and from its influence on mankind, as a pest that damages crops and granaries.

↔ SYMBOLS ↔

Due to its tiny size, its ability to hide and agility it is a symbol of understanding the small details, silence, shyness, discovery, invisibility, sneaking, constant movement, seeing the double meaning of things and learning the lesson of life. On the other hand it symbolizes the forces of darkness, tumult, restlessness and inexplicable anxiety. In Christianity the rat is described as a rodent that is gnawing the roots of the tree of life and a symbol of a devouring force - the devil. In ancient Greek culture the rat was attributed to Zeus and Apollo. In Jewish tradition the rat symbolizes hypocrisy and deceit.

Thus the rat has an ambiguous meaning. On one hand, it is a symbol of fertility and wealth, creating plentifulness, wisdom and intelligence and the ability to be invisible, and its sneaking ability is a symbol of defense. On the other hand it is the animal of plagues, a symbol of death, decay and degeneration, disease and feebleness – both physical and moral and the underworld. In Chinese symbolism the rat symbolizes evil and shyness and it is the first among the twelve animals of the earthly branches. In Christianity it is a symbol of evil. In Hinduism it symbolizes cleverness, prudence and foresight and it is the horse of Ganesha, who overcomes every obstacle and a symbol of successful efforts.

Raven

The raven is considered in many cultures and folktales to be a speaking bird and therefore it represents prophecy. Some see it as symbolizing the loneliness of the one who lives in higher planes. It is ambivalent as both a solar and lunar animal – as the darkness of evil on one hand and as wisdom and destruction of evil on the other. Ravens and wolfs are sometimes attributed to the ancient gods of death. In alchemist symbolism, the raven, due to its black color, is connected to the idea of the primary mater, the nigerdo, the initial stage of the matter in the "great work". As representative of the nigerdo stage it is allegorical to the maternal night, the initial darkness and the fertilizing earth. As connected to the earth, it represents in alchemy the phrase "ashes to ashes, dust to dust". Since it is connected to the atmosphere, the raven is a symbol of the creative power of the spiritual force. As a result of its flight it is considered in some cultures to be the messenger bird. The raven has cosmic meanings as well. In Native-American culture the raven is the "trickster", a folk hero and judge. Among the North-American natives the raven was considered the great civilizing force of the creator of the visible world. A similar meaning is attributed to the raven in the Celtic and Germanic tribes and in Siberia as well. In Celtic culture it is also an omen for the future. The "sacred raven" is the symbol of war and the goddesses of fertility. Morigan is the goddess of the raven and Badb, the "raven of war", symbolizes war, bloodshed, panic, cruelty, envy and malicious intents. When the raven is completely black it is a bad omen, but when it has even one white feather it is considered to be benevolent. In Scandinavian and Teutonic symbolism Odin/Wodin has two ravens on his shoulders. The first – Hugin, is thought and the second, Munin, is memory. They flew over the earth and returned with reports on what they saw. The raven is also the symbol of the Vikings.

In Classical cultures the raven does not have such a broad meaning, but it still symbolizes certain mystical forces and mainly the ability to see into the future. Therefore, it had an important role in fortune telling and various ceremonies.

In Christian symbolism, the raven is allegorical to loneliness (and therefore it sometimes symbolizes the reclusive monk), and symbolizes the devil who feeds on corruption. When it is depicted as plucking eyes it symbolizes the devil punishing the sinners. It is a symbol of sin as opposed to the dove that symbolizes the pure soul. The raven that was sent from Noah's ark symbolizes wandering, restlessness and impurity. In the symbolism of the "fall" – the banishment from paradise, the raven sometimes appears on the tree of knowledge from which Eve picked the fruit. In Chinese culture a black raved is a symbol of evil, wickedness, malice, hostility and bad luck. A red or a golden raven represents the sun as well as tradition passed on to future generations. The raven is one of the symbolic animals of the twelve earthly branches. It symbolizes power. A well-known symbol of the raven depicts a three-legged raven within the solar disc. In this shape it is one of the first symbols of the Chinese Empire, and represents the yang of the emperor's active life. The three-legged raven symbolized the three "legs" of the sun, the first light – sunrise, the peak – noon, and decline – sunset. In ancient Egyptian culture it symbolizes destruction, decay and wickedness, but a pair of ravens symbolized marital bliss. In ancient Greece the raven was consecrated to Apollo/Helios and was the messenger of the god of the sun, It was also the symbol of Athena, Chronous and Asclepius and symbolized longevity. In Mithridatic culture the raven symbolized the first stage of initiation and was considered to be the servant of the sun. In Jewish culture it is connected to dead corpses and symbolizes impurity, decay, destruction and deception. In Hindu tradition it is a symbol of Varuna. In Japanese culture the black raven is a bad omen and symbolizes bad luck, but in Shinto religion sacred ravens, the messengers of the deity, were connected to the temples. The broader symbolism of the raven today is based both on Native-American traditions and on a variety of symbols from different cultures. The raven is perceived as a symbol of life cycles, regeneration, recovery, rebirth and regaining and recovering hidden parts of the soul. It also symbolizes change in awareness, new events, self-acceptance, connection to the origin, introspection, casting light on shadows, understanding reflections, finding comfort in loneliness, respecting the ancient ancestors, magic and sorcery, fortune telling and eloquence.

Rhinoceros
The rhinoceros symbolizes connection to ancient wisdom and clever use of ancient wisdom – since it is a remnant of ancient life forms that were extinct. It also symbolizes the ability to learn and find comport in times of loneliness, knowing one's self and trusting one's instincts.

Robin
The robin symbolizes poetry, courtship and fatherhood. In Native-American symbolism it symbolizes the understanding of the power of the blowing wind and finding the personal song of the soul. In Teutonic culture it is connected to Thor and considered a storm bird. In Christian symbolism it symbolizes death and rebirth. According to Christian legend, the robin tried to remove the crown of thorns from Jesus' head when he was crucified. The robin could not remove it but its chest was pierced by a thorn during the attempt and started to bleed. This is why, according to the legend, its chest is red.

Salamander
The salamander is the mythological spirit of fire. In New Age symbolism the salamander represents the connection to the memory of the soul of the earliest days on earth. It is believed to promote the connection between the earth and water and symbolizes change, encouragement in the darkness and the ability to wear camouflage in face of danger. The salamander is usually depicted as a small lizard or a dragon, that jump from the flame and represents the element of fire. It is the animal of fire. It was considered to be sexless and therefore was identified with chastity and purity.

In Christian symbolism the salamander symbolizes the strong and continuos faith of the righteous man that the fire of temptation can not seduce. In Heraldic tradition it symbolizes courage and bravery that do not yield under the flames of pain. More on the salamander as a mythological animal see in "mythological animals".

↔ **SYMBOLS** ↔

Salmon

The salmon is a phallic symbol. It symbolizes fertility, the value of returning home for regeneration and regaining strength, swimming upward in the current of water and in the current of emotions in order to gain new insights. It is a symbol of the rebirth of spiral knowledge and understanding the messages of fortune telling. In Celtic tradition it is a symbol of wisdom, the early knowledge of the gods and knowledge from other worlds and knowing and understanding other worlds. It is connected with the sacred Celtic fountains and can replace the snake as symbolizing wisdom and connection with the forces of the other world.

Scorpion

The scorpion symbolizes death and rebirth, transformation of poison and returning dark and negative energy back to its sender. Its most common symbolism is mainly negative as a symbol of death, destructive force, disaster and darkness. In ancient Egyptian culture it symbolizes Set in its negative aspect and also Selk or Selket, as protector of the dead. Seven scorpions accompanied Isis in her journey in search of Osiris. In Jewish tradition the scorpion symbolizes poison, venom and death. In Mithridatic tradition the ox and the scorpion symbolize life and death and the rising and setting sun. In Sumerian and Semitic traditions scorpions, or scorpion men, were the gatekeepers of the god of the sun, the mountains of the east and the twin gates. Scorpions were connected to Ishtar or Nina. In Christian symbolism the scorpion symbolizes evil, torture, treachery and Judas Iscariot.

Shark

The shark has a somewhat ambivalent symbolism. On one hand, it is obviously a symbol of cruelty and mercilessness. But on the other hand it is also a symbol of the ability to live the moment and of spiritual, mental and physical self-acceptance. The shark is also a symbol of constant movement, work/movement in silence, the ability to defend one's self and connection to the past, a living fossil – a living organism whose closest spices have been extinct long ago. It is symbolically considered a "devourer" of negative energy, a recycler of energy that is never caught unprepared.

Sheep

The sheep symbolizes new beginnings, maintaining balance in dangerous situations, fertility, self-confidence, courage necessary to maintain balance, plentifulness and a sense of security in new areas and domains. On the other hand, a sheep that follows the flock without a thought of its own symbolizes blindness and foolishly following the ways of others. In Chinese tradition the sheep symbolizes life of seclusion. It is the eight of the symbolic animals of the twelve earthly branches. In Christianity the sheep symbolize the flock of Jesus, the loyal believers and the apostles.

Skunk

The more common and popular symbolism of the skunk stems from its unique ability to secrete a strong smell in times of danger. Therefore, the skunk symbolizes protection, repulsion and chasing away by smell. It is also a symbol of a smell that "sticks" to a person that is impossible to get rid of. Thus the skunk became a symbol of reputation. The skunk is also a symbol of courage, willpower, self-respect and self-confidence, knowledge and understanding how to find a personal course of action and sensuality.

Snail/slug

The most popular meanings of the snail are slowness and sensuality. It also symbolizes the ability to use slow motion as an advantage or to gain some benefit, the importance of mobility, leaving a trail, understanding the value of humor, defense through retreat and sensuality. Since the snail appears and disappears (from its shell) it symbolizes the moon. Its shell is a symbol of the labyrinth, the spiral and the big cave under the earth. In the Egyptian hieroglyph system, it is connected with the activity of the microcosmic spiral on matter. In Christianity it symbolizes sloth, sin and nourishing on mud and slime.

Snake

The snake is an ancient and meaningful symbol that appears in almost every culture in the world. Its symbolism can be very positive, but on the other hand it can also be the most negative symbolism in the world or symbols. The many meanings of the symbolism of the snake sometimes depict the snake as a whole and sometimes focus on its attributes such as its movement, sleekness, venom, the manner in which it attacks its prey, its hiss etc. Another reason that the snake is such a widespread and meaningful symbol stems from the very fact that it is so widespread – the snake can be found in almost every part of the world and it lives in many different habitats – on trees, in deserts, mountains, fields and in water. Therefore, it can be connected to all the elements. The connection to the element of the earth is obvious and natural and so is the connection to the element of since it is a reptile and since various species of snakes live in water.

The connection to the element of fire is depicted in the snake of fire and even the element of air is expressed in the symbolism of the snake – the feathered snake with the crown of feathers on its head in Aztec culture and in the symbol of the winged snake.

The snake symbolizes energy. It is one of the primary symbols of transformation, elusiveness, discovery of the mysteries of life, primordial and fundamental energy, creative power, immortality and super-sensual energy. On the other hand it is a symbol of destruction, ruin, evil, seduction, material and sexual temptations, sin, degeneration, the principle of evil that exists in the physical and material world and the cruel side of nature. Contrary to the symbolism of the negative earthly power of the snake, it can also appear as a symbol of high spirituality and profound wisdom. As a result of the shape of its body and movement that remind the waves the snake became in many cultures a symbol of the wisdom of the depths. Snakes were depicted as keepers of the fountains of life and immortality and as guards of treasures, symbols of hidden spiritual wealth.

There is a clear connection between the snake and the feminine principle, as it appears in the story of the Garden of Eden and in many mythologies. Many feminine deities around the Mediterranean are depicted as holding snakes in their hands (Artemis, Hecate, and Persephone) and feminine entities with snake hair (such as the gorgon Medusa). In Aztec culture there is a snake woman, Kuatlique, who wears a skirt woven of snakes and is the mother of the earth. In Central Europe there was a widespread belief that hairs ripped from a woman's head under the influence of the moon would turn into snakes.

The snake was a popular symbol in ancient Egypt. The names of the goddesses were composed of the hieroglyphic symbol that represents in its shape the movement of the snake and was also used in words referring to cosmic powers.

Like other reptiles, the symbol of the snake was used to signify the most primitive state of existence and the very beginning of life. Although the snake represents the forces of evil or demonic powers, it can also have a positive meaning – when these forces are learned, controlled and subdued and their user masters them and not vise versa, and uses them for a worthy cause such as the advancement of mankind. In this aspect the snake responds to the goddesses Nekhbet and Buto. The transformation the snake represents and the notion of turning its negative forces to spiritual ones and submitting them to the supreme celestial power are expressed in an ancient legend. This legend tells how the snake wrapped its body around Buddha seven times, but since it could not crush him, it became a young man bowing low before Buddha.

The snake's trait of shedding its skin turned it into the main symbol of transformation and a symbol of revival and regeneration. Philo from Alexandria was deeply impressed by the snake's ability to shed its skin and claimed that by doing so it also sheds its advanced age. He also believed that the snake can kill and heal (and indeed the remedy to the snake's venom is made from the snake's venom itself), and therefore it is a symbol of all the aggressive forces, both positive and negative. Philo also believed that the snake is the most spiritual of all animals.

Jung mentions that the Gnostics attributed the snake to the spinal column and spinal cord and saw it as an example of the way the subconscious expresses itself suddenly and unexpectedly and sometimes even in an aggressive and harmful manner. From a psychological point of view Jung saw it as a symbol of the tormented expression of the subconscious outbursts, i. e. the activation of the destructive potential of the subconscious.

The connection between the snake and the spinal column, spinal cord and power of vitality, is well expressed in the snake as the symbol of the condlini. In Yoga, the condlini, or snake, is wrapped in the shape of a ring (condla) at the bottom of the spinal column. But after intense training to elevate the spiritual frequencies the snake dissolves its ring and stretches up through the chakras until it reaches the chakra of the third eye. According to Hinduism this is the moment the individual rediscovers the sense of eternity. Some see this description as symbolic of the rising power that comes up from the genitalia and the basic chakra, sex, the physical world and the basic survival instinct to the realms of spiritual thought.

Some see the snake as a symbol of the force of life that determines both life and death and therefore it is connected to the wheel of life. The connection between the snake and the wheel of life is expressed in the Gnostic symbol of the ouroboros (see entry), the snake that bits its tail that is half white and half black (like the Chinese yin-yang symbol). It also expresses the snake's essential ambivalence since it depicts the two aspects of the life cycle (active and passive, positive and negative, constructive and destructive).

In African culture the snake was considered a royal symbol, a symbol of resurrection and a vehicle to eternal life. The celestial snake is also the rainbow. It surrounds the earth or guards the treasures or it is the spirit of the thunder and identified with lightening. The snake is connected to water and fertility, and can be a folk hero or ancient ancestor that gave mankind the first cob of corn. In Native-American culture, the snake is a creature of thunder and deliverer of rain and the enemy of the thunderbird. It is lunar and has powers of witchcraft. It is the spear of the gods, a symbol of eternity and an omen of death. The horned snake is the spirit of water, the fertilizing power of water. The snakes are the intermediaries between man and the underworld. Among the Australian Aborigines, the snake is the masculine principle, lightening, and the presence of the snake can be a sign of pregnancy.

Contrary to the widespread lunar symbolism of the snake, in Aztec culture the sun is symbolized by a feathered snake, a combination of the Kuatzel bird and the snake. It also symbolizes the wind, rain, thunder and lightening, the primordial movement of the wind and water, the breath of life, knowledge, an eternal creation, and an intermediary between man and god. The bird of prey that holds the snake-god from which the blood of humanity was created is a symbol of the breakup of the original unity and the emergence of division and differences in the material world.

In Buddhism the snake that appears at the center of the cycle of existence represents anger, with the pig it represents greed and ignorance and with the cock it represents carnal lust. The three together symbolize the sins that bind mankind to the world of illusion and wheel of existence. The snake is sometimes identified with Buddha, who turned himself into a snake (naga) in order to save people in times of plague and suffering.

In Celtic culture the snake is identified with the healing water and it is the symbol of Brigit as the mother goddess. In Chinese culture the snake is usually identified with the dragon, and only rarely it appears as a snake. When the snake is not identified with the dragon it is a symbol of evil, destruction, negativity, deception and deceit, and it is one of the five poisonous creatures. The snake is the sixth symbolic animal among the twelve animals on the earthly branches.

In Christianity the attitude towards the snake is ambivalent, but it is usually a symbol of evil. Sometimes it can symbolize Jesus as wisdom and Satan in its earthly aspect. It is the seducer, the enemy of god, that man has to overcome all by himself. When it is wrapped around the tree of life it is a positive symbol of wisdom, and when it is wrapped around the tree of knowledge it is Satan and evil. In ancient Egyptian culture the cobra is a celestial and superior entity that symbolizes royal wisdom and power, knowledge and gold. Apep, that is Set in its negative aspect, is the snake of mist, the "demon of darkness", destruction and ruin and the cruel aspect of the scorching sun.

In ancient Greek culture the snake symbolizes wisdom, the principle of life, resurrection and healing. As a symbol of healing, it is the symbol of Asclepius, Hypocrites and Hermes. It is consecrated to Athena as a symbol of wisdom. The snake is also a phallic symbol that symbolizes passions that revive both the feminine and masculine principle. In Hinduism the snake symbolizes the shakti, nature, cosmic power and chaos. As the cosmic ocean, Vishnu sleeps on a snake lying on the primordial waters, a symbol of the chaotic state before creation.

The snake was attributed with magnetic powers and protection from religious persecutions. This may stem from the fact that the snake was the most religiously "persecuted" of all symbolic animals and became the primary symbol of evil in various cultures– and still it could not be extinct, not physically and not in its positive symbolism.

The symbol of the eagle carrying in its claws a wounded snake symbolizes the triumph of the forces of the spirit over the low earthly forces. The deer trampling a snake with its hoof also symbolizes the triumph of good over evil.

Two snake symmetrically wrapped around the staff of Mercury, the caduceus (see entry), symbolize balance, and as a medical symbol it is often used in homeopathy and represents the principle of curing the illness by the very thing that causes it.

The snake of fire is a solar symbol that symbolizes purification and transcending from an earthly to a celestial state.

The sea snake combines the symbolism of the snake as a creature of the subconscious and the depths. If it has more than one head, the number of heads represents the symbolism of that number.

Winged snakes are a solar symbol and symbolize the union of mind and matter, the union of the eagle and the snake and the union of all opposites. They also symbolize quick understanding.

In Alchemy the winged snake symbolizes the changing principle and the wingless snake the stable principle. The crucified snake symbolizes the fixation of the changing or volatile. The alchemists also saw the snake as a symbol of "the feminine in the masculine".

Two snakes wrapped around each other symbolize time and fate, the two great binding forces.

The symbol of the snake as the rainbow that quenches its thirst in the sea can be found in French, Indian, African, Native-American and Aboriginal-Australian symbolism. The snake is the messenger of the rainbow snake (according to Native-American and Aboriginal tradition). The snake activates the lightening (according to Native-American tradition) and represents the principle of transformation (beyond spiritual and mental transformation – transforming the body of the shaman into an animal or another creature). It also serves the shaman as a magical rope that connects him to the world of the souls.

↔ SYMBOLS ↔

Spider

The spider symbolizes the great mother who in her aspect as the spinner of the threads of fortune is sometimes depicted as a huge spider. As a positive symbol the spider symbolizes wisdom, creativity, divine inspiration, transformation, understanding the patterns of illusion/Maya and feminine energy of the creative life force. But as a predator and somewhat mysterious insect it also has a rather negative symbolism (the term "negative" as appears in the yin-yang symbol, i. e. connected to the material world). There are three main meanings in the symbolism of the spider that sometimes overlap and sometimes mingle together. The spider's creative force as the spinner of its magnificent web, made it a symbol of the master spinner, spinning the threads of fortune, creativity and imagination. The spider's aggression turned it into a symbol of destruction and decay that is even connected to the idea of the illusion of the material, finite, world, in which death and finality are inevitable. The spiders, in the endless process of spinning webs and killing – construction and destruction, symbolize the constant transformation of the forces that the stability of the universe in which humans live depends upon. Therefore, the symbolism of the spider has a third and profound meaning. The spider symbolizes the transformation the individual undergoes in the course of his or her life, not just the earthly life, but also ending one life period on earth in order to reincarnate into a new life and start all over again – to spin again a new life.

The spider sitting at the center of its web symbolizes the center of the world, and therefore it was considered in India to be the Maya and the eternal spinner of the web of illusion (the illusion of the material reality and all its implications). It can also symbolize the sun surrounded by its beams and shining to all directions or the moon as the cycle of life and death of the material world, and the year that spins the threads of time.

The spider is a lunar animal, due to the passive nature of the moon – as it only reflects light, and due to its constant appearance and disappearance (in the sense of positive and negative situation). The spider is connected to the world of the senses (the world of illusion – the material world) and in the spiritual sense, it is connected to the imagination (as the moon). Therefore, since the moon controls the world of the senses it spins the threads of human destiny. This is why the moon is described in many myths as a huge spider.

All the goddesses of the moon are considered to be "spinners and weavers" of fate. And the cosmic spider, the great spider of the great spinner is also the creator who spins the threads of life from its own matter and connects all humans to itself by the thread of the umbilical cord and spins them into the web of the universe.

In Native-American tradition the spider symbolizes the wind and the thunder, and protection from harm. In ancient Egyptian culture the spider is attributed to Neith as weaver of the world. In ancient Greek culture it is attributed to Athena as spinner of the world and to Persephone and Hermina. In Roman culture the spider symbolizes cleverness, acute perception and good fortune. In Hinduism and Buddhism the spider spins the threads of the Maya, the world of illusion, and it is also the creator, spinner of the world from its own matter. In Scandinavian and Teutonic traditions, Holda and the Norns are the spinners of fate. In Sumerian and Semitic cultures it symbolizes Ishtar and Atargatis as the spinners of the world and faith. In Christian symbolism, the spider symbolizes the devil that traps the sinners in its web and the miser who makes the poor bleed.

Squirrel
The squirrel symbolizes collecting and storing, storing for the future, resourcefulness, change and rapid change of direction, discovery, the ability to solve riddles and problems, balance between giving and receiving, avoiding danger by climbing to high places and in some cultures even a sign of warning. In Celtic culture, together with the bird, it is a symbol of the Irish goddess Madb. In Japanese symbolism it symbolizes fertility and it is usually connected with the vine. In Scandinavian symbolism the squirrel is called Ratatosk and brings rain, water and snow. In Christianity it symbolizes avarice and greed.

Starfish
In Europe it is the "stella maris" that symbolizes divine love, the unconquerable force of love. In Christianity it is a symbol of the Holy Ghost, piety, charity and the Virgin Mary as stella maris.

Stork
The stork symbolizes creation, new beginnings, protection of the young, loyalty and devotion. Sometimes it symbolizes the traveler. Together with the eagle and ibis, it symbolizes the destruction of reptiles in their malicious aspect, and therefore it was considered a solar bird. But as a creature that is nourished by the sea and a fisher it is connected with the waters of creation. The children brought by the stork are a symbol of the fetus in the womb of mother earth and the creating water that is found by the fisher storks. The stork also symbolizes the coming of the spring and the beginning of new life and is considered a good omen. In Chinese symbolism it symbolizes longevity, happy old age, piety that is taught to future generations, the recluse and the nobleman who is distant and

aloof. In ancient Egyptian culture too the stork symbolizes piety taught to future generations and was considered to feed its parents when they reach old age. In ancient Greek culture the stork goddess represents the archetype of the woman, creator of life and nurturer. Hera is sometimes symbolized by the stork. In Roman culture the stork symbolized religious belief and piety, devotion of parents to children and children to parents and was attributed to Juno. A similar symbolic meaning can be seen in the Hebrew name of the stork "hasidah" (follower or strong believer – Hasidic). It symbolizes knowing the correct and natural way as opposed to not knowing the law of god. In Christian symbolism the stork symbolizes purity, chastity, piety, cleverness, prudence, alertness and vigilance. As a messenger of the spring it is a symbol of the new life after the Second Coming of Jesus.

Swallow

The swallow symbolizes hope, the coming of the spring, good luck, the power of life in a community or group, the value of the home and family life, protection, agility, light movement and maneuvering skills. It is considered to be related to the legendary thunderbird. In Chinese symbolism the swallow symbolizes infidelity, but also domesticity and maternal care. In Japanese art it is connected to the willow and waves. In ancient Egyptian culture it is consecrated to Isis as the great mother. In the Pyramid text the swallows are called "viable stars of the north" and are believed to fly over the tree of life. In the cultures of ancient Greece and Rome the swallow was consecrated to Aphrodite/Venus. In the Heraldic tradition it symbolizes young sons (who are not landlords). In Minoan culture it appears in Cretan art as connected to the great mother. In Sumerian and Semitic traditions it is the symbol and shape of the goddess Nina as the great mother. In Christian tradition it symbolizes the Second Coming of Jesus in the flesh and resurrection. Its return in the spring symbolizes new life.

Swan

The swan is considered to unify the two elements of water and air and therefore it is considered in many traditions as the bird of life. It symbolizes the beginning of the day, sunrise. The swan is a solar bird but it also has feminine meanings.

It also symbolizes loneliness and seclusion and is called the "bird of the poets". Its white color symbolizes sincerity. In Celtic tradition, the deities of the swan are solar and benevolent. These deities (mostly masculine) have the healing powers of the sun and water and are connected with the chariot of the sun and symbolize kindness, love, purity and magnificent music. The swan with gold or silver chains on its neck is the supernatural appearance of the deities. In Chinese tradition the swan is a yang bird, a solar bird.

In the cultures of ancient Greece and Rome the swan is an incarnation of Zeus/Jupiter as Leda's swan. It is consecrated to Aphrodite/Venus and Apollo as solar and as god of music. It symbolizes happy death. In Hinduism two swans together are "the couple of swans who are the Ham and Sha, who reside in the brain of the mighty one, who lives on the nectar of the blooming lotus of knowledge".

The swan also symbolizes inhaling and exhaling, breath and the wind. Brahma rides on a swan, goose or peacock and the swan or goose is his symbol. This is the celestial bird that laid on the water the cosmic egg, the golden egg from which Brahma emerged. The sublime swan is the universal earth, the self. In Christian symbolism the white swan symbolizes grace and purity and represents the Virgin Mary. The consecration of the swan to Apollo, as the god of music, created the popular belief that the swan would sing a marvelous song when it is on the verge of death. This is the source of the famous expression "song of the swan" that is a last magnificent masterpiece. The red swan is the symbol of fire.

In art and poetry the swan often appears as allegorical to a nude woman, symbol of pure nudity and unblemished whiteness. Some see it as a deeper symbol, since the swan's neck is long and phallic, masculine yet rounded and its silky body expresses femininity. This creates a hermaphroditic symbol, an androgynous, both masculine and feminine. It symbolizes the perfect fulfillment of desire and desire leading to death accompanied by a song. The alchemists were also familiar with this ambivalent symbolism and connected it with the philosophical mercury, the mystical center and the unification of opposites. It symbolizes the vehicle of the journey to the other world, and therefore it has a funerary meaning and supports the mythical idea (that is completely unfounded) of the song of the dying swan. It has some of the symbolism of the martyr or the tormented, tragic artist.

In New Age symbolism that is partly based on Native-American traditions and universal meanings of the swan, the swan symbolizes inner strength, understanding the symbols of dreams, looking into the future, fortune telling, pleasantness and grace in relationships with others and developing intuitive abilities.

Tiger

The tiger like many other predators has an ambivalent symbolism – it is both solar and lunar, creator and destroyer. On one hand it symbolizes cruelty, savagery and aggression, and on the other hand it symbolizes fearlessness, courage, power, energy, excellent timing, strength and willpower in face of plight and quick action without thinking and analyzing the situation in advance – whatever the consequences may be. When the tiger is depicted as fighting with the snake it is a celestial and solar power. When it is fighting with the lion or the oriental dragon it is lunar, earthly and harmful. Sometimes the tiger symbolizes royalty and can be the incarnation of mother earth. In Chinese alchemy the tiger represents lead and physical power.

In Aztec culture it symbolizes the sun setting in the west and negative and earthly forces of darkness. In Buddhism it symbolizes one of the three negative animals of Buddhism together with the monkey as greed and the deer as lovesick. In Chinese culture it symbolizes courage and fierceness in war, and is considered the king of the animals and the lord of all the animals of the earth. In Chinese symbolism, when it is yang, the tiger takes the lion's place in the west and symbolizes rule, courage, military forces and the zeal needed for defense. When it is in conflict with the yang, with the celestial dragon, the tiger becomes yin and earthly. Both of them together symbolize the opposite forces of mind and matter, The tiger is the third among the symbolic animals of the twelve earthly branches and it is the symbol of army officers of the fourth rank. It is also the symbol of gamblers. The god of wealth rides on a tiger that is considered the protector of coffers of money. The goddess of the wind rides on a tiger as well. The tiger is the guard of tombs and chases away the evil spirits. It can see in the dark and therefore it is associated with the forces of darkness. It is lunar when it depicts the growing power of the new moon that is symbolized by the child running away from the tiger's jaws. The child is the "father of the man", that is of mankind, and the tiger depicts the forces of darkness from which the new moon, the light, escapes. The white tiger is the western province, autumn and the element of metal, and it should always be depicted with its head facing south and its tail facing north. The blue tiger is the planet earth, the east and spring. The red tiger is fire, the south and summer. The black tiger is water, the north and winter and the yellow tiger is the center, the sun and the ruler. "Riding on a tiger" symbolizes the encounter and confrontation with dangerous forces and the powers of nature and it is also a symbol of success. In Jewish tradition the tiger is a symbol of valor. The tiger's spots symbolize eyes, and therefore it is called the "great watcher".

In Christian symbolism it symbolizes the devil, sin and antichrist. In ancient Greek culture it is attributed to Dionysos as creator and destroyer, and pulls the chariot of Dionysos/Bacchus. In ancient Egypt the tiger was the symbol of Osiris and was attributed to Set in its negative aspect. In the heraldic tradition the tiger symbolizes power, action, courage, hastiness and recklessness. In Hinduism it symbolizes the royal and warrior caste. Durga, as the destroyer, rides on a tiger and Shiva, as the destroyer, sometimes wear a tiger's skin. In Japanese culture the tiger symbolizes courage and is attributed to war heroes. In shamanistic traditions the tiger symbolizes super-natural forces and it is the messenger of the spirits of the forest and the gods and immortals and exorcists ride on it.

Toad

The toad is a lunar animal that is associated with the principle of humidity. Since it appears and disappears it is lunar and symbolizes resurrection. The toad can also symbolize evil, something loathsome and repulsive and death. In some cultures it symbolizes the earth, connection to various states of consciousness, change of fortune, longevity and disguising poison. Like the snake, it was said about the toad that it has a jewel in its head. In alchemist symbolism it symbolizes the dark side of nature. It is lowly but fertile. It symbolizes residue, debris and earthly matter. In Native-American tradition the toad symbolizes the dark Manito (universal spirit, super-natural force), the water of the moon, forces of darkness and evil that overpower the positive Manito.

In Celtic tradition the toad sometimes replaces the snake as the force of evil. In Chinese symbolism the toad symbolizes the yin principle, the lunar principle, the unattainable, longevity, wealth and making profits. The three-legged toad lives on the moon and its three legs symbolize the three states of the moon. In Iranian symbolism it symbolizes Ahriman, evil, envy, greed, avarice, but also fertility. In Mexican symbolism the toad symbolizes the earth and the sacred mushroom that gives enlightenment. In Christian symbolism the toad symbolizes the devil and greed. In witchcraft the toad symbolizes the witch and good luck.

Turkey

The turkey symbolizes self-sacrifice for a worthy cause, understanding the gift of giving, respecting mother earth and gaining rewards. It is connected to the thunder and rain since it grows restless before storms. It is considered a sanctified bird to the Toltecs and serves as food in ceremonial feasts.

↔ **SYMBOLS** ↔

Turtle

The turtle is considered to be the symbol of the earth and symbolizes mother earth, but it also symbolizes the water and the moon and it is sometimes a phallic symbol as well. But others see it as symbolizing the female vagina and its moistness. Some see its slowness as a symbol of earthly, natural development, as opposed to spiritual development that does not depend on time and space. The turtle appears as a clear symbol of earthiness, stagnation and materialism. On the other hand, it symbolizes the beginning of creation, time, immortality, longevity and connection to the center. It is a symbol of slowness, patience, smoothness, navigation abilities, borders, connection to the feminine, developing new ideas, the ability to cure women's illnesses, respect for the domain of others, spiritual protection, self-reliance, non-violent defense, stubbornness, fertility and regeneration. It is often depicted as supporting the world at the beginning of creation. In China the turtle was considered to have fortune telling abilities. In Alchemist symbolism the turtle represents the massa confusa (the prima materia, primary matter that needs to be processed). Among Native-Americans, the cosmic tree grew from the back of a turtle, but it also symbolizes the cowered, the sensual, the earthly and winter. In Chinese symbolism it is considered one of the four spiritually blessed or sanctified animals. It symbolizes the element of water, the yang principle, the winter, the northern province and the black color, the color of primordial chaos. When it is called the "black warrior" it symbolizes strength, endurance and longevity – it is often depicted together with the crane as a symbol of longevity. The turtle is considered to be the supported of the world, with its four legs in the Four Corners of the Earth. According to the legend, the pakua trigrams, that contain all energetic interactions in the world, were invented from watching the signs and stripes on the turtle's shell. In Christian tradition the turtle symbolizes chastity in marriage and women who remain at home as the turtle remains under its shell. But in early Christianity it appears as evil. In the cultures of ancient Greece and Rome it symbolizes the feminine principle, the fertility of water, and it is consecrated to Aphrodite/ Venus who came up from the sea. It is also a symbol of Hermes/Mercury. In Hinduism the turtle symbolizes the northern star. It is considered the first living creature, the incarnation of Vishnu, who preserves and symbolizes the power of water. The turtle's lower shell symbolizes the material world and the upper shell the celestial world. The turtle supports the elephant that holds the world on its back. The elephant is masculine and the turtle is feminine when they symbolize the two creative forces. In Japanese culture the turtle symbolizes longevity, good fortune and support. In Mexican culture the turtle symbolizes the great mother in its horrible aspect. In Australian Aborigine symbolism the turtle symbolizes the farmer, agriculture and successful harvest. In Sumerian symbolism the turtle is consecrated to Eaa-Oanes as god of the depths. In Taoism the shape of the turtle symbolizes the entire cosmos. Its back symbolizes the sky, the body in the middle is mankind or the earth, the intermediary, and the lower part of the shell symbolizes the water.

Whale

The whale is considered the keeper of knowledge, the one who possesses all the knowledge connected to sound. It is a symbol of beauty and movement, super-natural and telepathic powers, the power of water and all the aspects of the sea. Since the whale symbolizes the power of cosmic water it symbolizes regeneration, both cosmic and individual, but also the tomb that covers the body. The belly of the whale is a place of both death and rebirth and it symbolizes Jonah who was swallowed into the belly of the whale and entered the darkness of death and emerged after three days to a new life, to resurrection. In Christianity the whale symbolizes Satan. Its jaws are the gates of hell and its belly is hell. On the aspect of the whale as a mythological animal see in "mythological animals".

Wolf

The wolf, like many other predators has an ambivalent symbolism. It symbolizes death and rebirth, facing the end of one's life cycle with courage and dignity, spiritual learning, instincts connected with intelligence, social and family values and the ability to defend one's self and one's family and deceiving and overcoming enemies. It also symbolizes the ability to pass by without being seen, permanence and stability, the ability to make good use of changes and a guiding figure in dreaming and meditation. Nevertheless, it has an earthly and material symbolism of evil, devouring and voracity and rage, and together with the raven, the wolf is a companion of the ancient gods of death.

In alchemy the wolf, together with the dog, is the dual nature of the philosophical mercury and symbolizes intellect and knowledge. In Aztec culture, the wailing of the wolf is the god of dance. In Celtic culture the wolf swallows the sun, father of heaven, at nightfall. In Chinese symbolism the wolf symbolizes greed and voracity. In Christian symbolism it symbolizes evil, the devil that devours and harms the flock, stiff-necked people (there was widespread belief that the wolf can not turn its neck), cruelty, cunning and heresy. It is a symbol of St. Francis who tamed the wolf Gubio. In ancient Egyptian culture the wolf is a symbol of Kenti-Amenti and Aupuaaut. In the cultures of ancient Greece and Rome the wolf is consecrated to Ares/Mars as wrath, and it is also consecrated to Apollo and Silvanus. A she-wolf breast-fed Remus and Romolus, the founders of Rome and is often depicted in Roman art. The wolf also symbolizes courage and heroism. In Jewish tradition the wolf is the symbol of the tribe of Benjamin and a symbol of cruelty, bloodlust, and greedy lords are likened to a devouring wolf (Ezekeil 22, 27) and corrupt judges as well (Zephaniah 3, 3). In Scandinavian and Teutonic traditions the wolf is the messenger of victory. Odin/Wodin rides on a wolf. Penris, the cosmic wolf, brings evil.

Woodpecker

The woodpecker is considered a prophetic bird. It is called the "drummer of the earth" and it is the defender of kings and trees. It symbolizes forces of witchcraft and sorcery, connection to the earth and the ability to discover hidden layers and understand rhythms, patterns and cycles. It is connected to the god of thunder and it pecks until the truth is discovered and sometimes is a sign of warning. In Greek and Roman mythology it is consecrated to Zeus/Jupiter, Ares/Mars and Silvanus. It guarded the twines Remus and Romulos, the founders of Rome. In Christian symbolism, it symbolizes Satan and heresy, undermining the faith and human nature.

Worm

The worm has an ambivalent symbolism. On one hand it symbolizes the earth, regeneration, renewal, purification of the soul and the ability to find food in the depths or the ground. But due to the same reasons – the fact that it lives in the depths of the ground - it symbolizes death, separation, and decomposition (since it eats up dead corpses that were buried in the ground). Jung defined the worm as a symbol of the libidinal drive, sexual desire that kills rather than give life.

Mythological animals, Legendary Creatures and Monsters

Basilisk/Coctris

The basilisk is a monster that is a combination of a bird and a reptile. It has a pointed head, usually of a bird, bird claws with three fingers and a body of a snake. When its body ends with another head it is called Emfisbana. Its name means in Greek "little snake king". In Medieval descriptions it was said that it was born of an egg without a yolk, that it was laid by a cock and hatched by a toad on a surface of manure. It was depicted has having a tail with three ends, flashing eyes and a crown on its head, sometimes a crown with three points. According to other myths of the basilisk that tell the story of its birth it was born from a woman's menstrual blood, from the hair of a menstruating woman or from the snakes in the gorgon's hair. The substance of its birth is connected to the idea that the woman's menstrual blood is something mysterious. There was a belief that gaze of the basilisk is deadly and it can be killed only by looking at it in a mirror, just as Perseus killed Medusa. This belief is connected to the myth of the gorgon's head, and the notion of the "evil eye". The basilisk also appears in eastern cultures in which it is depicted as a combination of a cock, snake and toad. In Christianity the basilisk symbolizes evil, the antichrist and one of the four aspects of the devil.

According to the perception that mythological animals are actually a projection of different aspects of the human psyche, the basilisk is clearly related by its very nature to the inferno according to the trinity symbols it contains. It has a tail with three ends and legs with three claws that symbolize the opposite of the holly trinity (Like cerberos, the infernal dog), and two salient "evil" components, the snake and the toad. The basilisk is one of the many keepers of treasures that are often mentioned in fairytales.

Behemoth

The behemoth is probably the hippopotamus that symbolizes the quality of the earth as opposed to the whale that symbolizes the quality of the sea. Various commentators of the Bible believe that the behemoth is a hippopotamus and others believe it is an elephant. Some suggest that the behemoth is connected to the Hindu god Ganesha who has a human body and the head of an elephant and a huge belly. The behemoth was devalued in Christianity and turned into a demon with a huge belly, as a result of its description in the book of Job, in which almost two chapters are devoted to the description of the Behemoth. "Behold now the behemoth...his might is in his loins, and his force is in the muscles of his belly. He stiffens his tail like a cedar: the sinews of his thighs are knit together. His bones are tubes of brass; his limbs are like bars of iron. He is the beginning of the ways of God: let him that made him bring near his sword to him! He lies under the thorny bushes, in the cover of the reed, and fens...Behold, he drinks up a river...He trust that river will thrust some food into his mouth...His sneezings flash forth light and his eyes are like the eyelids of the morning. Out of his mouth go burning torches...Out of his nostrils goes smoke. In his neck abides strength...The flakes of his flesh are joined together. They are firm upon him; they can not be moved. His heart is as firm as stone..." (Job 40:41). No one can overcome the behemoth. Swords, spears and slingstones do not harm it and it is like a "king over all the children of pride".

Bukentaur

The bukentaur is a half-human half ox monster. In certain monuments Hercules is depicted fighting the bukentaur. Like the centaur, the bukentaur is an animal that symbolizes the dual nature of man – the material, earthly, instinctive forces that deteriorates man to the degree of an animal, versus knowledge, wisdom and divine spirituality that elevate man and bring him closer to god. Unlike the centaur, the bukentaur emphasizes the low and earthly element in man. The struggle of Hercules against the bukentaur is a well-known symbolic struggle, a struggle against the negative and earthly forces that are depicted as external to man. These forces actually represent man's earthly traits and the struggle against them is also an act of purification. The struggle of heroes against monsters such as the minotaur or the dragon should be interpreted as such as well, and this interpretation is also reinforced by the Jewish proverb "who is a hero, the one who overcomes his urges".

Centaur

The centaur is a creature with the body of a horse and an upper part of a human being. It sometimes symbolizes the animalistic or lower nature of man, human morality and judgement and the conflict between the two opposites – the human wild and savage nature and intellect. At the same time, the horse (the centaur's lower body part), that symbolizes powerful masculine solar energy is the greatest realization of the guiding spirit of man, a combination of the guiding spirit and blind force – beastly horsepower. The cantauer can be seen to some degree as a legendary creature that expresses the constant conflict in human life. Since it is endowed with reason and moral judgement the man-centaur can turn to the guiding spirit and use the great power of his body to move forward in his chosen path. But on the other hand, the "beastly" body, the lower nature does not necessarily obey to the laws of reason.

The image of the centaur was very popular in Greek mythology. The centaurs were considered to be a strong, wild and savage tribe. They used to share their property and any use of public property, even a barrel of wine, was prohibited without the consent of the rest of the centaurs. Any violation of this law could lead to conflict and bloodshed and punishment to the delinquent. The centaurs sometimes accompany Dionysos/Bacchus.

In Christian tradition, the centaur was mainly a personification of the animalistic or lower nature of man. Its image was similar to the image of the god Pan who was also half-human and half animal (goat legs), and was connected to the image of the devil in Christianity). Therefore, the centaur symbolizes sensuality, lust, adultery, brutal force, the heretic and an incarnation of the devil, and his bow and arrows are the arrows of the devil. But the centaur also symbolizes the man torn between good and evil and the combination of animalistic force and spirituality. Another aspect of the centaur is the antithesis to the knight, as an entity that is totally controlled by the lower forces, the cosmic power, instincts or the subconscious, when it is not controlled by the spirit.

When he is depicted holding a bow and arrow, the centaur also symbolizes the sign of Sagittarius in the zodiac.

Although the centaurs were considered to be very savage one of then is the famous centaur Cheiron, the symbol of multi-disciplinary wisdom and kindness. He was the teacher of the legendary hero Achilles, and the great physician Asclepius, the famous hunter Actaeon and many other heroes. According to certain traditions of the Greek mythology Cheiron asked to relinquish his immortal life in order to save himself from eternal torment – after Hercules unintentionally injured him. Hercules visited one of his centaur friends, Polus, and since he was not very clever and rather impulsive he asked, begged and seduced his friend the centaur to open for him a barrel of win from the joint stock of the centaurs. The centaurs were quick to punish the offender. Hercules fought to protect his friend and injured Cheiron who did not take part in the fight at all. Cheiron's wound caused him great pain and Zeus, father of the gods, agreed to grant him death in order to save him from his misery.

Cerberos

Cerberos is the giant dog with three heads and snakes around its neck. It represents the trinity of the underworld. As keeper of the gates of underworld of Pluto (of Hades) its task is to keep the confined souls of the underworld from climbing up to the intermediate world in which there is a possibility for reform and redemption.

Chi-Lin (Ki-Lin)

The Chi-Lin symbolizes the yin and yang and is sometimes identified with the unicorn. It symbolizes the connection of the male and female, wholeness and purity. The Chi-Lin (or Ki-Lin) is one of the four spiritually blessed creatures and it is the essence of the five elements. It is both a yin and yang animal and it symbolizes gentleness, generosity, goodwill, longevity and sound management. To ride on the Chi-Lin means to win glory. It was the symbol of high rank army officers and noble birth. Its body is made of five colors: red, yellow, blue, white and black, and its voice sounds like bells. According to the legend it lives a thousand years and is considered the noblest of animals.

Chimera

The chimera is the monstrous daughter of Typhoeus and Ekhidna. It has the head of a lion, a body of a he-goat and a tail of a dragon. Sometimes it has another head, of a he-goat or an antelope and its mouth spits flames of fire. It is a symbol of complex evil, storms and winds, dangers on the earth and at sea and the end of existence. Bellerophon, who rides on Pegasus (see entry), is the one who killed it.

Dragon

The dragon is a universal symbolic figure that can be found almost every culture in the world.

It seems that the body of the dragon is a combination of the external features of some of the most aggressive and dangerous animals such as snakes, crocodiles, lions and maybe even pre-historical animals as well. The dragon can be winged or wingless. In Eastern cultures it sometimes reminds a huge winged snake, while in western cultures it resembles a dinosaur (mainly the erect Tyrannosaurus rex), with two small bat wings.

The symbolism of the dragon is ambivalent and complex and it may represent the feminine or masculine principle, the sun or the moon, the benevolent celestial powers or the earthly power and the powers of evil. Since it combines the image of the reptile, or the snake, with the image of the bird (wings) some see it as a symbol of the combination between mind and matter. Its shape changes from one culture to another. Some see it as a winged snake that lives in water and can fly in the air. The dragon has huge jaws and it swallows people and animals after killing them with the blow of its huge tail. In other cultures the dragon is considered an earthly animal, its jaws are relatively small, its tail huge, heavy and powerful and it is an instrument of destruction and demolition when it flies and feeds on the blood of the animals it kills. In certain cases the dragon is considered to be amphibious and its head is the head of a beautiful woman with long flowing hair. In this shape it is no less horrible, and maybe even more so. Sometimes the dragon has a number of heads like in the revelation of St. John in which the red dragon has seven crowned heads and ten horns.

Originally the dragon was an absolutely positive symbol that represents the combination of the life giving water (the snake) and the soul of life (the bird). Therefore, the dragon was identified with the gods of the sky and with their earthly proxies, the kings. Later it became an ambivalent symbol, positive on one hand as the symbol of the life-giving rain that comes after the thunder and negative and dangerous on the other hand, as the destructive force of the flood and lightening. Another element that is part of the image of the dragon is the element of fire, which the dragon spits from its mouth.

In western culture the dragon is a symbol of earthly, negative, destructive and evil forces. Therefore the struggle of the knight or hero (see entry) against the dragon is a symbol of the struggle against the forces of evil, or the struggle of the human spirit against material, earthly forces. The dragons in western culture symbolize plagues that come upon the land (or the individual if the legend is interpreted from a psychological point of view). According to Schnaider, the dragon symbolizes disease and in any case it is the symbol of the monster.

It symbolizes celestial, supernatural forces, forces of wisdom, power and recondite knowledge, the force of the life-giving water and the emperor as the son of heaven. (In Celtic culture the dragon also symbolizes sovereignty and rule).

In Chinese culture the dragon is a popular positive and meaningful symbol. The dragon also symbolizes the most sublime spiritual power, the supernatural, eternity, the winds of change, the celestial power of change and transformation, the rhythms of nature, the law of creation, power, the sun, light and life, the sky and the masculine yang power.

In Chinese iconography there are four famous dragons.

The blue dragon, Lung has five claws and is the tallest dragon that lives in the sky and is the vital spirit. This is a celestial, supernatural and eternal power that dominates the earth as well. This power symbolizes the imperial power and the emperor. This dragon is in charge of the eastern side and the life-giving rain. The ordinary, common, dragon, Mang, has four claws and symbolizes earthly power. Lee, the dragon without the horn that lives in the sea and rules the depths is also the symbol of scholars. The dragon Chiao lives in the mountains or on the earth and represents the statesman.

According to Wang Fu, the dragon has nine formalistic traits: its horn is the horn of a hart, it head is like the head of a camel, its eyes are the eyes of a demon, its neck resembles a s snake, and its belly is made of shell. It has the scales of a carp, claws of an eagle, soles of a tiger and ears of a cow.

Two dragons facing one another represent the yin and yang principles, and all the complementary opposites and the celestial and earthly powers. Usually between them there is a symbol of the moon or sun. When they are depicted back to back they symbolize the yin-yang and eternity. When they chase one after the other's tail, they symbolize the creative bilateral action of the yin and yang forces. The images of the dragon and phoenix together symbolize the union of heaven and earth, the emperor and empress, the total celestial potential of all opposites, the interaction between the macrocosm and microcosm, the two aspects of the androgynous, the rhythms of development and degeneration, life and death. In Japan, the dragon with the three claws symbolized the Mikado - the imperial and spiritual power.

In Hinduism the dragon symbolizes the power of the spoken word. It is the symbol of Suma and Varuna, while Indra is the slayer of dragons.

In Sumerian and Semitic cultures the dragon is the "enemy", the force of evil.

In ancient Egypt, the dragon is the symbol of Osiris god of the dead. Apep, the dragon of darkness and chaos, is defeated every day by the god of the sun Ra.

In the cultures of ancient Greece and Rome and dragon is the symbol of Hercules as the slayer of monsters.

In monotheistic religions too the dragon is a symbol of the forces of evil, satanic forces or inferior and instinctive animal-like forces. There are only a few exceptions in which the dragon represents the logos, the reviving spirit or celestial omniscience.

In Christianity the dragon is sometimes identified with the devil. It represents the primordial snake and symbolizes death, darkness, paganism and heresy. The symbol of the dragon with the tied tail is a symbol of the triumph over evil.

In alchemy the symbol of the dragon is quite common and several dragons fighting one another symbolize the stage of putrefaction, the stage in which the elements are separated and mental disintegration takes place. The winged dragon in alchemy symbolizes the volatile or changing element, while the wingless dragon symbolizes the fixed element. In Chinese alchemy, the dragon symbolizes mercury, blood and semen.

In many legends the dragon appears as a primordial, total enemy and the struggle against it is the ultimate test. Apollo, Cadmos, Perseus and Zigfried fought against dragons and defeated them. They symbolize the hero, goodness and all human virtues. The struggle against the dragon symbolizes the struggle between the forces of light and darkness, good and evil and sometimes it even symbolizes achieving recondite knowledge. Saving the maiden from the dragon is liberating the forces of goodness and purity after destroying the forces of evil.

Sometimes the dragon is attributed with an acute eye and magnificent eyesight, and therefore some suggest that the source of its name is the Greek word derkein that means "sight". Therefore, the dragon sometime serves as the keeper of temples and treasures.

Some believe that the biblical tanin or tanim (crocodile) is actually a dragon and Eliezer Ben-Yehuda the reviver of modern Hebrew interprets these words as dragon or sea dragon.

Elf

The elf is a small creature with pointed ears that appears in many folktales. There are many kinds of elfs – the elf of the forests, mountains and home. The elf can be ugly or beautiful. In various traditions there was a belief that the elfs lived in "elf land", the counterpart of "fairy land".

In ancient European legends and cultures the elfs were treated positively and gifts of cloths and food were place in the creature's assumed whereabouts. Thus people created a supportive connection with the creature that secretly came to them during the night and help in the various house works. In the famous folktale about the old shoemaker for example, the elfs came to his workshop in the middle of the night and made for him wonderful shoes. (Originally the helpers were the elfs not the dwarfs). The elfs also appear in folktales about different craftsmen and they look after house pets and little children. From a psychological point of view, the elf in these folktales symbolizes the secret wish of the hard working man that a "little dwarf" will relieve him of some of his burden. The secret desire to wake up one day and see that all his work was done as though there was some magic involved. On the other hand, the elfs can also appear as harmful and destructive, in fairytales that some believe to be rooted in the context of the gifts that were given to the spirits of the dead. In these ancient times the elf symbolized the spirit of the dead person or the kinsman who passed away. The Icelandic elfs were identified with the spirits of the ancient ancestors or with pagan deities. In the Kormak saga it was said that they would cure illnesses if they received a gift of the flesh and blood of an ox in a pagan burial cave. Sometimes the elfs abducted people for a certain period of time or forever and there are legends about human babies being replaced with elf babies. Some see the elfs, like the dwarfs, as a symbol of subconscious desires and wishes.

↔ **SYMBOLS** ↔

Emfisbana

The Emfisbana is a monster identical to the Basilisk but it has one head on both sides of its body and therefore it can see to both directions. The Emfisbana is the keeper of the "great secret", according to a 16th century Italian manuscript. This symbol appears quite frequently in the heraldic tradition. It was also known to the Greeks, and its name stems from the belief that because of its two heads it can move backward and forward at the same ease. Sometimes it is depicted as having the wings of a bat and some see it as a symbol of the fear and pain caused by ambivalent situations.

Fairy

The fairy in fairytales is a tiny feminine creature with wings of a butterfly. They appear mainly in the Celtic folklore of Ireland, Wales, Britain, northern Europe, Scandinavia and Iceland. They are usually considered to be spirits of nature. Some believe that the origin of the legendary fairies is the cult of ancestors, i. e. the "revival" of the spirits of dead kinsmen in pagan cultures, like the elfs. This is probably the source of the "fairy godmother" who appears in fairytales (the most famous among them is the fairy godmother of the motherless Cinderella and Tinker Bell, the fairy godmother of Peter Pen). The fairy godmother's task was to protect and save her godchildren from trouble and she usually appears as a protective spirit. "Fairyland" was considered to be heaven on earth or the western paradise and even in Christian sources there is still a belief that such a place exists.

In Pre-Christian Europe, gifts of food and drink were placed for them near the house. When Christianity replaced pagan beliefs many attempts were made to portray the fairies as evil spirits, after the attempts to refute the belief that they were ancestral spirits succeeded. Nevertheless, this attempted failed and fairies are known as positive creatures although they might appear as deluding or as an illusion – like the symbolism of another winged and transparent creature – the dragonfly. It was in pagan times, and not as a result of the attempts of the church to denounce the belief in fairies that fairies were sometimes accused of wrongdoing, mainly replacing human children with fairy children. Healers who failed to heal sick children tended to use the excuse of the "fairy" when their treatment caused the death of a child, and thus the fairy resembles Lilith (see entry) who harms an infant or newborn baby. The child that was placed instead of the baby the fairies stole was called "changling", and it was a deformed baby that failed to grow. Often children with birth defects were considered in primitive cultures to be changlings and the legal authorities condoned the beating of these unfortunate infants – since according to the legend the only way to deal with the changling that is laying in the cradle was to hit him. And then the fairy would appear screaming, "I did not hit your child so why do you hit mine?" take her child and return the abducted child to his parents.

One of the most popular traits of the fairies is the ability to wear different shapes and transform and the ability of to disappear immediately. Many fairytales tell the story of a poor boy that helped an old lady he met in his way. This woman was a fairy who changed her shape. Thus the boy was given magical gifts that enabled him to obtain great riches and marry a princess. Fairies who wish to cause harm change their shape to a raven.

From a symbolical point of view, fairies symbolize little creatures of the psyche. They are a personification of hopes, dreams and daydreams and symbolize the hope for help from a supportive and benevolent force. Fairies were attributed with supernatural powers, and in fairytales they can transform a person into an animal or an inanimate object. On the other hand, in medieval fairytales the fairy appears as an ordinary full-sized woman who has supernatural knowledge and powers. Usually the fairies have a queen to whom they obey.

Gargoyles

The gargoyles are monstrous heads of a man, animal or mythological animal. They appear in Medieval Christian religious art as a symbol of universal forces or as demonic creatures of the underworld. They are also depicted as imprisoned – prisoners of the rule of sublime spirituality. Therefore they are always depicted in art as overpowered by angels or celestial creatures, and they never stand at the center. Some saw them as "evil spirits" who fly out of the church and others saw them as "banishing evil".

Garuda

 Garuda is the bird that in Hindu mythology is the vehicle of the god Vishnu. It is called the "bird of life" and is sometimes identified with the phoenix. The garuda symbolizes the sky, sun and victory. It hatches from an egg in full-grown state and nests in the tree of life, the tree that fulfills all wishes. The garuda fights with the nagas, the mythical snakes in Hinduism.

↔ SYMBOLS ↔

Gnome

The gnome is an entity that is connected with the element of the earth. Some believe that the source of the word gnome is the Greek verb *"gnome"* which is also the root of the word knowledge and since the gnomes are believed to have profound knowledge of the secrets of the earth, minerals and subterranean processes of creation. The gnomes, who appear in fairytales as smaller than people but usually bigger than dwarfs, live in mines, caves and rifts in the ground. They know the stones, rocks, metals, minerals and precious stones and mining techniques. The gnomes appear mainly in German folktales. They helped miners and blacksmiths. The gnome is usually depicted with a hammer in his hands, wearing boots, a heat and a beard. In certain areas in Germany there is still a widespread belief that gnomes live in deserted mines and hidden caves and can kill those who invade their territory by creating a landslide of rocks.

Gorgon

In Greek mythology there are three gorgons – women with snake hair. The gorgons symbolize fear and terror, and the great mother in her horrible and destructive aspect, as the destroyer. The most famous of the gorgons is medusa whose gaze turns those who look at her into stone. This trait did not cease to exist even after she was beheaded.

Griffon/Griffin

The griffon is a monster with the head and wings of an eagle and a body of a lion. The griffon also has a long snake-like tail. It is a combination of the two sublime animals that are connected to the sun – the eagle and the lion, and this combination symbolizes the creature's benevolent nature. The griffon also symbolizes the sun, sky and the light of dawn that turns into gold, the richness of the sun and the combined force of the lion and the eagle. As keeper of the treasures, it symbolizes vigilance, alertness and vindictiveness. In ancient Greece it was consecrated to Apollo as a solar animal, to Athena as wisdom and to Nemesis as revenge. Without wings, it is the male griffon. The griffon always guards the path to redemption when it stands beside the tree of life or a similar symbol.

From a psychological point of view, the griffon symbolizes the relations between mental energy and cosmic power. In Medieval Christian art, the griffon is a popular symbol that usually represents ambivalence. Thus it represents both the antichrist and the savior, or both the spiritual and earthly power of the pope. In earlier times the griffon symbolized in Christianity the devil and all those who persecute the Christians. In eastern cultures the griffon is identified with the dragon and likewise symbolizes wisdom and enlightenment.

Harpy

The harpies are monsters with the head and chest of a woman and claws of a bird of prey. The daughters of Neptune and the sea (Tetis) are also called the "dogs of Zeus" (since they have an awful foul smell). They are connected to sudden death, storms and tempests and symbolize the feminine principle in its destructive aspect. Some see them also as a symbol of the fear of men from a woman "with claws". Another psychological aspect of this mythological animal is the personification of evil or crime in the double aspect of guilt and punishment. On a more profound philosophical level, they were  defined as a representation of the "evil aspects of cosmic energies". Sometimes the emphasis is on their dynamic nature. In this case they are depicted as "hasty movement". In Medieval art they sometimes appear as the symbol of the sign of Virgo that has musical aspects.

Hobgoblin

The word "goblin" means wind. Hobgoblin is the spirit of the hearth (main fire in the house). The belief in hobgoblins started in Europe in ancient times when a dead kinsman was buried in the house under the threshold or the main fire. Therefore the hobgoblin was originally a protective spirit that protected the members of the family and the family home itself, like the protective spirits of the house in South Asian cultures. It continued to appear in this meaning even after people began to bury their dead outside the house. But when Christianity replaced the pagan beliefs, the hobgoblin was demonized and became a demonic figure like other mythical creatures that were not originally evil. (As a result of the very different perception of good and evil of the pagan world compared to the Christian or monotheistic view in general). Since there were no malicious legends in the pagan world about the hobgoblin, it did not become a "significant" demon but remained a small and "insignificant" demon without any extremely destructive powers.

Hydra

The hydra is a blind monster in the shape of a dragon or a snake with seven heads that symbolizes the animalistic vital force. The number seven is connected to cosmic series – days of the week, planetary gods, planets, seven good virtues, seven deadly sins etc. The triumph over the monster with the seven heads can symbolize triumph over the evil influences of the planets and man's lowest and basest forces.

Incubus and Sucubus

The source of the name Incubus is "to stay overnight" as well as to "brood" or "incubate". In ancient times temples usually had isolated, dark, womb-like (see entry) chambers with a similar meaning of initiation, in which people could stay overnight for healing purposes, initiation or waiting for a vision or enlightenment. The priests overseeing the temple and these rooms were the Incubi, who later, when the Christians started to forcibly convert the religions and minds of pagans, became the Incubus – threatening, frightening and shocking demons. The notion of the womb represented by the Incubi rooms joined the notion of the impurity of everything that does not coincide with religion. The primordial masculine fear regarding the uncertainty of one's paternity of the child in the woman's womb was added as well. And thus, when patriarchal Christianity replaced paganism with its strong matriarchal features, the Incubus became a horrible demon who seduces and impregnates women in their sleep. It was said about the Incubus that after he visited a woman a human male would no longer be able to satisfy her as a result of the Incubus's great lust and knowledge of the secretes of sex (sex in Christianity was a problematic issue). The feminine counterpart of the Incubus is the Sucubus or Sucuba, that has similar features with the Lilith (see entry) – she makes men dream erotic dream and steals their sperm in order to impregnate herself. Religious authorities debated extensively the question whether these creatures can have children. Some suggested that the Sucubus can change her shape and turn into an Incubus, and with the sperm she stole from the man she impregnates the human woman. From many years, erotic dreams and nightmares were believed to be caused by this pair.

Kobold

The kobold is a creature that lives in mines and appears mainly in German folktales. German miners used to tell that they saw the eyes of the kobold in the mine, but the kobold itself is never to be seen and so there is no description of it beside a pair of eyes glowing in the darkness. The kobold is not unequivocally different from the gnomes and dwarfs (since it is invisible).

Some believe that the origin of the name of the mineral cobalt is the kobold, and it is called so because of the legend that it is very difficult to melt ores with cobalt since they were bewitched by the kobolds in the mines.

Lamia

Lamia was a mythological queen, greatly admired for her beauty, who became a savage animal as a result of her cruelty. Ancient manuscripts relate to the lamias, in plural, as identical to the sirens, and they were believed to dwell in the company of dragons in caves and deserts. They are connected to the symbolism of the fish. In Gascony the belief in lamias existed for a long time.

The symbol of the lamias is a golden comb that is maybe connected to the fishbone with which they comb their hair. It was told of the lamias that they eat children, and it became a popular myth in some places. The source of the name of the lamias is "lamos" – depths.

Lycanthrop – man-wolf

This is the legendary image of the man who Satan or the powers of darkness covered with wolf skin and forced to wander at night and wail at the roadsides. Some see the  Lycanthrop as a symbol of the hidden irrationality in the lower and earthly side of man and the possibility that this power might take control over one's life.

Mermaid

The mermaid is a creature that is half woman and half fish. It is the image of the Syrian goddess Atargatis or Tirgata and it is also similar to Ymaya, the African mermaid with the long green hair of seaweed, whose jewels are sea conches.

Minotauros (minotaur)

The minotauros has the body of a man and the head of an ox. Its name probably stems from the words Minos – the name of the king who imprisoned it in a labyrinth and tauros – ox, the ox of king Minos. In order to confine the minotauros the famous Cretan labyrinth was build by the architect Daedalus. The minotauros ate meat and the defeated Athenians were forced to sacrifice to it every seven (some say nine) years seven maidens and seven young men. Some say that the Athenians were punished because Minos, the king of Crete that was a mighty kingdom in those days, sent to Aegieus king of Athens his only son, Androgeus for a friendly visit. Aegeus, king of Athens, did the unthinkable – he sent the guest Androgeus to a fatal mission – to kill the dangerous raving ox (hospitality was considered to be sacred by Zeus, father of the gods). Androgeus was killed by the ox and Minos did not forgive the Athenians and demanded this gift. The sacrifice of young men and maidens happened three times, but at the fourth time, the hero Theseus slashed the minotaurous's throat and found his way out of the labyrinth with the help of Ariadne and her magic thread.

The mythological legend about the birth of the minotaruous is no less fascinating. This gruesome creature was the son of a mortal woman – Pasiphae, wife of Minos, king of Crete. The father of the minotaourous was an extraordinarily handsome bull, the picture of perfection. The bull was given to Minos by Poseidon, god of the sea, to be sacrificed to him. But Minos was deeply impressed by the bull's beauty and instead of sacrificing it, spared it and kept it for himself. Since he disobeyed the god's command, Poseidon punished him and made Pasiphae, Minos's wife, fall deeply in love with the bull and this is how this mythological monster was born. The triumph over the minotaurous put an end to this dark and distorted family relationship, and it also happened "within the family". Ariadne who gave Theseus the thread that helped him find his way in the labyrinth was the daughter of Minos who fell in love with Theseus at first sight.

The triumph of the hero Theseus over the monster symbolically suggests a cosmic solution that in this case is social salvation. Some see it as the psychological struggle between the lower, bloodthirsty, cruel and animal-like nature of man and his more superior, spiritual nature. Usually the superior human nature is represented by the warrior or knight and the animal-like nature by a mythological animal with the body of an animal and the head of a man – centaur or bukentaur for example. In this case it is the opposite – the head is that of an animal and the body is the body of a man – which symbolizes the absolute dominance of the low, animalistic principle over the human body. This is also true in the story of the birth of the monster. Minos's greed (but some say his pity for the handsome bull and his infatuation with the misleading vision he saw), disobedience to the gods and lust that made his wife fall in love with an animal are all features of the lower animal-like side of human nature.

In sum, the minotauros is a clear symbol of the dominance of the most basic urges over the superior and spiritual nature of man, the personification of the man-animal. It symbolizes the person who is totally controlled by the most basic and animalistic urges – the urge to kill and destroy that harms society and the animalistic sex urge that is implied by the sacrifice of the seven maidens and seven young men. The story of the monster's birth also features the power of basic human urges. The defeated Athenians "catered" to the embodiment of these urges that was confined in the labyrinth (as nowadays we lock the body of such a person in prison in order to keep him away from society). The hero, who represents the superior side of man – the one who overcomes his urges and instinctive traits, including fear, is a person ready to enter into that labyrinth, find the monster and kill it. From a psychological point of view, we can see it as the demand of society from the "animalistic" man to kill the animal inside him.

The Hindu god of the dead, Yamah, was also a minotauros – with a head of an ox and a body of a man.

Nymph

The Greek name of the nymphs is connected to the words "bride" and "doll". The nymphs were considered to be the sources of the feminine creative powers of the universe. Later they became protective spirits, mainly of fountains and mountains. The nymphs accompany various mythological deities and symbolize ideas connected to these deities.

The nymphs are closely connected to the symbolism of the running water, fountains, ponds and waterfalls. Since they are connected to water they also symbolize ambivalence, birth and regeneration or decomposition and death.

Jung saw the nymphs from the point of view of his individualization theory as the independent manifestation of the feminine nature of the unconscious. Jung concludes that what Paracelsus called regio nymphidica, actually describes the

.relatively undeveloped stage of the individualization process, a stage that is connected to notions of seduction, transience, reproduction and decomposition. The most famous nymphs are the sisters of Tetis, the Nereides, who appear in the story of the Argonauts in Greek mythology.

Pegasus

The winged horse, a symbol of the sun, symbolizes the combination between high and low and the aspiration to reach as high as possible. There was a widespread belief that Pegasus leaped from the blood of the gorgon medusa when Perseus beheaded her with the magical weapon given to him by the gods. It was said of Pegasus that it is never exhausted when it flies in the air at the speed of the wind. The beloved fountain of the poets, Hipokerini, burst from the place where Pegasus's hoof hit the ground.

Pegasus was the heart's desire of Bellerophon, the handsome young who was blessed with all the virtues of Greek mythology. He succeeded to capture Pegasus, what no other mortal could do, with the help of dream he dreamt in the temple of Athena, goddess of wisdom. In his dream he saw Athena holding in her hand some golden object. When he woke up, beside him was a harness made of gold. When Pegasus saw the golden harness he surrendered itself to Bellerophon without any resistance. Afterwards, Bellerophon rode on Pegasus in his struggle against the Chimera. According to the legend both the horse the rider greatly enjoyed their relationship.

Pegasus has human qualities of reason and judgement although it does not speak, unlike most of the mythological animals in Greek mythology. These traits were manifested when Bellerophon committed the sin of hubris and decided that his place was at the Olympus among the gods. As a result of his pride he lost the wise Pegasus that threw him of its back on his way to the Olympus. Pegasus itself reached the mountain of the gods where it found an honorable place in the stables.

Therefore, Pegasus symbolizes man's aspiration to rise up in the world and human willpower that as long as it is harnessed to a good cause it is benevolent and brings happiness, inspiration and elation. But when a man succumbs to the sin of pride and sees himself as the son of gods as a result of this great grace of elation – he loses his spiritual power, and this is what happened to Bellerophon.

The Hippogriff that appears in Medieval legends is the counterpart of Pegasus and also symbolizes the aspiration to rise up and the desire to reach the sublime that exist in each and every one of us – the innate ability to reach the spiritual level of existence.

Phoenix

The magical bird that is as big as an eagle shares certain similarities to the pheasant. The phoenix is depicted as coming up from the flames and it is a universal symbol of resurrection and eternity, death and rebirth and revival by fire. According to the legend when the phoenix sees death approaching it builds a nest in a tree with a sweet scent and starts extracting resin in order to manifest the full power of the sunbeams, until it burns itself to flames and ashes. And then another phoenix comes up for the bone marrow of the previous one. The phoenix remains dead for three days before its revival (the three days symbolize the waning of the moon) and only then it emerges again from the ashes. Thus it is also a lunar symbol (the moon that appears and disappears), but it is a universal solar symbol since it is the "bird of fire" that symbolizes celestial royalty, nobility and uniqueness. It also symbolizes gentleness since it does not crash the things she lands upon and does not feed on anything alive, but only on dew (that symbolizes divine grace). The phoenix is connected with the rose in most of the descriptions of paradise in various cultures.

In Turkish tradition, the phoenix is called Kerkis and in Persian Simuge. It is a well-known symbol of the cycles of destruction and regeneration. In China the phoenix is considered to be the emperor of all birds and a solar symbol. In alchemy, the phoenix is connected to the color red, the regeneration of universal life and the successful completion of a process. It symbolizes the materialization of the magnum opus – the great work. In Maya, Aztec and Toltec cultures the phoenix symbolizes solar power, blessings, happiness and Ketzel, the friend of Ketzelkuatel. In Chinese culture the phoenix is the

Peng-Huang, that is called the "scarlet bird" or the "material of flames". It is one of the four spiritually blessed or sacred creatures, and like the dragon and Chi-Lin with whom it is connected, it is always both yin and yang. When it is male, it is called Peng. It is yang, solar and bird of fire. As female it is Huang, yin and lunar. The Huang symbolizes beauty, gentleness, emotion and peace. When the phoenix appears together with the dragon that symbolizes the emperor it becomes totally feminine and symbolizes the empress, and together they symbolize the two aspects of imperial power. It is also a symbol of marriage and represents "unbreakable friendship", not just of the married couple but also the mutual connection between the yin and yang in the universe and in the realms of duality.

Like the dragon and the Chi-Lin, the phoenix is also made of a number of different elements and represents the entire cosmos. It has the head of a peacock (symbolizing the sun), the back of a swallow (symbolizing the sickle of the moon), its wings are the wind, its tail represents trees and flowers and its legs are the earth. It has five colors that symbolize the five virtues. In an ancient Chinese ritual it was said on the phoenix that: "its color delights the eye, its tranquility is a sign of virtue, its tongue speaks the truth, its voice sings a tune, its heart obeys the laws, its chest contains the treasures of literature and its powerful claws are a mighty weapon against evildoers". The appearance of the image of the phoenix in any occasion was very impressive and symbolized peace and benevolent rule, or the appearance of a man of great wisdom. A pair of phoenixes symbolizes the combination of the emperor and man of wisdom.

In Japanese symbolism the phoenix symbolizes the sun, justice, loyalty and obedience. In ancient Egyptian culture the phoenix is identified with the Benu, the sunbird. As a solar bird it symbolizes resurrection and eternity and is connected with Ra. In Roman culture the phoenix symbolized the rebirth and continuos existence of the Roman Empire. In Christianity the phoenix symbolizes resurrection, the triumph of life over death and the resurrection of Jesus after three days. In general the phoenix symbolizes triumph over death, faith and continuity.

According to psychological interpretation the "phoenix" exists in each of us and enables us to live every moment and overcome every momentary death – sleep, dream or change.

Rock

The giant storm bird that the wind symbolizes the movement of its wings and the lightening symbolizes its flight. It symbolizes the sun and the sky. According to Arab tradition, the rock bird never lands on the earth, but only on top of the mountain Kaf, the axis mundi (axis of the world).

Salamander

The salamander is the mythical lizard-like wingless creature that bounces out from the flames. It is one of the most familiar symbols of the element of fire and there was a belief that it is born from fire. A reptile called salamander with the same physical attributes as the mythical creature indeed exists in nature (see: animals, salamander), and it suffered immensely because of the symbolism attributed to its mythical counterpart. For thousands of years people used to burn salamanders because they believed that salamanders were fireproof. Various scholars wrote in their books that salamanders live happily and joyfully in the fire, although they were burned into ashes in bonfires when people tried to demonstrate their miraculous qualities.

Satyr

The masculine spirit of nature that has the head and chest of a man, the body of a he-goat from the waist down and he-goat horns and beard. The satyrs accompanied the gods of nature Silonus, Faunus, Pan and Dionysos/Bacchus. The satyrs symbolize the undomesticated and uncivilized nature, passion and lust and carnal pleasures and mischief. Sometimes the satyrs wear ivy crowns that symbolize Dionysos. They are also depicted with bunches of grapes, baskets of fruit, skin bags of wine and snakes. The satyrs' partners in the Bacchanalias (the orgies to Dionysos) were the Maenads.

Siren

The siren usually appears in two forms – as a bird with a human head or as a woman-fish. She symbolizes feminine seduction, deception, diverting the individual from his true goal by earthly temptations that divert him from the spiritual path. She also symbolizes the soul trapped in carnal lust. In Greek mythology the sirens seduced mariners with their singing. The singing of the sirens was so sweet and seductive that the mariners (like Odysseus and his men,

for example) had to tie themselves to the mast of their ship in order to prevent themselves from jumping into the sea to follow the capturing voices of the sirens.

Some see the sirens as a psychological symbol expressing the fear of the seductive woman who diverts the man from his quest and attracts him to the water of emotion and death. (The sexual act itself is likened to death since it involves the loss of individual identity and exhaustion). Some see the siren as a symbol of the seductive forces of the senses and illusions. The sirens appear before mariners after a long stay at sea away from home, and they can also be creatures of the imagination born out of the mariners' sensual desires. Thus, by activating the senses and the sweet seduction of music the siren sweep the mariners to the realms of illusion in which human existence fades away.

Since they cause death by seduction, the sirens are connected to funerals. The sirens are also connected to the flutes and lyres (an ancient harp). In ancient Egypt bird-sirens symbolize souls that left the body. In Greek mythology they symbolized evil, bloodthirsty souls. The myth of the siren bird evolved into the woman-fish that is lurking to mariners between the cliffs and rugged islands, and acts like her bird-like sisters who are connected to the element of air.

This myth is so widespread and powerful that it continued to exist among mariners in certain cultures almost until the modern age.

Sphinx

This mythological creature has the head of a man or a woman, the body of an ox, the feet of a lion and the wings of an eagle. The sphinx combines the four elements and is made of four superior animals that represent the sacred animals and the four elements. The ox (represents the sign of the Taurus in the zodiac and the element of the earth), The lion (the sign of Leo, element of fire), the eagle (the sign of Scorpio and element of water), and man (the sign of Aquarius and element of air). Since it is made of these four "strong" animals and combines all the elements it is the key to cosmic secrets. Therefore it symbolizes the mysterious and enigmatic. The sphinx also symbolizes the power of the sun.

In Greek mythology the sphinx appears as an important figure in the story of the city of Thebes and king Oedipus. In this legend, the sphinx was a winged creature with the body of a lion and face and chest of a woman who stood at the entrance to the city of Thebes and asked travelers that wanted to enter the city a riddle. If the traveler could solve the riddle the sphinx permitted him to enter the city. If he failed – the sphinx would swallow him. Thus the city of Thebes was under siege and nobody could enter it. The seven great gates of Thebes, the city's pride, were locked as a result of this menace and famine began to spread.

Oedipus, who abandoned his home in Corinth because of the prophecy of the oracle of Delphi that he would kill his father and marry his mother, approached the gates of Thebes. Oedipus was an outcast who had no family or friends and therefor he did not spare his life and decided to confront the sphinx and its riddles. The riddle that the sphinx asked Oedipus was: "who is the creature that walks on four in the morning, on two at noontime and on three in the evening?" Oedipus's answer was: "A human being. In childhood he crawls on his hands and knees, in his youth he walks on two and in old age he is aided by a stick". True, this mythological riddle is not so difficult as it could be expected from the sphinx, but it is symbolic to the legend of the sphinx – it expressed the sphinx's sense of superiority over humans since they are ephemeral and subject to the physical changes that life brings upon them. While the sphinx is a creature that symbolizes the union of the elements and the power of nature embodied in them. And indeed when the sphinx heard this answer it killed itself.

The sphinx is one of the quintessential symbols of riddle and mystery. The sphinx is the keeper of ultimate knowledge that is supposed to be kept forever beyond the comprehension of humans. Jung saw the sphinx as a synthesis of the "horrible mythological mother" who takes back all the she gives.

Tihamath
Tihamath is the monster of the depths, a primordial monster from the times of chaos before the creation of the world. The origin of its Semitic name is close to its symbolism – monster of the abyss. It symbolizes the primordial chaos, water and the power of water, darkness, the blind forces of chaos and the feminine principle. In Sumerian and Semitic cultures, all life forms emerged from the sweet water – Apsu, and the salty water – Tihamath.

Triton
The triton is the man of the sea, half human and half fish, who holds or blows a horn or a conch and dominates the forces of water – seas or rivers. The tritons can create sea storms by blowing their conches. Cartographers in ancient times

considered them to be the partners of the mermaids and used to draw them on maps since they believed that seafarers could indeed meet them in their voyages.

Unicorn

This mythological animal has the body of a horse and a single horn at the center of its forehead. It symbolizes the feminine and lunar principle together with the lion that symbolizes the masculine and solar principle. It symbolizes grace, purity, rarity, virginity, perfect goodness and sublime virtues, the power of mind and body and the incorruptible. The unicorn also symbolizes the sword or the divine word. When the two horns are united into one, it symbolizes the unity of opposites and the perfect sovereign power. The universality of this animal that does not exist in nature is surprising. It can be found as a familiar cultural symbol in many different cultures both in the eastern and western world.

Jung, who studied the connections between psychology and alchemy, investigated the many aspects of this mythological animal. He concluded that in general it does not have one clear and definite symbolism, but a varied symbolism that characterizes animals with one horn, both real and mythological such as the swordfish and certain types of dragons. Jung mentioned that the unicorn changes sometimes to a white dove and suggested the possibility that on one hand it is connected to ancient monsters and on the other hand it represents masculine, pure and penetrating power. In alchemy the unicorn represents mercury together with the lion as sulfur.

In order to catch the unicorn the virgin had to wait for it in the field. The unicorn was caught because it would come and lie in her lap.

Jesus is sometimes represented by the unicorn, and the unicorn's sole horn symbolizes Jesus' invincible power since he is the only Son of God or the union between him and his father. As a solitary and isolated animal the unicorn also represents monastic life. As a symbol of purity, virginity and grace it symbolizes the Virgin Mary and is a symbol of all good virtues. On the other hand, in ancient traditions the unicorn sometimes appears as having evil traits and sinister intentions towards mankind. Jung noticed that the church does not recognize the negative attributes of the unicorn. The alchemists, on the other hand, used the ambivalent attributes of the unicorn to symbolize the Monstrum Hermaphroditum (monstrous hermaphrodite).

In Iranian tradition it symbolizes wholeness and all the moral virtues. In

Sumerian and Semitic cultures it is a lunar animal. It is attributed to the virgin goddess and appears with the tree of life.

In the cultures of ancient Greece and Rome the unicorn symbolized the sickle of the moon. It is attributed to all virgin goddesses and lunar goddesses, mainly to Artemis/Diana. According to heraldic tradition, the unicorn has the head and body of a horse, lion's tail, legs and hoofs of a deer and a contorted horn at the center of its head.

The unicorn appears sometimes in pairs, one on each side of the tree of life, as keepers of the tree. The conflict between the lion and the unicorn symbolizes the struggle between solar and lunar forces and the pairs of opposites. According to the legend the unicorn can detect poison in water with its horn, and purify it. It appears in many traditions as a white horse with a single horn, but in esoteric tradition it has a white body, red head and blue eyes. According to one legend the unicorn is never exhausted when chased but kneels on the ground in submission when a virgin approaches it. In China, the animal known as Chi-Lin (see entry) is identified with the unicorn but some claim that it is not so because it can have two horns. The unicorn, like the Chi-Lin, is one of the main symbols of Taoism and represents the essence of the five elements and virtues.

Whale

The whale in its mythological sense is a huge fish, a "giant snake", and an ancient monster of the sea and chaos. It symbolizes the snake and the power of the depths. Together with the behemoth it symbolizes the element of the earth. In Jewish tradition it was said on the whale that the righteous would eat its flesh in paradise. In Scandinavian mythology the oceans were created by a huge snake or dragon that swallows the water in order to spit it out. This creature is called midgardorm. The whale is the archetype of the primordial monster from the times of chaos, like the Mesopotamian Tihamath. Sometimes it is identified with the world or the world's preserving and reviving power. Some see the reference to the whale in the Jewish scriptures "this whale you made to play with" as an emphasis of the power of the one god over the entire creation, even the mighty forces of nature people used to worship in ancient times.

Symbolism in human images

Androgyne/Hermaphrodite

The androgyne is a mythical figure of a man and a woman in one body, but also a figure that exists in reality, since it is embodied in a physiological condition – an infant that is born with two sets of genitals – female and male. Such cases are rare but exist physiologically, sexually (bisexuality), psychologically and spiritually – especially since the beginning of the New Age in which we live, when certain people find the illusion of the separation between the female and the male to be blurred or unacceptable, or they develop and reach a state of a perfect combination between the female principle and the male principle on the mental and spiritual level. As a symbol, the androgyne symbolizes primordial perfection, the unconditional state, independence, the return to Eden, the oneness of the primordial female-male forces, the unification of heaven and earth – between the king and queen – when the two become one, mother of all and father of all, and a powerful symbol of ongoing creation. The hermaphrodite is also a symbol of intellectual activity that is not connected to belonging to a particular gender.

Some people consider the hermaphrodite or the androgyne to be the realization of the symbol of the number 2 in the person, which creates a personality that is blended and unified despite the duality. The hermaphrodite is also known in pre-Columbian Mexico, in the image of Quetzalcoatl, the god in whom the law of opposites and the separate sexes achieve final oneness.

The hermaphrodite is closely linked to the archetype of Gemini. In the *Symposium*, Plato declares that God initially created man in the form of a figure consisting of two bodies and two sexes. Similarly, there are Hebrew legends that indicate the primordial creation of man as a creature that combined man and woman in one body. The hermaphrodite is also a symbol of the idea that all the opposites unite to form one inclusive unity. The androgynous divinity is also known in China, Persia, Australia, and in various forms in many cultures of the ancient world, and echoes of the idea can also be found in the monothcistic religions. Hermaphrodite divinities are linked to the myth of birth, and are described in many ancient Egyptian monuments.

In alchemy, the *magnum opus* is creating the perfect androgyne, restoring humanity to its state of perfection. This idea is represented by a male-female image or the two-faced head of a king and a queen, or the red man and his white wife. Symbols of this state among the gods are the androgynes Zervayan, the Persian god of time without limits. In Greek mythology, Chaos is neutral from the point of view of gender. In other words, before the Big Mother, the asexual androgyne existed. Zeus and Heracles are frequently dressed as women. In Cyprus, it is the bearded Aphrodite. Dionysos has feminine characteristics. The Chinese god of night and day is an androgyne and the androgynous perfection is also represented by the yin-yang symbol and by the "spiritually blessed" yin-yang creatures – the dragon, the phoenix and the Chi-Lin may all be yin, yang, or both. Hinduism has the Shakta-Shakti and several divinities, especially Shiva, who are (sometimes) shown as half male and half female.

Other symbols of androgynes are: a lotus, a palm tree, a cross, an arrow, an anchor, a dot in a circle,a snake, and a bearded woman.

Angels

In most cultures, angels appear as the messengers of God and as the links between heaven and earth, man and God. According to the Hebrew tradition, they do not have free will and their entire desire is to serve God and do his bidding. They have superhuman powers, and through them,

God grants to the angels his goodwill, heavenly tidings, enlightenment, direction, divine protection, and so on. In contrast, they may also be God's messengers and executors of his commands concerning destruction and punishment. Since they praise God in song, they are linked to the symbolism of musical instruments.

Cherubs

Josephus Flavius wrote the following about cherubs: "Cherubs are winged creatures, but their form is not the same as any living creature observed by human beings." Cherubs symbolize the divine presence and they are guards of the sacred and door-keepers.

As Tetramorphs, the cherubs represent the four forces or elements that guard the center of the Garden of Eden. They combine the bull (Taurus, element of earth), the lion (Leo, element of fire), the eagle (Scorpio, element of water), and man (Aquarius, element of air). The four cherubs or the four-headed cherub also symbolize the four winds, and in Christianity, the four Evangelists. The cherubs are highest in rank after the seraphs among the nine orders of angels.

The word *cherub* originates from the Accadian word *kherbu*. The cherubs stood at the entrances of Assyrian temples and served as "door-keepers."

Child

The child is a symbol of the future. He symbolizes the physical realization of powers or their latent possibilities, as opposed to the old man who symbolizes the past. The child symbolizes renewal, innocence, naivety, simplicity, and future possibilities. He is also symbolic of the stage in the life of the old person at which he undergoes a transformation and assumes renewed simplicity. In that way, the child symbolizes a high level of transformation of individuality, the self that changes and is reborn toward perfection. Jung sees in the child a symbol of the supportive and protective forces that form the subconscious. A dream about a child frequently symbolizes a spiritual event or change that occurs in auspicious circumstances.

The mystical child, who solves riddles and imparts wisdom and knowledge, is an archetypal figure with the same meaning, but on the collective and general level. He also constitutes the heroic child who liberates the world from monsters. This archetype carries faith within him, because simplicity, innocence and purity ultimately prevail.

In alchemy, the child who wears a crown and a royal cloak symbolizes the philosophers' stone – the supreme recognition of the mystical identity with God, the divine and eternal spark that is in man.

Cyclops

The Cyclops was a mythological giant with one eye in the middle of his forehead. In contrast to Shiva's three eyes (including the third eye), which symbolize enlightenment and superhuman properties, the single eye of the Cyclops symbolizes abnormality that derives from the lowest forces of nature. It is linked to the mark of Cain, to the sign of otherness that brings suffering in its wake, and to extreme materialism – the tremendous body of the giant Cyclops blinds the person and prevents him from observing his external and inner world normally.

The myth of the Cyclops occurs in different versions in most parts of Europe and Asia Minor, but is unknown in the Far East. In northern Spanish folklore, the Cyclops was called Ojankano, and was thought to be a giant with red hair (a folkloric satanic symbol that was prevalent in the region). He was tall and had one light-colored eye and a maleficent gaze. The Ojankano was a symbol of evil and of the destructive forces that lay hidden in the low or regressive aspect of the person. It is interesting to point out that cases of a single eye in nature are rare but do exist as a birth defect. However, they are not usually linked to gigantism.

Dwarf

Like other mythological creatures of small size, the dwarf may appear as symbols of forces, which, because of moral standards, are not included in the circle of consciousness. In other words, the dwarf symbolizes the unconscious and immoral forces of nature. In folk-tales, he frequently appears as a naughty, sometimes mischievous, and even harmful creature. He has somewhat childish characteristics that stem from his low stature. But as a symbol of dual significance, the dwarf may also appear as a protective, supportive and helpful creature, or as one who reveals secrets about the earth, the forest, metals, minerals and treasures. Jung sees the dwarfs as the doorkeepers of the unconscious.

The smallness of the dwarf may represent some kind of distortion, abnormality and inferiority. This interpretation may explain the figure of "the dancing Shiva" in which a divinity is dancing on the flattened figure of the demon-dwarf, which symbolizes the "blindness of life," the ignorance of man, and his smallness. (In other words, in Hinduism, the dwarf beneath Shiva's feet symbolizes ignorance, blindness and smallness.) The triumph over this demon symbolizes the achievement of true wisdom.

In the ancient Egyptian culture, the god Bes is described as a dwarf. In the ancient Greek and Roman cultures, Hephaistos/Vulcan is sometimes described as a dwarf. Vishnu sometimes assumes the image of a dwarf. In the Japanese tradition, the river god is a malicious dwarf, and in Scandinavian symbolism, four dwarfs stand tat the corners of the earth and hold up the sky.

Father

The father represents the spirit/soul, the sun, and the male principle. He is linked to the conscious and the cognizant, as opposed to the subconscious, which is attributed to the mother. He represents the forces of law and order, in contrast to the female mother, who represents the intuitive and instinctive forces.

The symbolic representation of the father is linked to the elements of air and fire – the masculine elements, to the sky, to the light, to lightning and to weapons. The power that is ascribed to him is the power of rule (just as the power of heroism is attributed to the son). For this reason, and also because he represents the power of tradition (which he has to perpetuate by passing it on to his son), he represents the world of the moral imperatives and the prohibitions that limit the instinctive forces.

Father is also a common name for "celestial father," God. The male gods of heaven always appeared as "big father." In myths and legends, the image of the father symbolizes physical, mental and spiritual superiority.

Giant

The giant symbolizes the brutal forces of nature, primeval strength and force, darkness, night and winter. The giant per se is neither evil nor good, but rather an "amplification" of the human mass and of materialism. He may be beneficent and protective, as in many folk-tales in which the giant's help is often granted to the simple man. To the same extent, when confronting the tyrannical ruler, the giant may also be harmful and dangerous. The victory of the simple person over the giant is the victory of the spiritual over the material (as in the story of David and Goliath).

The deepest and most ancient myth of the giant is the existence of a primordial and gigantic creature whose sacrifice advanced Creation. This is the case in the story of the giant Prometheus, who brought fire to humanity in Greek mythology, and paid for his deed with enormous suffering. This cosmogenic myth was extremely widespread among ancient and primitive peoples, and he links it to the ritual of human sacrifice that was performed in order to summon the cosmic forces and create a beneficial change or advancement. Some people consider the myth of the giant to be a psychological projection of the fear of the "terrible father," since children tend to see their parents as giants.

Hero/Heroine

The symbol of the hero appeared as early as the prehistoric cultures, and from the dawn of humanity it expresses the need to extol and enumerate the values symbolized by the hero figure. In most of the legends, the hero starts out as low-born or as a person of high birth who is unaware of his high-born status. Every detail along his path and in his struggle has symbolic significance. The hero's journey is symbolic of the journey of the soul in the material world and of the struggles of the soul with the dark sides of the personality and with the illusions of this world. The hero encounters temptations and obstacles whose goal is to weaken his physical strength, which symbolizes his mental strength, or temptations that are meant to weaken his mind directly. The hero fights the figures that symbolize darkness, and, in a symbolic manner, fights the very fact of the inner darkness of human nature. The goal of the hero or the reward he obtains are mostly patently symbolic. Winning the hand of the princess or the beloved, or saving her from a dark or mysterious place such as the Underworld, from the tower where she is imprisoned, or from the figure that symbolizes evil, and being united with her, symbolizes the return to the coveted state of oneness of the soul, the primal state that existed prior to the descent into the material world and its struggles. Like the alchemists' gold, the prize or the achievement of material wealth in folk-tales symbolizes reaching the pure, pristine and enlightened state of the soul. Winning the monarchy or rule symbolizes the person who rules his mind and wins "self"-monarchy – the hero that conquers his evil nature.

The heroine in legends also usually starts off from a symbolically low social status. She frequently makes herself unattractive, and her ugliness is symbolic of the selfish nature of the person at the beginning of the journey. She sheds this ugliness and selfish nature when she completes her path successfully.

King/Queen

The king symbolizes the male principle, sovereignty, supreme achievement in the terrestrial world, earthly power and absolute control. The king is identified with the Creator and with the sun, and in many cultures he is considered to have "divine" or "solar" authority for his majesty, since he carries out the word of heaven on earth. The king is also thought to be identified with the earth in the realm of his sovereignty and with the people under his rule, and his state affects and is affected by the state of those two. The king and the queen together symbolize perfect oneness, the two halves of one whole, perfection and androgyny (see Androgyne). Since they are the sovereigns of the earth, they are represented by the rulers of the sky – the king is a symbol of the sun and the queen is a symbol of the moon. The king is a symbol of heaven, of gold and of the day, and the queen is the symbol of earth, of silver and of the night.

In alchemy, the king is symbolized by sulfur and the queen by mercury. Some of the king's symbols are the sun, the royal scepter, the crown (which is reminiscent of the shape of the sun), arrows, the royal throne, the raven and the sword.

Knight

The knight is a symbol of intellectual strength and moral fortitude that transcends low, earthly and bestial aspects, even of human begins. The knight is a symbol of the logos, a symbol of the hero who overcomes his evil impulse, which is embodied by the animal, the horse he is riding – the bestial element in the submissive person that is controlled and directed by the knight for lofty purposes. The horse is also the symbol of the physical element the knight transcends.

The knight is a symbol of the spirit's superiority to matter, and for this reason, in folk-tales, he is able to conquer and subdue physical masses that are greater than his own. As mentioned above, his spiritual strength is superior to his physical strength, and, in parallel, he has the agility, intention and persistence to accomplish his goal. His war, which is waged on the forces of earthly, dark, inferior forces, culminates in the victory of the knight's spirit. This is the symbolic meaning of the knight's battle with the dragon. The battle can be interpreted psychologically as a war on the person's inferior side, a war on the dark sides of his personality, which ultimately results in the triumph of the mind, of the power of the spirit, and of the lofty side of the person.

Nowadays, this symbolism gains mainly from a historical distance. In the past, the image of the knight was a concrete image, most of whose training was physical training in order to bolster physical strength. However, fortifying and strengthening the body do not contradict the spiritual expression of the symbol of the knight, since the powers of the body contribute to the powers of the mind and vice versa.

Lilith

According to Hebrew legends, Lilith was Adam's first wife. According to the sources, they broke up after a quarrel about who would be "on top" during intercourse. After her separation from Adam, Lilith went over to the other side, and became the wife of the chief of the demons, Ashmadai, and the queen of the demons. According to folklore, she is a nocturnal menace that mainly harms women in childbirth and newborns. In character, she resembles the Greco-Roman Lamia. She can also be identified with Brunhilde in the Nibelung saga, and as the opposite of Grimhilde (who can be compared to Eve). Lilith is a blatant symbol of the "terrible mother," of the terrible female aspect. Her characteristics make her comparable to the figure of the Greek Hecate, who demanded human sacrifice. Her image is that of a seductress who tries to extract semen from men while they sleep. She symbolizes jealousy and vindictiveness. In astrology, the Lilith is the moon when it cannot be seen from earth, and whose astrological influence is different than that of the visible moon.

Mother/The Big Mother/The Mother Goddess

The mother symbolizes ambivalence because she represents two aspects: on the one hand, the great, nourishing, life-giving mother, Mother Nature, Mother Earth, and on the other, "the terrible mother," an image that symbolizes death. She has a dual nature: creative and destructive, nourishing, protective, providing warmth and shelter, but she also possesses forces of destruction and death. She creates and nourishes all of life, but also buries it. "The return to the mother" is identical to dying. Jung adds that "the terrible mother" is not just a symbol of death, but also of the cruel and harsh side of nature, which is indifferent to human suffering. He sees the mother as a symbol of the collective subconscious, of the left and nocturnal side of existence, and as a source of the waters of life. He stresses that the mother is the symbol of the anima – the female principle in the male – that the person casts onto the feminine figures in his life: his mother, sister, and beloved.

The mother is the archetype of femininity, the source of all life, the principle of containing, the symbol of all states of cosmic life, the unification of all the elements, both celestial and terrestrial. She is the queen of heaven, the mother of God, the keeper of the keys of fertility and the gates of birth, death, and rebirth. Apollius relates to the mother in the following words: "The universal mother, mistress of all the elements, the ancient child of time, sovereign of all spiritual things, queen of the dead and queen of the immortals, the only materialization of all the gods and goddesses, who rules the shining heights of the sky, all the winds of the sea and the silence that saddens the nether world with a nod of her head. She is admired in many aspects, known by many names, and worshipped in many ways in various ceremonies."

As the goddess of the moon, the mother is a symbol of constant renewal that creates the seasons and controls the life-giving waters and the growth within the fertile earth. She is linked to the symbolism of the moon and of time. As such, she is considered to be the spinner of time and fate, and all the mythological "Big Mothers" are spinners and weavers, spinning the webs of life and their patterns in the thread of fate, symbolizing the binding power on the one hand and the liberating power on the other.

Mythologically speaking, the Big Mother, "the virgin mother" or "the mother of God" is simultaneously the mother and bride of God, in other words, of the divine force. Spiritually speaking, she is the archetype of perfection, self-existence, wisdom, self-development and redemption via enlightenment and transformation. As wisdom, she embodies the transformation of the person's condition from the most basic and inferior level into the highest.

In alchemy, the Big Mother is the dynamic symbol of fire and heat, the force that changes shape, purity, digestion and destruction. In Buddhism and Taoism, she is the passive and static principle, wisdom and understanding, and her symbol is the lotus and the open book of wisdom. In the Kabbala, "mother" is the name of the third sphere, the sphere of wisdom, which moves the entire universe and contains it within her. In her beneficial and positive aspect, the Big Mother is represented by goddesses such as Hat-hor, Isis, Kibela, Ishtar, Lakshami, Parvati, Tara, Kwan-Yin, Demeter, Sophia and Mary, mother of Jesus. In her terrible aspect, she is represented by the goddesses Astarte, Kali, Durga, Lilith, Hecate and the Black Virgin, who is sometimes described as having hair of serpents or a frightening appearance.

The pattern of matriarchal society (as opposed to that of patriarchal society) is based on family ties and blood relations, covenants, friendship and the passive acceptance of the laws and phenomena of nature, in contrast to patriarchal societies, which extol laws and human deeds, the preference for works of art rather than agriculture and nature, and obedience to hierarchy.

The symbols of Mother Earth, are water, stone, cave, night, the home of the depths, the home of the mothers, and the home of strength/wisdom. Other common symbols are the crescent moon, the crown of stars, a blue robe, cow's horns, the spiral, all the pools of water, wells, springs, and so on, everything that protects and serves as a shelter – a house, a wall, a gate, a temple, a church, a city, and so on – all the vessels with the capacity to contain and the vessels that are connected with feeding, abundance and the principle of receiving, such as the cup, the basket, the horn of plenty, the vase, the yoni, and so on, and everything whose source is in water, such as the pearl, fishes, and shells. Among birds, the symbols are the swan, the partridge, the swallow, the goose, and so on, and among the plants and flowers are the lotus, the lily, the rose, the peony, and incense trees. In her positive and supportive aspect, she is associated with all the animals that provide nourishment, whether via their flesh or via their milk. In her negative and destructive aspect, she is represented by the deadly cobra, the lioness, and is identified with the female praying mantis and the black widow spider, which devour their mates during copulation. As a protector of her young and as an avenger, she is identified with the lioness. The symbol of her virginity and her purity is the unicorn.

From the astronomical point of view, the Big Mother is identified with the Big Dipper. The number associated with her is 7 and her day of the week is Friday, when a fish is sacrificed and consumed in her honor. In several cultures, she also appears as the goddess of the hunt and the queen of the wild animals and is accompanied by a broad range of animals.

Person
In certain cultures, the person symbolizes the jewel of creation. Its symbol is number 5. Regarding the first person, the name "Adam" comes from the Hebrew

word for earth, *adama*, in order to emphasize the earthly forces inherent in him, as well as the fact that man originates from the earth, and his very existence depends on it. Unfortunately, this link does not seem to be understood today.

It is said about the first man that his body was all light, and after the original sin in the Garden of Eden, it became skin. Man was thought to be the link between low and high: an earthly body, which decays and returns to dust, and a divine, immortal soul.

In the Kabbala, in alchemy, in gnosticism and many other theories, man is a macrocosm and contains the entire universe within him. For this reason, he can learn about the universe and what is beyond earthly realms to a certain degree, with the help of his inner being and his experience in the concrete world.

In the Kabbala, each of man's organs is attributed to one of the spheres. Eve, the first woman, is the completion of the man's androgenous state (see Androgyne/Hermaphrodite). According to Hebrew commentaries, the first man and woman were created as one body with two qualities, the masculine and the feminine, which were subsequently separated. Plato also states that when God first created man, the latter contained both sexes. This idea occurs in many ancient cultures.

Prince/Princess

The prince and the princess symbolize the potential for sovereignty, since they are the heirs to the throne. They also symbolize the power and the necessity of young monarchy. The prince is linked to the king as a symbol of the fertility of the people and the earth. The prince sometimes appears as a hero in legends. His main attribute is intuition and he is generally completely positive, devoid of the properties of judgment and law that are attributed to the king.

In many tales, winning the hand of the princess symbolizes the aspiration to rise up to a lofty and exalted position or a higher spiritual plane, the path to which is fraught with danger and may even lead to the death of the warrior who is trying to win the princess. Winning her hand, therefore, occurs after a long, exhausting journey, which symbolizes a mental and spiritual journey.

In the last centuries, with the repression of spiritual aspirations, the "ailments" are coming back, gaining momentum and becoming everyone's ailments, while in the past, they were mainly the province of certain classes only. The prince and the princess now symbolize the unattained in the material, emotional and status realm – the dream princess, the prince on a white horse. The cynicism that accompanies these concepts symbolizes rationality, the focus on the status and materialistic aspects of existence, and the absence of belief in the importance of the mental and spiritual journey to transcendence and unification on the higher levels.

Symbols in the plant kingdom

Acacia

In Mediterranean countries, the acacia symbolizes life, immortality, platonic love and withdrawal. Since the acacia has both white and red flowers, it symbolizes life and death, death and rebirth. The thorns of the acacia represent the rays of the half moon.

In the ancient Egyptian culture, the acacia was a solar tree that symbolized rebirth, eternal life, initiation and innocence. It symbolized Neit, it was considered to be a sacred tree, with its white and red (pink) flowers linked to the sacred principle of red-white.

In the hermetic doctrine, the acacia symbolizes the declaration of Hiram, which teaches that "man must know how to die in order to live again in the eternal world."

In the Hebrew tradition, the acacia is the tree that is sacred to the Temple. It symbolizes a life of morality and innocence. In the Christian tradition, the acacia symbolizes a life of morality.

Almond/Almond Tree

The almond tree symbolizes sweetness and delicateness. It is one of the first trees to bloom, so that late frost is liable to damage it and destroy its blossoming. This led to the symbolism of delicateness on the one hand and awakening on the other. It symbolizes virginity, production from within the self, and the yoni – the vagina – because of its shape.

In China, the almond symbolizes feminine beauty, courage in the face of sorrow and adversity, alertness and wakefulness.

In Christianity, the almond symbolizes divine grace and authorization, as well as the purity of the Virgin. In Hebrew, the root of the word for almond, *shaked*, relates to alertness and diligence. Aaron's almond orchard represents a miracle of renewal and resurrection, since buds emerge from the the cultivated orchard. In the Persian tradition, the almond symbolizes the tree of heaven. Similar symbols that are linked to the almonds are the mandorla and the *vesica piscis*.

↔ SYMBOLS ↔

Aloe
The aloe is a decorative plant that symbolizes bitterness as well as honesty and wisdom. It is dedicated to Zeus/Jupiter.

Apple
Because it is completely round, the apple symbolizes totality, absoluteness and union, as opposed to the plurality symbolized by the pomegranate. It is also the symbol of earthly passions, or of the pleasures of this kind of passion.

Inexplicably, the apple has become the symbol of the fruit from the Tree of Knowledge in the Christian world, too, even though there is no basis in the scriptures (where the fruit of the Tree of Knowledge is described as "fruit" without any indication of the nature of the fruit). Consequently, the apple has become the symbol of the passion for the material versus the divine command that forbade eating it. For this reason, it symbolizes both knowledge and the passion to know. In addition to this connotation, which, as mentioned above, is not based on any of the scriptures, but rather on some kind of interpretation, the apple also symbolizes love, fruitfulness, gaiety, heavenliness, luxury, but also deception and death – as can be seen in its relation to the story of the Garden of Eden.

It is possible that the appearance of the apple as the fruit in the Garden of Eden stems from the fact that it was the forbidden fruit of the Golden Age. During the Golden Age, it was the fruit of the Tree of Life that gave its redness to the gods. In the Celtic tradition, too, the apple has a similar meaning. It is the fruit of the other world. It also symbolizes fertility and marriage. Halloween, the festivity of the apple, is linked to the death of the old year.

As the apple of Hesperides and the fruit of the garden of Freia, it symbolizes immortality. In various cultures, the offer of an apple symbolized a declaration of love. Like the orange, which represents fertility, apple blossoms are used to adorn brides. In the Chinese traditions, the apple symbolizes peace, compatibility and agreement. In Christianity, there is an ambivalent attitude toward the apple as a symbol. On the one hand, it is the fruit of temptation and of the sin that led to the fall of man; on the other, when it is described as being in the possession of Jesus or the Virgin Mary, it is a symbol of the new man and of redemption. A monkey with an apple in his mouth symbolizes the fall (the expulsion from Eden).

In the ancient Greek tradition, the apple is dedicated to Venus, as love and passion, a symbol of marriage and a proposal of marriage. "The unharmonious apple" was given to Venus by Paris. The branches of the apple tree are attributed to Nemesis and to Artemis, and are used in rituals for Diana. In addition, it served as a prize in a race, just as the olive branch served as a prize in the moon maiden race. The apple of Dionysos was the quince. The apple tree is linked to health and immortality and is dedicated to Apollo. The apple blossom is the Chinese symbol of peace and beauty.

Apricot
Since it is self-fertilizing, the apricot symbolizes androgyny. In the Chinese tradition, it symbolizes death and bashfulness.

Ash
This is a symbolic Semitic tree that is linked to the feminine aspect of the divinity, especially Astarte or Ishtar, who are mostly represented as a sacred tree. For this reason, the ash appears in the Bible as idolatry. Moreover, it sometimes appears as a phallus or as a sign of a tree god.

Aspen
This tree symbolizes fear, uncertainty, eulogy and lamentation. In Bach Flower Remedies that are used for treating the various layers of the mind energetically, the aspen symbolizes unknown and incomprehensible fear, and is used for treating paralyzing and all-enveloping fear from an unknown source, which seizes the person for no apparent reason.

Aster
In the Chinese tradition, this plant and flower symbolizes beauty, personal charm, humility and elegance. In Greece, it is a plant that is dedicated to Aphrodite, and symbolizes love.

Bamboo
Bamboo symbolizes grace, resilience, bending while preserving strength, pliancy, good reproductive ability, long-lasting friendship, longevity, an elderly but strong person, the whole person who bends with the storm and then straightens, strong and bold, when the storm passes.

In the Chinese culture, bamboo symbolizes longevity, piety, preservation of the tradition from generation to generation, and the winter season, together with the plum tree and the pine tree as the three winter friends. It is the sign and mark of Buddha, and the scholar who deports himself upright but humbly. Bamboo with seven knots symbolizes the seven stages of initiation and prayer. Bamboo

.with a sparrow symbolizes friendship. Bamboo with a crane symbolizes longevity and happiness. In Japan, bamboo symbolizes devotion and sincerity.

Barley
The grains are all symbolic of the renewal of life, resurrection and fertility. In Egypt, barley that was sprinkled on the body of Osiris sprouted and became "new life after death." Sometimes, a figure of Osiris was created out of earth and barley, and the growth of the barley symbolized the resurrection of the spring and his return to earth. The Greeks used sheaves of barley for describing fertility and fruitfulness. Barley is linked to the god Kor, to Demeter and to the moon goddess.

Basil
This is a plant that was used in funerals and funerary rites. It was considered to be a plant that was mentally encouraging, clarifying and thought-provoking.

Bean
The bean symbolizes immortality, total change, bewitching power and phallicism. According to the Romans, the bean was dedicated to Silvanus. In the Teutonic tradition, it symbolized eroticism and sexual pleasure.

Beech
This tree symbolizes prosperity and soothsaying. It was dedicated to Zeus and is the symbol of Denmark.

Buttercup
In the Greco-Roman traditions, the buttercup symbolizes mockery, scorn, malice, resentment, a wish to harm, madness. Moreover, it symbolizes Ares/Mars, the gods of war.

Camellia
The camellia mainly symbolizes stability. In the Chinese tradition, it symbolizes health, beauty and mental and physical strength. In Japan, in contrast, the camellia symbolizes sudden death.

Cedar
The cedar is a symbol of power, nobility and justness. It is the symbol of Lebanon. In Christianity, it symbolizes glory, splendor, exultation, beauty and

sometimes Jesus. In the Hebrew tradition, the cedar symbolizes the sacred tree of Solomon from which he built the temple. In the Sumerian tradition, it symbolizes the cosmic tree, the Tree of Life, and magic properties are attributed to it. It was dedicated to Tamuz.

Cherry
Since it bears fruit before leaves, the cherry tree symbolizes man, who comes into the world naked, without any assets, and returns naked to the earth. In the Chinese tradition, the blooming of the cherry tree symbolizes spring, as well as hope, youth, virility, feminine beauty and the male principle. In Japan, the cherry symbolizes prosperity, wealth and growth. In Christianity, the cherry is thought to be the fruit of paradise and the fruit of the blessed. It symbolizes good deeds and sweetness and sometimes describes the infant Jesus.

Chestnut
In Christianity, the chestnut symbolizes virtues, purity and modesty. It is "surrounded by thorns but they do not touch it." The chestnut serves as a symbol for overcoming temptation.

Chrysanthemum
In the Chinese tradition, the chrysanthemum symbolizes the spring, retirement, comfort, the cool brightness of the sun, scholarship, cheer and joy, harvest, wealth, longevity, and the person who survives the cold. In the Japanese tradition, the chrysanthemum symbolizes longevity and happiness, and is thought to be the flower symbol of Japan.

Citron
In the Buddhist tradition, this is one of the three sacred fruits of China, together with the peach and the pomegranate. In the Hebrew and Roman traditions, the citron symbolizes love and an ornament for the wedding room. In the Hebrew tradition, the citron is one of the four species for the festival of Tabernacles, and it symbolizes the person in whom there is both taste and smell – that is, both good deeds and commandments.

Clover
Clover symbolizes celestial properties, the three aspects of life – body, mind and spirit. The clover symbol in playing cards represents tremendous power and sometimes serves as a phallic symbol.

In the Chinese tradition, it symbolizes the summer. In Christianity, clover is the symbol of the holy trinity, and it is the symbol of St. Patrick in Ireland. The clover symbol in playing cards represents the betrayal of Jesus.

In the Celtic tradition, it symbolizes the weapon of Dagda as the lord of life and death. In addition, it symbolizes tremendous power and appetite. The clover symbol in playing cards was used in the Greco-Roman tradition as a symbol of Heracles/Hercules, and in the Semitic tradition it symbolized the "destroyer and grinder of the world," the symbols of Ba'al and Ninurta.

Convolvulus
The convolvulus symbolizes clinging, humility and low spirits, uncertainty and creeping doubt. In the Chinese tradition, the convolvulus symbolizes love and marriage, dependence, dawn, impermanence and transience.

Coral
Coral is organic matter that originates in the sea and is found in a range of colors – black, white, pink, red and blue. Unique activities are attributed to each color. Coral is a symbol of the provision of a life-giving environment for everything, symbiosis, the understanding of the need for variety, communal life and a shared life. It also symbolizes the sea tree of the mother goddess, the moon, and the fertility of the water. In Chinese symbolism, coral is a symbol of longevity and advancement. According to the Greek legend, corals sprouted from the blood of the Medusa and the Gorgon. Coral is thought to be the sacred stone of the Tibetans and the Native Americans. It symbolizes life force energy, flow and hardness together. It was used as a protection against spells and the evil eye (especially red coral). Some people claim that when a person who is wearing coral suffers from a shortage of energy or blood, the coral becomes pale. Properties of bone-strengthening, renewal of bodily forces and spinal recovery are attributed to it. It is thought to spread a feeling of tranquillity and harmony and to stimulate the imagination, intuition and diplomatic skills.

Black coral is thought to help the person cope with the dark sides of his personality and release repressed emotions. Qualities of improving communicative abilities are attributed to blue coral. Pink coral is thought to stimulate unconditional love and admiration, and helps strengthen the intuitive sides of understanding love. Red coral is thought to inspire a feeling of harmony and understanding toward the forces of nature, to encourage practicality, to help dispel depressions and dependencies, and to get rid of fears. White coral is imbued with qualities of dispelling negative thoughts and distraction. Coral is thought to be a stone that stimulates mystical abilities and is used in channeling with powerful spiritual figures from the past. Black coral is reputed to protect its owner from negative energies and dangers. Horn coral was used in order to understand and amass knowledge about ancient cultures and to link up to one's personal totem and strength animals.

Red coral is thought to balance matter and spirit and helps the person link up to supreme sources of information and wisdom. White coral is used for developing prophetic and predictive abilities. Coral is linked to Pisces, and black coral is thought to be especially suitable for people who belong to the sign of Scorpio.

Corn

The ear of corn is a symbol of abundance and fruitfulness and is linked to the sun. It symbolizes the idea of reproduction and growth – potential development, the shift from theory to practice.

The sheaves of corn have symbolic significance that is similar to that of the single ear of corn – it combines merging and control, which is symbolized by the "cluster, sheaf" and the notion of fertility or abundance that exists in the single ear.

Cyclamen

In the Christian tradition, the cyclamen symbolizes the Virgin Mary. The red dot at its center is the symbol of Mary's bleeding heart. In Israel, the name of the cyclamen is linked to bashfulness and humility, because it is hidden and bent, as if hanging its head bashfully.

It is a Celtic fairy flower, and in Europe it symbolizes purity, youth and gaiety.

Cypress

The cypress is a phallic symbol. It has a widespread significance of death and burial. Possibly because of the fact that the ancients attributed anti-decomposition properties to it, it was planted in cemeteries. Since it is linked to both the sun and the moon, it symbolizes androgyny. In Chinese tradition, the cypress symbolizes kindness, happiness, and also death. In Christian symbolism, the cypress symbolizes patience and the stoicism, and for this reason it symbolizes "the Christian." Moreover, it symbolizes persistence in good deeds, the honest and kind person, and also death and mourning. In Greco-Roman symbolism, the cypress is the symbol of Zeus, Apollo, Venus and Hermes, and so it is thought to grant life. As a symbol of the gods of the underworld and of Hades/Pluto.

Daisy

In the West, the daisy symbolizes innocence and purity, a symbol of the nymph Blades. It is a solar flower, and some people claim that the name *daisy* comes from the words, "day's eye."

Date

The date symbolizes fertility and abundance. It appears as a male symbol, a symbol of male fertility, while the grape represents female fertility.

Elm

In Christian tradition, the elm symbolizes respect and status. Its extensive branches and abundant growth symbolize the power and strength of the scriptures for believers.

Fennel

The fennel plant is dedicated to Sebazeus. In rituals devoted to this god, the believers would wear wreaths of fennel. Huge fennel bulbs were dedicated to the fire-producing gods. According to Greek mythology, the Titan, Prometheus, who brought fire to mankind, brought it in a fennel bulb. During the Middle Ages and the Renaissance, fennel began to be linked to paganism, and therefore to witchcraft (since Christianity linked the two together). It is told that in Northern Italy, witches who called themselves "the walkers of God" held mock battles with a gang of wizards who were called "the walkers of evil." Apparently, these "battles" were agricultural ceremonies whose aim was to prevent agricultural disasters. The weapons of both sides were fennel bulbs.

Fig

The fig tree and its fruit symbolize life, fruitfulness, prosperity and peace. Sometimes, the fig tree is described like the Tree of Knowledge, and it combines symbols of both the female and the male principles, with the fig leaf representing the male principle, or lingum, and the fruit representing the female principle, or yoni. The fig leaf symbolizes passion and sexuality. Plutarch wrote: "The fig leaf symbolizes drinking and movement and is supposed to represent the male sexual organ." A basket of figs represents fertility and represents the woman as a goddess or as a mother. It is linked to the grapevine as a place of peace and tranquillity – "each man under his vine and under his fig tree." Because of the shape of its fruit, which resembles female breasts, the fig tree is identified with the female chest, and is sometimes called "the many-breasted tree."

In the Buddhist tradition, this is the sacred Bodhi tree, under which Buddha was granted enlightenment. In Christianity, the fig tree sometimes takes the place of the apple tree as the Tree of Knowledge in the Garden of Eden. In the Greco-Roman cultures, the fig tree is dedicated to Dionysos/Bacchus, Priapus, Jupiter and Silvanus. It is a phallic symbol. In the Hebrew tradition, the fig tree symbolizes peace, prosperity, abundance, and is a symbol of Israel, together with the grapevine. In Islam, it is described as the celestial tree that is sacred because Muhammed swore an oath on it. In the Oceanian cultures, it symbolized mainly the Tree of Life, and played an important role in spiritual rituals.

Fir
The fir tree symbolizes daring and honesty. In Chinese symbolism, it symbolizes patience and the chosen person. It is dedicated to Pan in Greek mythology, and to Odin in Celtic mythology.

In connection with the Christmas tree, this evergreen tree symbolizes the winter solstice (the shortest day of the year), New Year, and a new beginning. It is the tree of rebirth and immortality, the tree of paradise of light and gifts, that shines at night. Every light on the tree is thought to be a soul, and the lights also symbolize the sun, the moon and the stars that shine between the branches of the cosmic tree. Parallel to it is the pine tree, which is dedicated to Attis, Atargatis and Cybele, upon which silver and gold ornaments were hung. With a sacred bird between its branches and ritual gifts beneath it, the tree was burned after the ceremony. The fir was also the sacred tree in a similar context to Odin/Wodin.

Fleur-de-lis
This plant belongs to the heraldic tradition, and does not exist in reality. Its shape resembles that of the schematic lotus, lily or water-lily. As a flower of light and life, the fleur-de-lis symbolizes the flame of light and life, the kingdom of heaven and the royal trinity of God, the flower of the Holy Trinity, royalty. The fleur-de-lis is also linked to the androgyne, to the trident – the three-pronged fork, and to a thyrsus – a stick wreathed with a vine, ivy or ribbons, with a pinecone at its end. Since its shape is reminiscent of a spearhead, it contains phallic symbolism, and represents male and military strength.

The fleur-de-lis has served as a symbol of the aristocracy since ancient times. As a symbol, the base of the fleur-de-lis is an inverted triangle representing water upon which there is a cross (which symbolizes spiritual connection and achievement) and two additional, symmetrical leaves wound around a horizontal arm. The central arm is straight and points upward, toward the sky. During the Middle Ages, the fleur-de-lis was thought to be a symbol of enlightenment and was attributed to God.

Fruit

The fruit symbolizes immortality, the essence, the peak of one situation and its consequences, and the seed of the next. First fruits represent the best that is offered as a tribute or as a sacrifice. The fruit has a symbolism that is similar to that of the egg in tradition symbolism, since at the center of the fruit is the pit that represents the source. It is also a symbol of earthly passions and lust.

In Christianity, Jesus is thought to be "the first fruit" of the Virgin. The fruit of the Tree of Knowledge led to the expulsion from the Garden of Eden. Iit is considered to be the seed of the fall – since together with it came self-knowledge that includes the recognition of the separation from God, and the very recognition is what created this separation. The fruit of the Tree of Life is immortality.

Gardenia

In the Chinese tradition, the gardenia symbolizes feminine kindness, delicacy and artistic qualities.

Garlic

Garlic symbolizes protection against spells, against the evil eye and lightning (because of its pungent odor).

Grapevine

In ancient times, the vine leaf was one of the most powerful symbols of life. The grapevine symbolizes fertility, the Tree of Life in certain traditions, and the Tree of Knowledge in others. In biblical commentaries, it is suggested that the Tree of Knowledge was a grapevine, and the fruit that was eaten by Eve and Adam was the grape. The fecund grapevine symbolizes fertility. The wild vine sometimes symbolizes disloyalty. The grapevine also symbolizes passion, such as in Buddhism, in which the twisted grapevine of greed and lust must be eradicated. In Christianity, Jesus is the "true vine," and his apostles are the leaves. It also symbolizes the church and the believers. In the ancient Egyptian culture, the grapevine was dedicated to Osiris. In the Greek and Roman cultures, the grapevine was dedicated to the god Dionysos/Bacchus, and also to Apollo. In the Hebrew tradition, along with the fig tree, the grapevine symbolizes peace, plenty and prosperity and it also serves as a symbol of the people of Israel. In the Sumerian and Semitic cultures, the grapevine was dedicated to Tamuz and Ba'al, and it is in the symbol of Geshtinana, the goddess of the vine.

Grass

Grass symbolizes usefulness, submissiveness and obedience. As a lawn, it symbolizes the earth of the motherland. A handful of grass symbolizes victory, the conquest of land, submission. In Rome, a crown of grass was awarded to a top-level military hero who succeeded in saving an entire army. Pliny remembers only seven heroes in his time, who were honored with a crown of grass. Apparently, the importance of the crown of grass stemmed from the fact that in ancient days, the vanquished ruler gave the conquering general a handful of grass as a sign that the entire land or country was now handed over to him.

Hyacinth

In Europe, the hyacinth represents wisdom, caution, intelligence, serenity, celestial aspirations and revival in the spring. In Greek mythology, a flower called the hyacinth was created after the death of a beautiful youth of this name. However, this is apparently not the hyacinth that is familiar to us nowadays, but rather a flower that resembles a water-lily with a deep crimson color that sprang from the blood of the youth. The youth Hyacinth died tragically, and every year he would be commemorated at the hyacinth festival that lasted a whole night.

Hyssop

Hyssop is a powerful symbol of purification. In Christian symbolism, it symbolizes repentance and penitence, humility, the restoration of innocence, and sometimes baptism. In the Bible, hyssop appears in purification rituals and special rituals: A bunch of hyssop was used to spread the blood on the *mezuzot* of the Israelite houses prior to the plague of the killing of the first-born sons. Hyssop was used for purifying the contamination of the dead by dipping it in water and sprinkling the water over the tent in which there was such contamination, as well as on the people and vessels that had been contaminated. In the ceremony of burning the red cow, the priest cast a cedar tree and hyssop and crimson yarns into the burning of the cow. The priest also used the cedar tree, the hyssop and the crimson yarns, together with two birds for purifying leprosy of the house (a plague that spread over the walls of the house), leprosy in the clothing, scales, psoriasis, and typhus. A leper who was cured of his affliction was also purified with hyssop, two birds, a cedar tree and crimson yarns. Hyssop appears with the cedar also as a dual symbol of greatness in contrast to smallness. It is said about Solomon that he spoke to the trees, "from the cedar that is in Lebanon even unto the hyssop that springs out of the wall" [I Kings 5:13] The proverb, "If cedars have caught fire, what will the hyssop on the wall do?" also symbolizes the smallness of hyssop in contrast to the power of the cedar.

Iris
The iris, which symbolizes the strength of light and hope, has a symbolism similar to that of the lily. In the Chinese culture, the iris symbolizes kindness, affection, and the beauty of being alone. In Christian symbolism, it is thought to be the flower of the Virgin Mary, along with the lily. In ancient Egypt, the iris symbolized power and strength, and in the ancient Greek tradition, it was the symbol of the female messenger of the gods (the counterpart of Hermes, the male messenger) and the psychopomp (that accompanies the soul to the next world).

Ivy
Like all evergreen plants, ivy symbolizes immortality and eternal life. In addition, it symbolizes joy and exaltation, clinging, dependence, bonds, constant affection and friendship. In Christian symbolism, ivy symbolizes eternal life, death and immortality, and loyalty. In the ancient Egyptian culture, ivy is the flower of Osiris and symbolizes immortality. In the ancient Greek culture, ivy was dedicated to Dionysos, who wore a wreath of ivy on his head and possessed the "ivy goblet." In the Semitic tradition, ivy was dedicated to the Phrygian Attis and symbolized immortality. The ivy leaf is a phallic symbol and symbolizes the male threesome. On the other hand, it may generally appear as a female symbol that indicates strength that needs protection..

Jasmine
In Chinese symbolism, jasmine symbolizes femininity, sweetness, kindness and attraction. In Christian symbolism, it symbolizes kindness, elegance and the Virgin Mary.

Juniper
In the Greco-Roman cultures, the juniper symbolized protection, safety and

initiative, and was dedicated to Hermes/Mercury. In pagan cultures, juniper bushes were thought to be the home of pagan spirits. Farmers would offer their tributes to the juniper bush, appealing to the fairies and elves among their branches. Many folk-tales that were pagan in origin located the entrance to the other world next to a juniper bush. In Estonia, it is said that Jesus rose up to the sky from a juniper bush. It was customary to burn juniper at funerals in order to banish the evil spirits, and, up to this day, juniper is also thought to help treat many female ailments and imbalances in the feminine cycle, as well as skin diseases. Juniper berries were used for producing the alcoholic beverage, gin.

Laurel

Laurel leaves symbolize victory. As an evergreen, the laurel represents immortality, eternity. In the Greco-Roman symbolism, it is a symbol of victory, peace and truth – it is the symbol of the victory that comes from motivation, struggle, and knowing the objective. The concept, "resting on one's laurels," has a similar meaning – the rest following victory and the knowledge that comes after the struggle. The laurel is dedicated to Apollo, Dionysos, Juno, Diana and Sylvanus, and represents the forest nymph, Daphne, whose was turned into a laurel tree. She was a young huntress, the daughter of the river god Peneus, and she fled from love, until one day Apollo saw her and began to pursue her. She fled from him, and when she felt that he was already breathing down her neck, she implored her father, the river god, to save her. At that moment, a kind of slumber came over her, her feet were rooted to the ground, bark began to cover her body and leaves grew from within her – she became the laurel tree. Apollo, who was disappointed that he had lost his love, turned her into his tree and declared that the conquering heroes would be adorned with the leaves of the tree, and she would have a part in his victories, so that they would both always be remembered in one breath. In Christianity, the laurel wreath became a symbol of the martyr's crown and the symbol of the death of saints.

Lemon

The lemon symbolizes sourness and sharpness. In Christian symbolism, it symbolizes fidelity in love.

Lily

The lily is a symbol of purity, peace, redemption and nobility. The lily represents the fecundity of the earth goddess and the gods of the sky. In the West, the symbolism of the lily is similar to that of the lotus in the East. A branch of lily flowers symbolizes virginity, renewal and immortality. As an artistic symbol, the lily was widespread mainly in Christianity during the Middle Ages, as a symbol of the Virgin Mary. The lily is generally depicted standing in a jar or vase, which symbolize the female receiving principle. In art, a white lily on one side and a sword on the other symbolize innocence and guilt. In Byzantium, the lily served as a symbol of nobility. In alchemist symbolism, the white lily represents the female principle. In the ancient Egyptian culture, the white lily symbolized bearing fruit, but was rejected as a symbol in favor of the lotus, which was more common in Egyptian symbolism. In the ancient Greco-Roman cultures, the white lily symbolizes purity. It springs from the milk of Hera, and symbolizes Hera/Juno and Diana as modesty and purity.

In the Bible, the lily appears as a carved ornament in the process of constructing the Temple, and concludes the act of building the columns of the Temple, Boaz and Yachin. " The "lilies" that appeared in the *Song of Songs* were interpreted as relating to the people of Israel, and as the people who studied and memorized the Torah. In Islam, the hyacinth symbolizes the same thing as the lily. In the Sumerian and Semitic cultures, the lily symbolized fruitfulness, abundance and prosperity.

Lotus

The symbol of the lotus in the East is like the symbol of the rose in the West – that is, it contains very significant symbolism. It is more symbolic than all the other flowers, and it is the most widespread flower with symbolic significance in those regions. Some people see the lotus as a natural symbol of all the forms of development. It appears both as solar and as lunar in symbolism. It symbolizes life and death and appears beside the Indian and Egyptian sun gods, with the celestial moon gods and with the "Big Mother" as a lunar goddess. Since it is both solar and lunar, it symbolizes androgyny, self-existence and perfect purity. It is considered to be the flower that first appeared on the primordial waters, a symbol of existence itself, which develops, reveals its beauty and disappears. Consequently, it is a symbol of the universe that rises from pre-cosmic chaos, and the sun was thought to rise from the lotus during the first days of the universe. It is called the "flower of light", the result of the interaction between the great creative forces of the fire of the sun and the lunar power of the water.

As a product of the sun and the moon, the lotus symbolizes spirit and matter like fire and water, the source of the whole of existence. It is the symbol of renewal, immortality, fertility, creation, and perfect beauty. Some people see it as a symbol of perfection, since its flowers and fruits create the shape of a circle. It symbolizes spiritual revelation, because its roots grow in the swamp and mire, it grows upward through the waters of the swamp, and its flower blooms in the light of the sun and the sky.

The roots of the lotus symbolize stability and steadfastness, its stem symbolizes the umbilical cord that links man to his source, the flower symbolizes the rays of the sun, and its seed symbolizes the fecundity of creation.

The lotus is also a symbol of a sublime person or of celestial birth that emerges pure and pristine from the mire. Gods that rise from the lotus petals symbolize the world rising from the element of water, with the lotus symbolizing the sun rising from the primal waters of chaos.

A flame that rises from the lotus flower is a symbol of celestial revelation and the unity of the dual forces of fire and water, sun and moon, male and female.

In Egypt, the lotus symbolizes the beginning of the development of life or the first appearance of life. During the Middle Ages, the lotus was identified with the mystical "center" and with the heart. Since it is both lunar and solar, both female and male, it sometimes appears in combination with various animals that characterize one of these principles or forces, and then its gender changes accordingly. When a bull appears beside it, it fulfills the male principle and symbolizes the sun and the sun gods. When a cow appears beside it, it is female and lunar and symbolizes the moon goddesses. Some of the other animals that commonly appear beside the lotus are the goose, the lion, the stallion, the deer and the swan. The symbol of the swastika sometimes appears beside it, too. When the cobra appears with the lotus, it symbolizes the Big Mother, the one who grants both life and death, the duality of existence, and the tension between opposites in the process of transformation into perfect oneness.

In Buddhism, the lotus is a symbol of primordial waters, of the potential of the material world and of man who exists in it, a symbol of flowering, thriving and spiritual revelation, of wisdom and Nirvana, and is dedicated to Buddha. It is one of the valuable things or treasures of Chinese Buddhism. "The heart of the lotus" represents solar fire, time, the invisible and all-consuming, the revelation of the entire universe, peace, harmony and unity. Because of its circular shape, the full bloom of the lotus symbolizes the circle of existence.

In Chinese symbolism, the lotus symbolizes perfection, purity, spiritual benevolence, peace, summer, and fertility. It also symbolizes the past, the present and the future, since the same plant bears blossoms, flowers and seeds. It also symbolizes the lord who emerges from the murky waters, but is not polluted by them.

In the ancient Egyptian culture, the lotus symbolizes the fire of wisdom, creation, fertility, rebirth, immortality and royal power. It also symbolizes the Upper Nile, with papyrus as a symbol of the Lower Nile. When they appear together, they symbolize the unity of the two. The lotus is dedicated to Horus. It is solar when it is linked to Amon-Ra and lunar when held by Hator. As the symbol of Isis, it symbolizes fruitfulness, but also virginity and purity. In the ancient Greco-Roman cultures, the lotus was the symbol of Aphrodite/Venus.

In Hinduism, the lotus symbolizes the universe in the passive aspect of manifestation, the highest form or the highest aspect of the earth, the one that moves on water, the one that creates itself, the one that begets itself, the immortal and spiritual nature of man, the revelation of all the possibilities, a superhuman source, purity, beauty, longevity, fame and wealth, especially for children. Brahma and Ajni were both born in the lotus and emerged from it, and it is linked in one way or another to many other Indian gods. The lotus at the threshold of a temple symbolizes the seat of the celestial powers and the state of purity and freedom from earthly passions that is required for the believer entering the temple. The chakras are drawn and described as lotus flowers, because they are associated with a wheel (the word chakra means "wheel" in Sanskrit) and because when they are stimulated, they open like the petals of the lotus.

In the Persian culture, the lotus symbolizes light and serves as a solar symbol. In the Mayan culture, it symbolizes the earth and the material world. In the Sumerian and Semitic cultures, the lotus is a solar symbol when it appears with the sun gods and lunar when it appears with the Big Mothers. It symbolizes creative power, but also serves as a funerary symbol. In this way it symbolizes both life and death, immortality and resurrection. In Taoism, it symbolizes the heart, the cosmic wheel of manifestation, spiritual revelation, and it is the symbol of Ho Xien-Ku, one of the eight immortals in Taoism.

As a work of art, the lotus is linked to the mandala and its meaning changes according to the number of petals. In India, the eight-petal lotus is thought to be the "center" in which Brahma resides, as well as the visible manifestation of his magical activity. The number eight symbolizes the merging of the earth (four, or the square) with the sky (the circle). The thousand-petal lotus symbolizes the final revelation. In the middle of it, there is usually a triangle in which there is "the vast emptiness," the symbol of amorphism. It also symbolizes the sun, and in man, it symbolizes the skull. Two lotuses symbolize the upper waters and the lower waters.

The lotus flower that blooms in the navel of Vishnu symbolizes the universe that grows.

In the Assyrian, Hittite, Phoenician, Greek and Roman cultures, the lotus is a funerary symbol that relates to burial, and symbolizes death and rebirth, resurrection of the dead and future life, as well as nature's renewed creative forces.

Magnolia
In Chinese symbolism, the magnolia symbolizes the spring, self-esteem, boastfulness and ostentation, beauty and feminine charm.

Malva
In the Chinese tradition, the malva flower symbolizes quiet, tranquillity, humility and rusticity.

Mangrove
The mangrove is the symbol of the Big Mother, the giver of life. It is an extremely magical plant, which symbolizes the power of the spell in sorcery. Many legends have been spun around it because its root resembles the human form. Moreover, the belief that whoever extracts the root of the mangrove from the earth is liable to die is widespread. For this reason, it was customary to tie the plant to a dog so that the latter could pull it out of the earth. In the Hebrew tradition, the mangrove is mentioned as a flower of love, both in the *Song of Songs* and in the story of Jacob, Rachel and Leah, and it represents pregnancy and fertility.

Marigold
This flower mainly symbolizes loyalty. In Chinese symbolism, it symbolizes longevity, and is called "the ten-thousand year flower." In Hinduism, it is the flower of Krishna.

Mould
In the Chinese tradition, mould symbolizes longevity, immortality, continuity, and appears with cranes and bats as a symbol of longevity and happiness. This is the food of the Taoist immortals.

Mulberry
The three colors of the three stages of the ripening of the mulberry – white, red and black – serve to symbolize the three stages of initiation, as well as the three stages in human life: white – the pure, innocent child; red – the active age; and black – old age and death. In the Chinese tradition, the mulberry symbolizes

the Tree of Life, and magical powers against the forces of darkness are attributed to it. In addition, it symbolizes industriousness. In the ancient Greek tradition, the mulberry symbolized bad luck in love, and features in the mythological story of Pyramus and Thisby. According to the legend, in ancient times, the fruit of the mulberry tree was completely white, and not red. The change in the color of the fruit occurred as a result of the tragic story of the two lovers, who had loved each other from childhood and lived near each other. Their parents, however, did not permit them to see each other. They decided to run away and meet near the mulberry tree. Thisby arrived first and waited for her beloved. While she was waiting, she saw a lioness that had just finished devouring her prey, her jaws dripping with blood. Thisby ran to hide, leaving her cloak behind. The lioness ripped the cloak and stained it with blood. Pyramus, who arrived shortly afterwards, discovered the blood-stained cloak with the lioness' footprints around it. He was sure that Thisby had been devoured. In his terrible grief, he carried the cloak to the mulberry tree, the symbol of their love, kissed the remnants of fabric, and plunged his sword into his chest. His blood spurted all over the fruit of the tree and stained it. When Thisby plucked up the courage to return to the tree, she no longer saw the mulberry tree with its white fruit. The fruit was all red, and beneath it lay the dead Pyramus. She took his sword and killed herself. Since then, according to the legend, the blood-red fruit of the mulberry tree became the memory of the love of the two young people.

Myrrh
In general symbolism, myrrh symbolizes suffering and sorrow. In the Bible, it appears as a perfume and incense plant.

Myrtle
Myrtle symbolizes merriment, peace, calmness, happiness, victory, the female principle, ...?, a fragrance that revives the spirit. It is called "the flower of the gods," an enchanted plant. In the Chinese tradition, it symbolizes fame and success. In Christian symbolism, myrtle symbolizes the peoples who convert to Christianity. In the ancient Egyptian culture, myrtle is dedicated to Hathor, and symbolizes love and joy. In the Greco-Roman cultures, it symbolizes love for Aphrodite/Venus, Artemis and Europa. In the Hebrew tradition, it is the plant of the temple, and symbolizes marriage, because of the custom of the sages to make couples happy on their wedding day by holding myrtle branches. It is one of the plants that is used during the *havdalah* service (that ends the Sabbath day) and one of the four species used during the festival

of the Tabernacles. According to the *Berakhot* tractate (the first tractate of the Talmud), if someone sees myrtle in his dreams, it is a sign of material success.

Nut
Since it is hidden inside its shell, the nut symbolizes hidden wisdom. It is also a symbol of fertility and longevity, and is served at Greek and Roman weddings as a symbol of those properties. The nut tree symbolizes strength in the face of adversity, but also selfishness, since nothing grows beneath it.

Oak
The oak symbolizes strength, protection, courage, resistance, stability, truth, man, and the human body. It is mainly linked to the gods of thunder and to thunder, and it symbolizes the gods of the heavens and the fertility gods, and for this reason it may also symbolize lightning and fire.

In the Native American tradition, the oak is dedicated to Mother Earth. In the Celtic tradition, it is dedicated to Dagda, the Creator, and is considered to be a sacred tree. In Chinese symbolism, it symbolizes virility, but also the weakness in strength that resists the changes of life, and ultimately breaks in the storm, as opposed to the strength of the willow and bamboo – the strength in weakness – that bend with the wind, make themselves pliant, and survive. In Christian symbolism, the oak is the symbol of Jesus as strength in times of adversity and distress. It symbolizes stability in faith and in virtues. In the Druid tradition, it is a sacred tree together with white mistletoe that grows on it and symbolizes the female principle. In the Greco-Roman cultures, the oak was sacred to Zeus/Jupiter. Jupiter's marriage to the goddess of the oak, Juno, was celebrated every year in an oak grove, and the believers adorned their heads with wreaths of oak leaves. Such a wreath was also awarded as a prize for saving a life and as a sign of victory in the Pathian games. The oak symbolizes Cybele and Sylvanus. The Darias were the oak nymphs. In Hebrew symbolism, the ark of the covenant was made of oak. In the Scandinavian and Teutonic traditions, the oak was Thor's Tree of Life and was also dedicated to Donar. Oak groves were places where Germanic rituals and ceremonies took place.

Olive
The olive tree symbolizes peace, immortality, fruitfulness, marriage, fertility and abundance. The olive branch, especially when borne by a dove, is the outstanding symbol of peace and of the Golden Age. It was the prize in the moon maiden's race, in parallel to the apple that was awarded to the victor in the race.

The olive tree is the seat of peace and a symbol of the moon. The olive leaf symbolizes the renewal of life.

In the Greco-Roman cultures, the olive symbolizes achievement and peace. The olive tree of the Acropolis bore the life and the fate of the people. It served as the symbol of Zeus/Jupiter, Athena/Minerva, Apollo and Cibele. At the beginning of Athens' history, when the two gods, Apollo and Athena, wanted to be the patron gods of the city, Athena won in the "miracles" contest when she caused an olive tree to grow on the salt water that Apollo had drawn from a rock. In Hebrew symbolism, the olive symbolizes power, beauty, and safe journeys. In Chinese symbolism, the olive symbolizes tranquillity, continuity, kindness, delicacy and sensitivity. In Christian symbolism, the olive is considered to be the fruit of the church, the belief of the righteous, and peace. The Angel Gabriel is described as carrying an olive branch when he announced the imminent birth of Jesus to Mary.

Onion

Since it consists of many layers, the most common symbolism of the onion is that of removing layers in order to reach the core – removing the mental and conscious layers in order to reach inner truth. The spherical-elliptical shape of the onion made it into a symbol of the cosmos and of the primal cause that was visualized as wrapped in mysterious layers in the concrete world. It symbolizes unity, the many in the one, eternity, revelation by means of the removal of the layers, and is considered to be a protection against the lunar powers of evil.

Orange

The orange blossom is the symbol of fertility and fruitfulness. In the Chinese tradition, the orange symbolizes immortality and good fortune. In the Japanese tradition, the orange blossom symbolizes pure love. In the ancient Greek culture, the orange is the symbol of Diana. Oranges were considered to be the golden apples of Hesperides. In Christianity, the orange symbolizes purity, modesty and virginity. When it is painted in the Garden of Eden, it symbolizes the "fruit of the fall" (the expulsion from Eden) and can be a substitute for the apple in the hand of the child Jesus.

Palm tree

The palm tree is a classic symbol of fruitfulness and victory. It is a sun symbol, and symbolizes happiness, righteousness, glory, things that sprout and grow straight along the entire path. It is considered to be the Tree of Life, and because it is self-fertilizing, it is a symbol of androgyny, as well as being a blatant phallic symbol because of its obvious phallic shape. As a phallic symbol, it symbolizes male virility and fertility, but when it is represented with dates, it is a female symbol. Because it produces tasty fruit even when it is very old, it symbolizes longevity and abundant and productive old age. In Arab symbolism, it is thought to be the Tree of Life. In the Chinese tradition, it symbolizes retirement, respect, and fertility. In Christian symbolism, the palm tree symbolizes the just man "who will bloom like a date palm." In addition, it symbolizes immortality, the blessing of heaven, Jesus' entry into and conquest of Jerusalem, the victory of the martyr over death, and paradise. The palm branches symbolize glory, victory, resurrection, triumph over sin and over death. For the first Roman Christians, it was both a funerary symbol and a symbol of a person who completed the pilgrimage to Jerusalem. In the ancient Egyptian culture, the palm tree symbolizes the calendar tree – one branch for each month. In the ancient Greek culture, the palm tree symbolizes Apollo at Delphi. In the Hebrew tradition, it symbolizes the just man and his fate – "a just man will bloom like a date palm." In the Sumerian and Semitic cultures, it symbolizes the Tree of Life, the symbol of Ba'al-Tamar, the lord of the palms, and of Astarte and Ishtar. In Jung's opinion, the palm tree symbolizes the anima – the female principle, the inner personality.

Pansy
In Europe, the pansy symbolizes remembering and recollecting, deliberating and meditating, and thought. In Spanish, the word for *thought* is *pensamiento*, which is reminiscent of the word *pansy*. The pentagonal shape of its petals contributed to or created this symbolism, since the number five symbolizes man, and thought is considered to be the unique strength of human beings. The pansy is also linked to the Greek goddess, Venus. In the Hebrew culture, it symbolizes the love of Amnon and Tamar, since the flower generally blooms in pairs, with slightly different colors for each flower in the pair.

Parsley
In the European tradition, parsley is considered to be a mystical plant and represents the feminine principle.

Peach
In Buddhism, along with the lemon and the pomegranate, the peach is considered to be one of the three blessed fruits. In Chinese symbolism, it

symbolizes immortality, the Tree of Life, an enchanted fruit, spring, youth, marriage, wealth, quality of life, and good wishes. In Japanese symbolism, too, it symbolizes the tree of immortality. The peach blossom heralds the spring. It symbolizes marriage and feminine charm. In Taoism, it is the Tree of Life, it grants eternal life and nourishes the immortals. The peach with the phoenix is the symbol of Siwang Mu, the goddess of the tree of eternal life and the queen of heaven. Peach pits are carved and serve as amulets. In the Christian tradition, the peach is called the fruit of salvation. When a leaf is attached to a peach, it symbolizes a single truth in both heart and mouth, and the virtue of silence. In ancient Egypt, the fruit was sacred to Hator.

Pear
The pear symbolizes hope and good health. In Chinese symbolism, it symbolizes longevity, justice, beneficial rule and correct judgment. In Christianity, the pear symbolizes the love of Jesus for humanity. Visually, some people see it as a symbol of the female body – the waist and buttocks.

Peony
In the Chinese tradition, this flower symbolizes the yang principle (one of the only flowers to do so), masculinity, light, love, good fortune, fame, happiness, spring, and the joy of youth. It is considered to be an imperial flower that is untouched by insects other than the bee. In most cases, it is linked to the peacock. In the Japanese tradition, it symbolizes spring, fertility, marriage, fame, merriment and happiness.

Persimmon
In china, the persimmon symbolizes joy. In Japan, it symbolizes victory.

Pine
Like the other evergreen trees, the pine is a symbol of immortality, of eternal life. It symbolizes uprightness, honesty, sincerity, a strong character, vitality, fertility, silence and solitude, and is also a well-known phallic symbol. It preserves the body from decay, and for this reason is planted in cemeteries and is used for preparing coffins. The pinecone symbolizes fire, because of its shape that is reminiscent of flames, and it is also a phallic symbol and represents creative virility, fertility, and good fortune.

In the Chinese tradition, the pine symbolizes courage, loyalty and devotion, longevity, resilience in the face of adversity and distress, and constitutes a symbol of Confucius. In the Japanese culture, it symbolizes longevity. In the ancient Egyptian culture, it is a symbol of seraphs. In the ancient Greek culture, the pine is the symbol of Zeus, and is also associated with Dionysos, Artemis, and Aesculapius. In Rome, the pine symbolizes Jupiter and Venus as *pura arbor* – "the incorrupt tree" – and virginity. It is also associated with Diana and Mithras. In the Semitic tradition, the pinecone is a symbol of life. It symbolizes fertility, and the tree is dedicated to the Phrygian Attis and his mate Cybele.

Pineapple
The pineapple symbolizes fertility.

Pinecone
The pinecone is a phallic symbol. It symbolizes fertility and fruitfulness and good fortune. In the Greek tradition, it symbolizes Dionysos, and is called "the heart of Bacchus." Similarly, it symbolizes Sebazeus, Seraphis, Astarte, and Byblos. The white pinecone is a symbol of Aphrodite. It is considered to be a creative and reviving force.

Plane tree
In the ancient Greek culture, the plane tree symbolizes study, analysis and scholarly disputes – academic discussions were held under plane trees in Athens. In the Persian tradition, it symbolizes learning, majesty and splendor. In the Minoan culture, it is dedicated to the cult of Zeus the Cretan. In Christiantiy, the plane tree symbolizes the all-embracing love of Jesus, kindness, and moral superiority.

Plants (general)
Plants symbolize vitality and life, and they are the expression of the manifestation and of the birth of forms in the physical universe. The annual cycle of many plants made them the symbol of the cycle of life, death, and rebirth. For this reason, the main symbolism of plants as a group is that of the life force and the cyclical nature of life, and is linked to the Big Mother, the earth goddess, Mother Earth, and to the fruitfulness of the life-giving waters. Plants and trees are sometimes thought to be mythological ancestors. Plants that are born from the blood of a god or a hero represent the mystical union between man and plant and the emergence of life from death, life that flowers from one situation to the next, for instance, the violets that bloomed from the blood of Attis, wheat and grasses from the body of Osiris, the pomegranate from the

blood of Dionysos, the anemone from the blood of Adonis, and red lilies from the blood of Jesus. Since water plants come from the cradle of primeval life, they are the symbol of development at the beginning. In India, cosmic images are described as being born of the lotus.

The fertility of the fields is one of the most powerful symbols of cosmic, material and spiritual fruitfulness.

Regarding life that ended violently, there is a widespread belief that it will continue following a metamorphosis to a plant form.

Plum

In Chinese symbolism, the plum tree symbolizes the winter, beauty, longevity, purity and a life of abstinence. Since it blooms in the winter, it symbolizes strength, endurance and victory. The plum tree, bamboo and pine are called "the three friends of the winter."

In Christian symbolism, the fruit of the plum tree symbolizes independence, loyalty and a lack of dependence.

Pomegranate

The shape of the pomegranate, round with many segments, made it into a symbol of the plurality and the difference that exist in one visible unit. For this reason, it appears as the symbol of the oneness of the universe. It is a symbol of eternal life, constant fertility, fruitfulness and abundance. In Buddhism, the pomegranate is one of the three blessed fruits, along with the peach and the lemon. In Chinese symbolism, it symbolizes abundance, fruitfulness and a happy future. In Christian symbolism, the pomegranate symbolizes eternal life, spiritual fertility and the church. In the Greco-Roman cultures, it symbolizes the spring, renewed youth, immortal life, fertility, a symbol of Hera/Juno, of Ceres and of Persephone as the seasonal return of the spring and the fecundity of the earth. In addition, it is considered to be the plant that rose up out of the blood of Dionysos. In the Hebrew tradition, the pomegranate symbolizes renewal, fruitfulness and numerous scholars. It appears on the priest's robe together with the bell.

Poplar

The two sides of the poplar leaf are in different shades of green. As a result, it symbolizes the Tree of Life – light green on the water side, symbolizing the moon, and darker green on the fire side, symbolizing the sun. For this reason, it occupies an important place among the bipolar symbols, since it symbolizes the positive pole and the negative pole. In general, it is thought to be a water tree. In the Chinese tradition, its leaves symbolize yin and yang, the lunar and the solar, and duality. In the Greco-Roman cultures, the white poplar symbolizes the Elysian fields (paradise), while the black poplar symbolizes Hades (hell). The poplar is dedicated to Sebazeus, and it was carried during ceremonies in his honor. In addition, it serves as a symbol of Zeus/Jupiter and Hercules, who wore a wreath of poplar when he descended to Hades.

Poppy

The poppy is a symbol of the "Big Mother" as one and as many, the mother and the virgin. It symbolizes the night and is dedicated to all the lunar and nocturnal divinities. It symbolizes fertility, oblivion, sloth, idleness and death – the four latter meanings are connected to the drugs that are produced from the poppy, such as opium, morphine and heroin. Poppy decorations appear in paintings of the Etruscan Island of the Dead. The reason why the poppy is thought to be a fertility symbol stems from its numerous seeds. In Chinese symbolism, the poppy symbolizes retirement, rest, success and beauty, but as opium, it symbolizes evil, absent-mindedness and debauchery. In the Greco-Roman cultures, the poppy symbolizes the period of sleep and death of the plant world, a symbol of Demeter/Ceres, Persephone, Venus, Hypnos and Morpheus. The leaves of the poppy were dedicated to the mother of the gods, Hera, and served for soothsaying. In Christianity, the poppy symbolizes sleep, ignorance and indifference. The poppy that is as red as blood symbolizes Jesus' *Via Dolorosa* as well as the sleep of death.

Pumpkin

Pumpkin is a symbol, like the letter X, of the hourglass and the pair of drums. It symbolizes the link between the two worlds, the upper and the lower, and the principle of inversion that regulates the pattern of events of the cosmic phenomena of day and night, life and death, shame and disgrace in contrast to elevation and exultation, sadness as opposed to happiness.

In the Chinese tradition, the pumpkin symbolizes Li Tie-Kui, the second of the eight immortals, a mythical figure characterized by his ability to leave his body and visit the kingdom of heaven. In Chinese alchemy, the pumpkin symbolizes the cosmos in miniature, the creative power of nature, and the original unity of the ancestors, while a double pumpkin symbolizes yin and yang.

In Roman symbolism, the pumpkin symbolizes foolishness ("pumpkinhead), an empty head, and madness. In the Native American tradition, the pumpkin represents women's breasts.

Quince
The quince is the Greek symbol of fertility, the food of brides, is considered to be the apple of Dionysos, and is dedicated to Venus.

Reed
The reed symbolizes documented time. In Chinese symbolism, it symbolizes successful management that leads to prosperity. The rapid growth of reeds symbolizes advancement. In the ancient Greek culture, the reed is a symbol of Pan. According to the myth, Pan was in love with one of the nymphs, who did not want him, and when he tried to catch her, her sisters turned her into a reed. Pan said, "Even so, you'll be mine!" and used her to produce his famous flute. For this reason, the reed symbolizes harmony and music in the Greek culture. In ancient Egypt, the reed symbolizes majesty and the fruitful Nile. In Christian symbolism, the reed symbolizes the death of Jesus, humiliation, and the believer who lives beside the waters of righteousness. It also serves as a symbol of John the Baptist.

Rice
In the West, rice has a symbolic meaning that is similar to that of grain, but in the East, as a basic food, it is thought to have a divine source. It may be enchanted and provide supernatural nutrition, like manna, or it may renew the supply of grains magically. It is a symbol of abundance and celestial provision, and according to the belief, people were forced to grow it themselves only after the expulsion from the Garden of Eden and the separation between earth and heaven in the divine sense. Rice symbolizes eternal life, spiritual nutrition, primal purity, solar strength, knowledge, abundance, happiness and fertility. The latter is reflected in the tradition of throwing rice on brides at weddings, a custom that is widespread to this day in East and West alike. In Chinese alchemy, red rice is linked to the mineral cinnabar. In Islamic esoterica, it is linked to red sulfur.

Rose
The rose is a complex and ambivalent symbol. The single rose is a symbol of perfection, attainment of celestial perfection, completion, the mystery of life, the heart of life, beauty, grace and the unknown, but it is also a symbol of earthly

passions, sensuality, seduction and lusts of the flesh, and it is linked to the yin. It simultaneously symbolizes time and eternity, life and death, fertility and virginity. Its symbolism is the same as that of the lotus in the East. In the symbolism of the heart, the rose is found at the central point of the cross, at the point of union. As the flower of the female divinities, the rose symbolizes love, life, creation, fertility, beauty and virginity.

The wilting of the rose symbolizes death and sorrow. Its thorns symbolize pain, blood, and "martyrs." As a funerary symbol, it symbolizes eternal life, eternal spring and resurrection. The rose also symbolizes silence and secrecy. A rose hanging in a secret room symbolizes discretion and secrecy. The golden rose symbolizes perfection. The red rose symbolizes passion, lust, gaiety and beauty. It is the flower of Venus and the blood of Adonis and Jesus. The white rose is the "flower of light" that symbolizes innocence, virginity, spiritual revelation and magic. The red and the white roses together symbolize the union of fire and water, the union of opposites. The blue rose symbolizes the unattainable, the impossible. The rose with four petals symbolizes the division of the cosmos into four. The rose with five petals symbolizes the microcosm, and the rose with six petals symbolizes the macrocosm.

"The rose of the winds" is depicted by a circle surrounding a double cross and symbolizes the four winds and the four directions between them.

The rose garden is a symbol of paradise and it is the place of mystical marriage, the union of the opposites.

In alchemy, the rose is wisdo. This is also the birth of the spirit after the death of matter.

In Chinese symbolism, the rose symbolizes fragrance, prosperity, the sweetness in dismantling and in ending. The metaphysical symbolism represented by the rose in other cultures is represented by the lotus in this culture.

In Christian symbolism, the rose is the flower of paradise, and symbolizes fragrance and perfection. The white rose symbolizes innocence, purity, modesty and the Virgin Mary.

The red rose represents martyrs and grows out of the blood of the crucified Jesus. A bunch of roses is the symbol of a celestial blessing and of the Virgin Mary as the rose of the heavens. The rose of the Sharon (apparently a corruption of the biblical "water-lily of the Sharon") is a symbol of the church. The thorns of the rose are the sins of the Fall (the expulsion from the Garden of Eden), and the "rose without thorns" is the mystical rose and symbolizes the Virgin Mary.

The golden rose is the symbol of the pope and symbolizes his special blessing.

In the ancient Egyptian culture, the roses were dedicated to Isis and symbolized pure love that was free of fleshly lusts and served the mystery of Isis and Osiris.

The other symbolism of the rose is attributed to the lotus.

In the Greco-Roman tradition, the rose symbolizes love, gaiety, beauty and passion. It was the symbol of Aphrodite/Venus.

The Romans would grow roses in their funeral gardens as a symbol of renewed resurrection and eternal spring. The Roman emperor wore a wreath of roses on his head.

A red rose grew out of the blood of Adonis. The rose symbolizes Aurora, Helios and Dionysos.

In the Kabbala, the center of the rose is the sun and the petals are infinity, the harmonious variety of nature.

The rose issued from the Tree of Life. In Hinduism, the lotus is parallel to the symbolism of the mystic rose as a spiritual center, especially in the chakras. In Islam, the rose symbolizes the blood of the Prophet, as well as his two sons, Hassan and Hussein, his two "eyes" or his two "roses." In the Rose of Baghdad, the first circle symbolizes the law, the second the path, the third knowledge, and the three together truth and the names of Allah.

When the rose is round in shape, it reacts to the mandala symbolism. The rose with seven petals reacts to the septenary pattern (seven directions, seven days of the week, seven planets, seven degrees of perfection). The rose with eight petals symbolizes renewal.

Rosemary

In Europe, the smell of rosemary is linked to remembering, loyalty, and devotion to a particular memory. In aromatherapy, a great ability to solve memory problems and improve the memory is attributed to rosemary. In addition, it is thought to be a funerary plant and is dedicated to Ares.

Sycamore

The sycamore tree is the Egyptian Tree of Life. "The lady of the sycamore" symbolizes Nut, the goddess of the heavens. The fruit of the sycamore produces a kind of milky liquid, so it is linked to the mother goddess, Hator, like a cow that nourishes. It is also a symbol of renewal, fertility and love.

The tree is also linked to the many-breasted images of Artemis of Ephesus, since the fruit of the sycamore is produced on the tree itself, and not on the branches.

Straw
Straw symbolizes emptiness, barrenness, fruitlessness, death, worthlessness, debility, and impermanence and transience.

Strawberry
In Christian symbolism, the strawberry symbolizes the righteous person, the fruits of good deeds and the fruits of the spirit. When it is accompanied by violets, it symbolizes the humility of the righteous person. In modern symbolism, it symbolizes sensuality and sexuality.

Sunflower
The sunflower symbolizes worship, being an enchanted person, blind adoration and following the sun blindly. Since it constantly changes the direction it faces in accordance with the sun's position, it symbolizes unstable or imagined wealth.

In the Mithraic culture, it symbolizes the sun god, Mithras. In Greek symbolism, it symbolizes Cliti, who fell in love with Apollo, the sun god. He did not see anything in her that could spark his love, and ignored her. In her love for him, she sat on the ground outside her house and followed him with her gaze as he sailed through the heavens. Because of the way she watched him, she became a sunflower, which always turns its gaze in the direction of the sun. The sunflower is also a symbol of Daphne.

In Chinese symbolism, it symbolizes longevity and is thought to have magic powers.

Thorn
The thorn is a symbol of defensiveness, misanthropy, vindictiveness and self-mortification. Thorny plants generally symbolize the rays of light of the crescent moon.

The rose and the thorn together symbolize a combination of pleasure and pain, joy and suffering. In Christianity, the thorn symbolizes sin, grief, sorrow and wickedness.

The thorns also symbolize Jesus' walk along the *Via Dolorosa*, wearing a crown of thorns. In the Bible, the thorn appears as a symbol of infertility, of the drudgery of manual labor, of the curse of the earth (Genesis 3:18). In Egypt, wheat thorns are the symbol of Neit, the mother goddess. The thorn is also linked to the axis of the world, and consequently also to the cross.

Tulip
The tulip is the Persian symbol of perfect love. In addition, it symbolizes Holland.

Verbena/Vervain
In the Celtic tradition, verbena is thought to be the plant of magic, sorcery and spells. In the Persian tradition, it is believed to make wishes come true. In the Roman culture, verbena is dedicated to Mars and Venus and symbolizes marriage and protection against spells and sorcery. In Bach Flower Remedies, verbena (vervain) symbolizes the type that concentrates all his energy on a particular objective, to the point that he becomes fanatic about a particular opinion, and sometimes imposes his opinion on those around him, all the while expending a great deal of energy outward without nourishing his inner energy.

Wheat
Grains and sheaves of wheat symbolize the divinity of wheat, mainly in the secret Greek traditions, and symbolize the fertility of the earth, abundant life in the spring that emanates from the death of the winter, growth and reproduction by means of the power of the sun, and abundance. The golden sheaves of wheat are the offspring of the marriage of the illuminating sun with the virgin earth. The goddess of wheat is identified with the constellation of Virgo. Wheat and wine together, like bread and wine, symbolize the balanced yield of man's agricultural endeavors and means of life. The bunch of wheat symbolized the yield of fruit, abundance. In funerary rites, wheat symbolizes abundance in the next world. In the Native American tradition, the representative of grains was corn, and an ear of corn with all its kernels symbolized the people and the things that exist in the universe. In the Christian tradition, sheaves of wheat symbolize the body of Jesus as well as abundance, kindness and divinity. In ancient Egypt, the sheaf of wheat symbolized Isis, and a bunch of barley symbolized the seraphs. In Greco-Roman tradition, the grains symbolized fertility, abundance, life that grows out of death, creation, and the symbol of Demeter/Ceres, Gaia (the goddess of the earth) and Virgo. In the cult of Cybele, Attis is "a reaped golden sheaf of wheat." For the Romans, sowing wheat symbolized the strength of the dead for the living in a sacred manner. In the Mexican tradition, corn with a hummingbird symbolized the hero of the sun and awakening growth. In the

Sumerian and Semitic traditions, wheat was dedicated to Cybele, who ate the bread in her ritual feast. In addition, it symbolizes Tamuz/Dumuzi. Dagon, the Philistine god, was the god of the earth and wheat in Ashkelon and Gaza.

White mistletoe

White mistletoe is a parasite that is linked to the oak tree. It symbolizes the essence of life, celestial matter, universal healing and immortality. Since it is neither a tree nor a bush, it symbolizes that which is neither the one nor the other – the indefinable – and for that reason it symbolizes freedom from limitations, so that everything that is found beneath the white mistletoe is free from limitations but also free from protection, and therefore chaos enters the world. White mistletoe is the golden branch of the Druids, and represents the sacred female principle in conjunction with the oak as a male principle. The Druids would gather it for use in their fertility rites. It symbolizes new life and rebirth on the shortest day of the year. The belief that it was created by lightning that struck the branches of the oak is widespread, and it is considered to contain special spiritual properties, among them that of discovering treasures.

Willow

The willow is an enchanted tree that is dedicated to the moon goddess. The weeping willow symbolizes lamentation, unhappy love and funerals. In Buddhism, it symbolizes humility, a demeaned spirit, submissiveness and obedience.

In Chinese symbolism, it is lunar, yin, and symbolizes the spring, femininity, a demeaned spirit and humility, goodness and a charming personality. In the Japanese culture, it symbolizes patience and safeguarding the existing. Moreover, there is a belief that the spine of the first person was created from the willow. The Celtic tradition links the willow to Eos, is described as a willow beam.

In the Greco-Roman cultures, the willow is dedicated to Europa and is the symbol of Artemis. In the Hebrew tradition, it symbolizes lamentation and weeping under the willows of Babylon during the Exile. The willow, tasteless and odorless, is one of the four species of the festival of the Tabernacles, and symbolizes the person who is devoid of the Torah and good deeds. In the Sumerian and Semitic cultures, the willow symbolizes Tamuz, victory, merriment and joy. It is the cosmic tree of Akkadia and was dedicated to the Akkadian Zeus.

In Taoism, it symbolizes the strength in weakness. It is linked to the pine and the oak, which resist the gale and are broken by it, while the willow is pliant, bends, lets the gale pass, straightens up again and survives.

Wormwood

Wormwood symbolizes bitterness, distress, danger, sorrow and torture. It is dedicated to Ares/Mars, the god of war.

Yarrow

Yarrow is considered to be the specific plant to counteract witchcraft. The sticks of the Chinese *I Ching* that were used for guidance and future prediction were made of yarrow.

Symbolism in objects

Alcohol

In alchemy, alcohol symbolizes *aqua vitae*, the water of life, since it is a blend of the elements of fire and water. For this reason, it symbolizes the link between fire and water, the link between and completion of two opposites, the *coincidentia oppositorum*. Water is a female element and fire is a male element, so alcohol, which is called "fire water," symbolizes both the male and female elements, the active principle and the passive principle that are inherent in a state of simultaneous creation and destruction.

Anchor

The anchor was an important symbol especially to the early Christians and to the seafaring nations. In regions in which shipping and fishing were the principal occupations, the anchor symbolized safety, stability and good luck. For the early Christians, the anchor was a symbol of hope and of correct and steadfast belief, as well as a common symbol of Jesus. This is expressed in the Epistle to the Hebrews (6:18-19): "…we might have a strong consolation, who have fled for refuge to lay hold upon the hope set before us: Which hope we have as an anchor of the soul, both sure and stedfast, and which entereth into that within the veil."

Ark

The ark symbolizes the force of preservation and of renewal both on the spiritual and on the physical plane – the preservation of all the things and the promise of their rebirth. This symbolism stems from the belief that the essence of spiritual and physical life may be concentrated and contained inside a seed until the moment in which the conditions for rebirth are suitable, and then this life will emerge in the external world. The ark is linked to the symbolism of the sea, water and the moon. Generally, it is drawn like a half-crescent. It symbolizes the female principle, the bearer of life, the heart and the womb. It is considered to be the life principle's vessel for conveying and moving, the ship of fate. The ark is closely linked to the rainbow. During the Flood, the ark floated on the "lower" waters while the rainbow, in the region of the "upper waters," was a symbol of restoring order – the same order that was preserved in the belly of the ark. The two symbols, which complement each other, complete a circle of unity. Together, they symbolize the two parts of the cosmic egg.

The ark and the flood are almost universal symbols that appear in many cultures. In the Torah, the ark appears as a symbol of containing life and preserving it, life that needs practical action by the just man in order to be saved. In this myth, the man is an active participant in the interaction between the lower waters and the upper waters, and his function as a person with free choice and will power is significant in preserving the natural surroundings, which were "punished" and destroyed mainly because of man's deeds.

In Hinduism, the ark was built by Satyavrata under the orders of Manu, and it carried the seeds of life. In the Torah, the ark carried human beings and animals. In both cases, the ark carried the principle of life that symbolizes stability and continuity. Some people see the ark also as a symbol of the human body, as a microcosm. In Christianity, the ark symbolizes the church, through which man was saved and in which he sailed safely over the waters of life. It also symbolizes Jesus as a redeemer, and the Virgin Mary as carrying Jesus in her womb. In the ancient Egyptian culture, the ark of Isis is the mother's womb that bears life.

Arrow

Since the invention of the arrow, its graphic symbol has been used as a sacred symbol. The arrows carried by the goddess Artemis represented her power of control over the hunt and over wild animals. The arrow of Eros/Cupid symbolizes the invasive nature of falling in love, which is liable to pierce the heart of the one who loves like an arrow and make him "lovesick." It is a symbol of the look in the eye that bears a message of love and invades the heart of the person falling in love. A symbol of an arrow piercing a heart has become the traditional sign of the union of lovers and sexual union. The arrow itself is a phallic symbol, which reflects the male principle that penetrates and is a symbol of war and of lightning. Arrows became a symbol of the god of war, Mars, and his Scandinavian counterpart, Tyr. With the development of the warrior societies, arrows became the tools of all the male gods and their followers, especially of soldiers and military men. The arrow also symbolizes the belt of lightning of the Balkan storm god. Several Native American tribes displayed a great deal of respect for the arrow as a symbol of male power. "The holy medicine arrows" of the Cheyenne represented the dominance of the Cheyenne warriors over the other tribes and over the animals they hunted. Women were not supposed to look at these holy arrows or even listen when the men discussed them. Nowadays, in the language of symbols that is familiar to most people ("Follow the arrow"), the arrow has become a symbol of directions, a hint as to the direction in which one's heart's desire can be found.

An arrow discharged from a bow symbolizes action – sometimes hasty – that cannot be contemplated in retrospect and changed. The arrow is the symbol of the warrior as well as a solar symbol that symbolizes the sun's rays that penetrate the clouds. It has this meaning in the Native American tradition. In the ancient Egyptian culture, two crossed arrows on a shield comprise the symbol of Neit, the warrior goddess. In the ancient Greek culture, the arrow is the symbol of Apollo, and it is analogous to the sun's rays that can bestow blessings and fecundity on the one hand and inflict damage on the other. In Christianity, the arrow is a symbol of the suffering of the martyrs.

The flight of the arrow is a symbol of speed and quickness and it appears with this meaning in the Bible: "As an arrow flies from the bow." It can also be seen as a symbol of an aspiration for rising upward and touching the sky. Because of haste and speed, this may backfire and lead to injury and a tumble back to earth.

In Hinduism, the arrow is a symbol of Rudra, the god of the earth, lightning and storms, who wreaks death and destruction on human beings and animals. Besides being dangerous and harmful, he also brings rain. The arrow also symbolizes Indra as a god of the sky. In Islam, arrows symbolized the wrath of god who punishes his enemies. In Shamanism, the feather-bedecked arrow symbolizes the flight of the bird into the sky as well as rising above the terrestrial condition.

Ax

The ax is a solar symbol and a symbol of the power of light. It generally symbolizes the celestial gods. The power represents thunder, the fecundity of the rain, the celestial gods, ritual, support or remaining. Some people also consider the ax to be a symbol of death by order of the divinity.

The double ax is a common symbol in symbolic art in many parts of the world. It is linked to the letter t [tau], and frequently appears above the bull's head, between his horns. In this case, it symbolizes the mandorla (because of the shape created by the bull's horns), and the role of the sacrificial ritual in the relationship between those below and those above – earth and heaven. Some people perceive it as a symbol of the sacred unity between the sky god and the earth goddess, between thunder and lightning. In Africa, the double-headed ax of Yoruba symbolizes the sky god's magic powers and bolts of lightning.

In Buddhism, the double-headed ax destroys the cycle of life and death. In Hinduism, the ax is associated with the god of fire, Ajni. Vishnu grasps an ax and chops down the samsara tree, the dual Tree of Knowledge. In the Celtic culture, it symbolizes the divine being and the chief of the warriors. In the Scandinavian culture, too, the ax accompanies a divine being – the chief of the warriors or the warrior. In Chinese symbolism, it symbolizes justice, law, sovereignty and penalty. An ax in a ritual symbolizes the death of the non-conscious person, who lives in the world of the senses only. In Christian symbolism, it symbolizes martyrdom and destruction. In the ancient Egyptian culture, it is considered to be a solar symbol. In the ancient Greek culture, the ax is the symbol of Zeus. In the Minoan culture, the double-headed ax has an important symbolic role, and many shards bearing this symbol have been found in Crete. The double-headed ax evidently symbolized sovereignty, power and the divine presence, and it seems that supernatural powers were attributed to it. In the Sumerian and Semitic cultures, the ax is the symbol of Tamuz. The double-headed ax is the symbol of Teshuv, the sun god and the lord of the heavens, and it symbolizes sovereignty.

Bag, pouch, sack
Since the bag, pouch or sack are objects that contain and cover, they symbolize containing, secrecy and concealment, as well as the winds. The gods of thewinds generally carry a sack ofwinds. The sack of the Celtic sea god, Mananan, contains all the treasures of the world.

Ball
The ball symbolizes the sun.
Ball games in ancient times were linked to sun and moon rituals. Throwing a ball symbolized the power of the gods to throw meteors, carry the globe, and lead the stars around the universe.

Basket
The basket is a symbol that mainly characterizes the seasons in their agricultural context.
It symbolizes the female principle of containing, fecundity, prosperity and abundance. A basket full of fruit symbolizes first fruits, first crops, full bloom, abundance and fertility. A basket whose contents are overflowing symbolizes the end of the fruit season. The symbolic meaning of being contained in the basket is fleeing from death or new life – as in the story of Moses in the bullrushes. The Tripitaka, or the triple basket, comprises the Buddhist canonical scriptures. In Chinese symbolism, a basket of flowers symbolizes longevity, reaching a ripe old age.
In the ancient Egyptian culture, the basket is the symbol of Baset, the goddess with the cat's head. In the ancient Greek culture, the basket is linked to Dionysos

and Ceres. A basket adorned with ivy represents the Dionysian mystery. Jung considers the basket to be a symbol of the maternal body.

Bell

The symbol of the bell derives from both its shape and its sound. The sound of the bell is an expression of the creative force. Since the bell hangs, it is part of the symbolism that represents objects that are suspended between heaven and earth. Its use in prayer reinforces this symbolism, since as an instrument of evoking prayer both in the lower beings (the worshippers) and in the upper beings (at whom the prayer is directed), it serves as an intermediary between earth and heaven. Its shape also makes it a part of the symbolism of the sky because it is reminiscent of the dome of heaven.

The movement of the bell and of the clapper inside it symbolizes the movement of the elements. The bell was also used to exorcise evil spirits and destructive forces. Its movement from side to side, like that of the pendulum, symbolizes the movement between the extremes of good and evil, death and immortality.

Small bells that chime in the wind symbolize the sweet sounds of paradise. The tolling of the bell indicates both an assembly (for prayer, for a meal, for communal study) and a warning of danger.

In Buddhism, the bell symbolizes the pure sound of the doctrine of pure wisdom. In Buddhist Tantra, the bell symbolizes the female principle, while the Durja symbolizes the male principle.

In Chinese symbolism, the bell is thought to chase away evil spirits and the evil eye. The ceremonial bell symbolizes a link between man and heaven. The bell also symbolizes respect, obedience, loyal ministers and warriors who are prepared to fight until their last drop of blood.

In Hinduism, the bell symbolizes status and honor. As a symbol of the yoni, it expresses virginity.

In the Greco-Roman culture, the bell was linked to phallic symbolism, and was used in ceremonies as such. It was customary to tie bells to statues of Priapus. On the high priest's tunic, there were bells and pomegranates. Some people view the pomegranates as a symbol of the four elements, and the bell as the fifth element. Bells also symbolize virginity, since they were worn until marriage.

In the Teutonic culture, the bell is a symbol of honor. In Christianity, the church bell announces the presence of Jesus at Mass.

Church bells summon the believers, and are thought to expel evil spirits. The hollow of the bell was compared to the preacher's mouth, and the clapper to his tongue.

Belt

The belt is a symbol of guarding the body. It links up to the symbolism of "virginity," not only in the physical sense but also in the sense of preserving moral values and virtues in general. This can be explained by the symbolism of tightness, stopping and blocking that are attributed to the belt because of its action. Preserving virtues is supported by the qualities of restraint, frugality and blocking the baser instinctive urges. This symbolism contains duality – when the belt is linked to Venus, its symbolism is erotic and fetishistic. Other meanings that are attributed to this symbol are linked to obligation toward power, status or position, devotion, realization, victory, power, values and virtues. Thor's belt doubles his strength.

Bonfire

The bonfire symbolizes the sun's power, the place around which the tribe gathers for holy ceremonies and therefore sacred unity, and the encouragement of the forces of light and good.

Book

The book symbolizes the universe. An open book describes the book of life, the study of the spirit of wisdom, and the revelation and wisdom of the writings. The book is linked to the symbolism of the tree, and the book and the tree together symbolize the entire universe. In the symbolism that describes the Holy Grail, the book may symbolize the quest for the lost world. In Buddhism, the book symbolizes the wholeness of wisdom, language and expression. In the Chinese tradition, it is a common symbol, one of the eight "valuable things" of Buddhism, a symbol of power that can eliminate and get rid of every evil spirit. The pages of the book symbolize the leaves of the cosmic tree. A book may also represent scholarship.

In Christianity, books symbolize the Apostles who teach and disseminate the Word. In Islam, the book symbolizes creative, static matter, while the pen symbolizes the creative principle. The sacred book is the name of God, truth and mercy.

Bottle

The bottle is a uterine symbol that represents the principle of containment. It is considered to be one of the symbols of redemption because it is linked to the ark and the boat. In Buddhism, the bottle represents the nature of the Buddha.

Bow

The bow is a symbol that combines a female component – its shape, which is reminiscent of the shape of the crescent moon, and a male component – the penetrating shape of the arrow and the action of shooting. The movement of the arrow discharged from the bow is symbolic of the movement of sperm, which explains the powerful male symbolism that accompanies the symbol, despite the blatant female shape of the bow itself. The bow is linked to the idea of "tension" and to the life force, as well as to spiritual force. It has this symbolic meaning in Buddhism, where it symbolizes will power and the mind that shoots the arrows of the five senses. In Chinese symbolism, drawing the bow is a symbol of male courage and skill. The bow and arrow together symbolize offspring and fertility. As stated above, the fertility symbolism stems from the combination of the male and female symbolism, which cooperate in creating tension and movement.

In Hinduism, too, the bow symbolizes will power, and is also linked to the symbolism of love-passion-fertility; the bowstring of Kama, the god of love, is made of bees, as a symbol of the "sting" of love itself – sweet pain. Shiva's bow, like the lingam, is a symbol of the power of the god. In Islam as well, the bow symbolizes the power of God. In the Sumerian and Semitic cultures, the bow symbolized Ishtar's weapon as the goddess of war. In Taoism, the bow symbolizes the Tao, which humiliates the proud, elevates the humble, removes surfeit and meets needs. In the ancient Greco-Roman culture, the bow of Artemis/Diana symbolizes the crescent moon. Arrows and bows are linked mainly to Apollo and represent the suns' rays, the sun, and its fertilizing and purifying force. Eros has a bow and arrows, and, since they are associated with him, they join the symbolism of love and passion – the arrow that penetrates the lover's heart at the moment of falling in love, discharged by a celestial go-between. The bow and the quiver of arrows are also attributed to the hunting giant, Orion.

Box

The box is a female symbol that represents the principle of containing, safeguarding and carrying, as well as the womb. As a symbol, the box relates both to the physical body – which contains the divine spark, the soul – and to the unknown, that is "guarded" inside a closed box, like the myth of Pandora. In this myth, the unknown occurs as unexpected, destructive and undermining existing stability. These properties are attributed to the unknown. Moreover a person's investigation of the unknown is fraught with various perils. The box also symbolizes cover and concealment.

Bread

Bread symbolizes life, the food of the body and the soul, and visible and concrete life. Bread symbolizes unity, since it is composed of many grains that create a whole, and the action of slicing bread and sharing it out among the people sitting in a circle or around the table symbolizes a joint and united life. Ritual bread was usually marked with a cross, not just in Christian ceremonies, but also in Sumero-Semitic and Mithraic ceremonies (in other words, the differentiation of ritual bread by means of the symbol of the cross does not originate from Christianity).

In ceremonies, bread usually appears with wine. Wine is considered to be ecstasy or celestial devoutness, and bread is the physical manifestation of the spirit. From this arises the symbolism of unity between man and God. Wine is thought to be a male symbol, while bread is thought to be a female symbol, a combination of the liquid with the solid, which may symbolize the androgyne. In Christianity, bread is thought to be the sustainer of life. Ritual bread symbolizes the body of Jesus, while wine symbolizes his blood. In the Sumerian and Semitic cultures, breaking the bread is thought to supply food for the souls of the dead. It also symbolizes the unity of the group. In the Hebrew tradition, bread is the most basic food, and can appear as a symbol of all foods as well as of man's work in the material world in order to obtain nutrition for his physical survival.

Bridge

The bridge symbolizes a connection and a link between two worlds – a world of a connection between different people or nations, and a world of a connection between man and God. In various folk-stories, crossing the bridge is a test the hero has to undergo in order to reach his desired destination and accomplish his mission – self-realization. This bridge is the link between the unconscious and the conscious, between the person and God, and between the person and the God within him, between the individual and the Other. In various cultures, the bridge is a symbol of the passage between what is grasped and what is not grasped. Even without mystical meanings, the bridge is always a symbol of a passage from one state to another state. The arch is a natural symbol that is linked to the bridge. It is the bridge between heaven and earth, between God and man, between this world and the next, which is longed for. Rabbi Nachman of Breslav uses this symbolism in order to describe man's passage through this world:

"The entire world is a very narrow bridge, and the main thing is not to be at all afraid."

Brush

In Chinese symbolism, the brush symbolizes wisdom, intelligence, "brushing away" all the worries and difficulties. In Japanese symbolism, the brush or broom made of grass serves to represent purification during the spring ceremony.

Bunch of flowers, wreath

A bunch of flowers symbolizes devotion, sanctity, interweaving (for creating unity), respect, esteem for a guest or a hero, a happy destiny and good fortune. It is linked to the concept of binding together. It is said that all things in the universe are bound together like a wreath. The ancients hung wreaths at the entrance to temples on festivals and holy days as a sign of brotherhood (bond and unity).

They were used during initiation ceremonies, and also adorned sacrificial animals.

Sometimes, prisoners of war were decorated with wreaths as a sign of victory over the other side.

The Egyptians, Greeks and Romans would place a wreath on their guests' heads during feasts as a sign of respect. In funerals, wreaths symbolize the life beyond, fruitfulness and happiness, symbolism that is identical to that of flowers during funerals.

Candle

The candle symbolizes the individualization of light, the life of the individual, enlightenment, light in the darkness, the light of the spirit/soul in the darkness of life, the person's soul, and the ease with which life changes and ends (as easily as a candle goes out).

The candle symbolizes the person – the flame of the candle, as the light of the soul, consists of consumable matter, wax, and the wick of life has a given length and reaches its end at a certain point.

In the Hebrew tradition, the candle is compared to a little light by means of which it is possible to light many lights without jeopardizing its power to give. Since it is one of the most clear-cut symbols of light, and light is a symbol of the manifestation of the divinity, candles are used in many religious ceremonies in numerous different cultures, as much today as in ancient times.

Chain

The Egyptian hieroglyph in the shape of a vertical chain with three links is represented by two interwoven lines with the fourth link open at the bottom. The chain has a dual symbolism. On the one hand, it is the symbol of the caduceus (the twisting serpent on the wand, the symbol of medicine) of Mercury, which represents the dual currents of the universe: degeneration and development. On the other, it symbolizes bonds, knots and communication.

On the cosmic plane, the chain is the symbol of the marriage between earth and sky (or between the terrestrial aspect and the celestial aspect) like other similar symbols such as the arrow that is shot from the earth and pierces the air, the whistle of the stone flung from the sling, a shout of pain (the biblical cry for help). On the terrestrial plane, it is a symbol of marriage (unity), and every link reacts actively or forcibly to blood ties – mother and father, sons and daughters, siblings. In the broader sense, it is linked to the symbolism of interweaving, that is, physical or social union with a component that is secondary but very important for the strength of the material.

Among the Gauls, pairs of comrades-in-arms would bind themselves together during battle so that if one of them was killed, the other would also be. Words that stress the spiritual meaning of the chain were said by Louis XI, king of France, to the brave warrior, Raoul de Lanoy, when he gave him a gold chain as a tribute to his heroism in battle: "My friend, you are so fierce in battle that you must be bound with a chain, since I do not want to lose you, lest I need your assistance again." The chain also symbolizes office, serving in a high or key position (such as a mandarin or a prime minister), since it binds the person to the position and to the power. The links of the chain symbolize communication and marriage.

In Buddhism, the links bind the person to continued existence in the world as perceived by the senses. In Islam, the chain of existence is the hierarchical order of things in the universe. The chain also symbolizes bonds, limitation and slavery. The chain is also a symbol of the chain of command and of the head of that chain, who is "bound" to his post when it is a high position, like a commander, mandarin, and so on.

Chariot

One of the basic analogies of the universal symbolism in relation to the human being is that of the chariot. However, it is also the symbol of many gods and a symbol of the link between the ones above and the ones below. It is a symbol of direction, of leading and controlling the forces that are symbolized by the animals that are harnessed to the chariot. The shape of the chariot, its colors, and the animals harnessed to it, always have a symbolic meaning.

The driver of the chariot symbolizes the "self" of Jungian psychology, the mind, wisdom or the spirit that drives the body, and the chariot is the human body and also thought in relation to terrestrial matters. The horses are the life force, and the reins symbolize the wisdom and will power by means of which the rider leads his life.

The chariot is a common concept and symbol in various esoteric doctrines. The "chariot of the sun" is the vehicle of esoteric Buddhism and is called "the great vehicle." The chariot of fire is a symbol of dynamic strength that has the ability of the wise mind. The chariot of the sun and the chariot of fire are sometimes identified as one and the same, and their meaning is so powerful that they are found in almost every mythology in the world. When the rider of the chariot of the sun (or of fire) is the hero, he almost always symbolizes the body of the hero who acts as a serving vessel for the calling of his soul. The appearance, nature and color of the group of animals pulling the chariot is symbolic of the hero's qualities, positive or negative, and of the motives that propel his chariot forward. The horses of Arjuna in the Vedic epic are white, and symbolize the purity of the rider. According to an ancient Polish legend, the chariot of the sun is pulled by three horses – one silver, one golden, and one made of diamonds. The number of animals drawing the chariot represents the numerical symbolism that relates to the hero or the god, or to their objective (see Numbers). Chariots that are drawn by golden or white horses or griffins, are a symbol of the gods of heaven who drive the chariot of the sun across the sky.

The chariots of fire rise into the sky by means of the power of the wind or the celestial power of holy people (such as the prophet Elijah in the Bible). White horses symbolize both spirituality and purity as well as the sun. Cats, as with Freya's chariot, are lunar and symbolize witchcraft and magic. The chariot can also serve as a symbol of war, when heroes, warriors or victors drive it. In Christianity, the chariot symbolizes the church that is compared to a vehicle that conveys the believer on high.

In the Greco-Roman culture, the chariot is a symbol of all the sun gods, who drive a chariot harnessed to white horses. Apollo drives the chariot of the sun, and Poseidon's white horses symbolize the element of water and the foam of the waves. A chariot and horses are also the symbol of the god of war, Ares/Mars.

Cybele drives a chariot harnessed to lions, Poseidon's chariot is sometimes harnessed to tritons blowing conches. Venus' chariot is harnessed to doves, while Diana's is harnessed to deer and Juno's to peacocks. Hephaistos/Vulcan and Eros/Cupid drive a chariot that is harnessed to leopards or rams, and Pluto drives a chariot harnessed to black horses.

In Hinduism, the chariot symbolizes the self-management of the physical world. The driver of the chariot is the "self" who directs the horses and controls them. He is symbolized by Krishna the driver, but is not involved in the action or battles around him. The axis of the chariot's wheels is the axis of the world, and two of the wheels are heaven and earth. Suma drives the three-wheeled chariot of the moon harnessed to a speckled antelope or to ten white horses. The dawn drives a chariot harnessed to red cows or horses. Shiva drives a chariot harnessed to lunar deer or to an antelope. Indra drives a golden chariot.

In the Persian tradition, the chariot of the magi is harnessed to four war horses that symbolize the elements and are dedicated to the four Persian gods. Anahita, the goddess of fertility who appears with Mithras, drives a chariot harnessed to four white horses – wind, rain, cloud and hail.

In the Scandinavian and Teutonic cultures, Thor's chariot is harnessed to celestial stallions or rams, and Freja's chariot is harnessed to lunar cats.

Chimney
The chimney, and sometimes the fireplace connected to it, or any other opening in the roof of a house or a temple, a tent, and so on, symbolize the escape route to the sky, the gate of the sun, and the escape from the momentary to the eternal, from the limited to the unlimited. Santa Claus, who enters the house through the chimney, symbolizes celestial gifts that are conveyed straight from heaven to the person through a terrestrial gate or opening.

Comb
The comb is thought to be the gift of wondrous female beings such as mermaids and sirens. It symbolizes fecundity, rain and the sun's rays. Because of its action on the hair and its purpose, it also symbolizes complications and embroilment. It is attributed to Venus, and since it is linked to her and the sirens, and also because of its shape, it is the symbol of music, too.

Cradle
Because of its shape that is reminiscent of a boat or a barge, the cradle is thought to be a symbol of the ship of life that rocks on the surface of the

primeval ocean. The function of the cradle made it into a symbol of new beginnings and new life. The archetypal cradle is made of wood, and this point is extremely important. The tree provides shelter and protection during birth both to the people in ancient times who would give birth under a tree and to the animals that would give birth under a tree. Later, the offspring would be transferred to a wooden cradle or to a shelter that would protect the newborn. In the next stages of life, the tree gives life, both on the physical and on the spiritual level. Afterwards, it provides shelter and protection at the time of death, whether as wood for cremating the body in various cultures or as a coffin.

Crossroads

The crossroads symbolizes choice, but also danger. It is the meeting-place of time and space, a place in which it is necessary to make a choice that may lead to completely new paths and change the face of reality. For this reason, mystical meanings were attributed to crossroads in the folk-tales of various cultures, in which it was customary to bury criminals, suicide cases or vampires near to crossroads in order to confuse them. The ritual of sacrificing dogs at crossroads is well known, but its origins are unclear. The crossroads is linked to Janus, the two-faced god.

Crown

The crown symbolizes honor, extraordinary spiritual and sovereign power, devotion, lofty achievement, perfection and the endless cycle of time. It can symbolize a man with extrasensory powers, and as such is linked to the symbolism of the aura. The crown is linked to the gods of the sun, and the points of the crown symbolize the sun. Crowns, including those made of various plants, such as the laurel wreath dedicated to Apollo, the olive wreath dedicated to Zeus, and so on, are a significant symbol of success, and as such were worn on the heads of the winners in the games and contests of ancient Greece. The symbolism of the crown stems from the symbolism of the head on which it is placed, and is linked to the symbolism of the aura. The head is the person's highest organ, and for this reason the crown is an extension of humanity into loftier domains.

In alchemy books, there are diagrams of the inferior metals bowing down like slaves before the lofty metal – gold – that is wearing a crown. After alchemical transmutation, the inferior metals also earn crowns, as witnesses to the spiritual evolution they underwent by means of the transmutation, a symbol of the victory of the higher forces over the lower forces, the victory over base instincts for the sake of spiritual elation. For this reason, Jung sees the crown as a clear-cut symbol of achieving the highest goal in evolution, victory over instincts and urges, in the form of "Who is the hero?" – "He who overcomes his urges." Overcoming the basic urges is what crowns the person with the spiritual crown and earns him a crown of immortal life.

The Pharaohs in ancient Egypt were crowned with a double crown – the white crown of the south and the red crown of the north, symbolizing the lofty world and the lofty mind and the inferior world and the inferior mind (from the spiritual point of view, but needed for the Pharaoh's activity in the material world). In Chinese symbolism, the crown symbolizes imperial power, superiority. A crown that covers the eyes with a veil of precious stones suspended from it symbolizes not seeing what is not worthy of being seen, and a crown that covers the ears symbolizes not hearing what is not worthy of being heard.

In Christianity, the crown symbolizes the righteous person, victory over death, achievement and the reward of the martyrs. In Hinduism, a crown at the top of the central column of the temple is a common architectural symbol that symbolizes the celestial world and creates a point of exit from the material world into the celestial world. In the Sumerian and Semitic cultures, the crown of feathers symbolizes sovereignty, celestial power, strength, and is attributed to Marduk and to Shamash.

The crown shaped like a tower is attributed to all the mother goddesses of the Middle East, and it symbolizes the sovereignty of the Big Mother – nature.

Dagger
Like the spear and the sword, the dagger is also a phallic symbol, symbolizing the penetrating and cutting male principle. It is attributed to the Greek god of war, Mars, to Mitra and to Melpomene.

Dice
Because of their role over the years, and because they display numerical values that possess cosmic significance on the one hand and "determine" the fate both of the gambler and of the querent who consults a dice soothsayer on the other, dice have become a symbol of fate and luck. Casting the dice mainly symbolizes fatefulness and immutability. In addition, as a characteristic of both fate and gamblers, it symbolizes irresponsibility, instability and capriciousness with regard to man and his actions.

Cutting the die in two symbolizes a covenant, a contract, or a renewal of friendship. In Christian symbolism, the die symbolizes Jesus' *Via Dolorosa*. In Hinduism, dice have a symbolism identical to that of the shape of the die, which concentrates on the number four that appears on it.

It symbolizes the Holy Four and the things that appear in cycles of four, or in a process consisting of four parts, such as the four seasons, the four yoga cycles, and so on.

Distaff, spindle

The distaff and the spindle are known in many cultures as symbols of time, spinning the threads of fate, creation, and fatefulness. They are linked to all the goddesses of spinning and weaving. Clotho is called "the spinner" or "the turner of the spindle," and Athene is the patroness of spinning and weaving. The symbolism of the distaff and the spindle is also linked to that of the spider and spinning.

Doll

Because of the doll's shape, it is usually a symbol of human beings, a symbol of a human figure , so that the doll becomes symbolic of the person's body, mind or soul.

One of the best-known symbolic uses of the doll that is reflected in this symbolism is in the use of black magic, such as voodoo, in which the doll symbolizes the person who is going to be harmed. In order to cause injury to various parts of the person's actual body, sharp objects such as pins are stuck into the identical places on the doll's body.

Alternatively, cuts with a knife are inflicted on the doll, or parts of its body are burned or split. In the Kabbalic *pulsa denura* ceremony, too, a wax doll is used as a symbol of the person who is to be cursed.

The burning of dolls in the image of a loathed figure reflects a similar desire for revenge that is directed toward the image of the person, even when he is dead.

In many ancient cultures, it was customary to hang dolls on a pole or a string on a farm in order to expel witches, evil spirits and harmful influences until the following harvest-time. Afterwards, the doll would become a scarecrow that was placed in the fields.

The use of the doll crops up in psychopathology as well as in symbolism. There are several mental illnesses in which the patient makes a doll and keeps it well hidden.

Some people see this as a projection of the patient's personality onto the doll.

SYMBOLS

In other cases, this has been diagnosed as erotomania or a perversion of the maternal instinct.

Door

The door is considered a female symbol. Its symbolism is the opposite of that of a wall, and is similar to that of a hole, a tunnel or an opening. It symbolizes opportunity, hope, an opening, entering a new life, initiation, a passage and a path from one state or world to another. It also symbolizes the protective shelter of the Big Mother. An open door symbolizes freedom, liberation and a new opportunity.

In Hinduism, divine images are etched and carved into the doorjambs, indicating the divinity through which the person enters the sublime presence. The door symbolizes the entry into the seven realms of paradise and the cave of initiation. In the ancient Roman culture, Janus was the god of the threshold, and held the key for opening and locking the door. In Christian symbolism, the door symbolizes Jesus, as is stated in the New Testament: "I am the door."

In the sign of Cancer in the Zodiac, the door symbolizes the longest day of the year, and it is called "the door of man" and symbolizes the wane and decline of the sun (since from now on the sun will shine for a shorter length of time each day), the *Fanua inferni*. The shortest day of the year, during the sign of Capricorn, is called "the door of the gods," and symbolizes the increase in the strength of the sun as well as the rising sun, the *Fanua coeli*. These doors are also linked to the entrance to and exit from caves of initiation as well as to souls that enter and leave the world. In Hinduism, the *Fanua inferni* is called *pitri-yana*, while the *Fanua coeli* is called *deva-yana*.

Drum

The drum symbolizes the ancient sound, power, the ability to utter sound and speech, celestial truth, revelation, tradition, and the rhythm of the universe. It is thought to inspire tradition and magic (witchcraft). In many cultures, drums were used during holy rituals, especially to get the tribal healer or shaman into a trance. Of all the musical instruments, the drum is thought to have the most mystical symbolism. It is identified with the ritual altar, and for that reason, ancient as well as modern cultures consider it to be an intermediary between heaven and earth, between the upper beings and the lower beings, but because of its shape and because of the animal skin stretched over it, it responds more to the element of earth. It is linked to all the gods of thunder. In Africa, the drum is linked to the heart and symbolizes it and also the powers of magic. In Buddhism, the drum is the voice of the law. It symbolizes happy news. The drumbeats of the dharma rouse the ignorant and the slothful. In Chinese symbolism, the drum symbolizes the voice of heaven and the Taoist immortal, Chang Kuo-Lau. In Japan, the drum summons people to prayer and is linked to the rooster. In Hinduism, the drum is attributed to Shiva and Kali, who were perceived as destroyers, and also to Durga. The goddess of arts and music, Sarasvati, is also found in the drum. Shiva's drum produces the ancient sound of the creation. In the ancient Greek culture, the drum symbolized orgies and was used during ecstatic dancing. In the Shamanic tradition, the drum is very important. It symbolizes the powers of magic and witchcraft, and is used to summon spirits. Symbolically, it is constructed from the cosmic tree. The secondary symbolism of the drum derives from its shape. There is an enormous range of shapes of drums, but the three basic shapes are the hourglass-shaped drum, the round drum, and the barrel-shaped drum. The hourglass drum symbolizes opposites or opposite order, and the relations between the two worlds, the upper and the lower. The round drum is thought to be the shape of the world, and it therefore symbolizes our world. The barrel-shaped drum is linked to thunder and lightning.

Ewer (jug)

The ewer symbolizes purity, hand-washing, and purification. It is also the symbol of Dionysos, the god of wine.

Fan

The symbolism of the fan relates to two common types of fan. The first, which is widespread in the East and Africa, is the large fan shaped (usually) like a kind of heart, and sometimes decorated with feathers. The second is the well-known European folding fan.

There are two common meanings for the large fan as a symbol. One is that it symbolizes the element of wind, moving air, the spirit of man, with the feathers that adorn it giving it celestial symbolism. When this is its meaning, it appears as the symbol of the first among the eight immortals in Taoism, Chung-Li Tsuan, who is said to have used a fan in order to revive the spirits of the dead. In Taoism, the fan is linked to birds and their flight as liberation from the material world and beyond into the realm of immortality. In Chinese symbolism, the fan appears in this context as a symbol of the power of air, which can breathe renewed life into the dead. It also symbolizes delicacy of emotion. In Japan, the white-feather fan symbolizes the power of the winds that blow. In Hinduism, in contrast, the fan is linked to the power of fire, as a symbol of Ajni, the Vedic fire god, and is also linked to Vishnu.

The second meaning of the large fan is that it represents status, honor and authority. In the cultures of the East and Africa particularly, the fan is a symbol of royal honor or status.

The reason is that a fan of this kind is large, and has a long pole for a servant to hold, and there were servants and slaves whose permanent function was to wave the fan over their master's or ruler's head.

In Chinese symbolism, it sometimes has this meaning, as well as being a symbol of the mandarin's honorable status and of authority in general. In Japan, it is a symbol of authority, mastery, and power. The fan has this meaning nowadays as well – with the pope.

The second fan, the Western one, is a fan that opens from one point and spreads out.

It symbolizes life that starts out from the focal point and spreads as the experiences of life expand. It is linked to the moon and its phases (since it opens and closes, fills out and shrinks, like the moon).

For this reason it is linked to the lunar changes, to the imagination, to change and to femininity. This may be the basis of the name that is given to an abandoned woman in China – "autumn fan."

The different stages of the fan when it is opened symbolize the phases of the moon – invisible, appearing, waxing, full, and waning until it disappears. All of them appear like a kind of continuous flow, like the movement of the opening fan.

Another symbolism is attributed to waving the fan, which, in various cultures, is thought to be a way of chasing away and expelling the forces of evil.

Flute

The flute occasionally appears in the context of mourning customs, lamentation and emotional extremes. In the Chinese culture, the flute is the symbol of Huan Xieng-Chu, one of the eight immortals in Taoism, who symbolizes harmony.

In the Greco-Roman cultures, it symbolizes the sirens as an expression of emotionalism and seduction, and it is one of the most blatant symbols of the god Pan, the player of pipes. In Hinduism, Krishna's flute was "the voice of eternity weeping to the inhabitants in time." In the Phrygian culture, it symbolized Cybele.

The duality in the symbol of the flute comes from the fact that it is phallic in shape, but its sound is linked to the inner feeling, intuition, the feminine, the anima. Moreover, the flute is linked to the orchard and to water.

Furnace, kiln
A furnace is a place in which fire is processed. Here, its power is increased and made more efficient in order to accomplish useful goals. The furnace has a female nature, "the womb of fire."

Gate
The gate symbolizes the entry into new life, a passage from one state to another, communication, communication between the world of the living and the world of the dead. It symbolizes the protective and sheltering aspect of the Big Mother. The gate as a passage symbolizes initiation – the entry of the unconscious person, or the "sleeping person" through the gate, and his exit on the other side as a conscious person, as a new person.

The gates in mythology and folklore were always guarded by dragons, dogs, animals and fantastic monsters. From the esoteric aspect of many of those legends, on the other side of the gate lay the coveted thing, and it was necessary to pass through the gate in order to reach it. The action of passage from one state of consciousness to a higher state involved a struggle or battle with the "monsters of the mind" or with the baser layers of humanity. The passage was manifested in the struggle with the monsters, animals or fantastic beasts that guarded the gate. The gates of Osiris' house were guarded by goddesses, each of whom guarded one gate. In order to enter, it was necessary to know the name of the goddess. This is similar to the fifty gates of wisdom in the Arabic tradition and in the Kabbala, which require knowledge of the special spiritual "keys" in order to pass through them. The gates of the East and the West are the gates through which the sun passes in the morning and evening. The symbol of the gate is linked to knowledge and wisdom. The gates of the city were the place where judges and kings sat in judgment over the people. The elders of the city and the "preacher at the gate" would also sit at the entrance to the gates. As a passage from one state to another, there are the "gates of heaven," "the gates of paradise," and, conversely, "the gates of hell."

Glass, goblet, cup
The shape of the cup as a container of liquids has made it into a female symbol that represents openness, acceptance and passivity. In addition, it symbolizes abundance, the potion of life and immortality. In many initiation

ceremonies, the symbolism of the sacred cup appears. An inverted cup symbolizes emptiness. The symbolism of the cup is similar in meaning to that of the goblet and the Holy Grail, and in Buddhism, it is similar in meaning to the symbol of the bowl.

In the ancient Greco-Roman cultures, it is linked to Hercules/Heracles. In the Celtic tradition, the goblet or the cup symbolizes the heart, life. In Hinduism, the four goblets of the sacrifice of the Veda (on the four books included in it) symbolize the four rivers of paradise that create the crossing of terrestrial life, the four elements, the cyclical periods of development, the four ages, the four castes, and the four seasons. A cup or goblet placed on some kind of supporting surface symbolizes the person who offers himself in the service of the forces of heaven and receives supreme grace and abundance from above. In the Islamic culture, the yamshi goblet, into which the Sufis gaze, symbolizes a mirror of the world.

Guitar

In Buddhism, the guitar is symbolic on two planes: on the social plane, it is a symbol of excellence in the arts and sciences; on the spiritual plane, it is a symbol of the harmony of existence in the higher worlds.

Hammer

The hammer generally appears with one of the two following meanings: shaping and creating or crushing, vengeance and judgment. As the blacksmith's tool, the hammer is granted the mystical power of creation. It is considered to be a symbol that represents formative power and is linked to all the gods of thunder. The hammer and anvil together are the formative forces of nature, two complementary facets of creation: the male – active, and the female – passive.

In the sense of striking and crushing, it symbolizes justice, law, and vengeance. This meaning is represented by the double hammer appears, also called the "tau cross." In ancient Egypt, it is the symbol of the god Ptha, the "grinder" or "avenger."

The hammer and tongs and double hammer – the tau cross – are linked to all the gods of thunder, but especially to Hephaistos, Vulcan and Thor. In the Greco-Roman culture, the hammer symbolizes thunder and vengeance. It is a symbol of Hephaistos/Vulcan and also of the god of the sky, Zeus/Jupiter. In Hinduism, the hammer symbolizes thunder. A stone hammer, an ax, is the symbol of Parashu-Rama. In the Scandinavian and Teutonic cultures, Thor's thunder hammer was called "the destroyer." Thor throws his hammer, which never misses, and always comes back to him after striking and crushing. It can also resurrect the dead. In Chinese symbolism, the hammer is used in the sense of creation and giving form, and symbolizes the celestial art of shaping the universe. Here too, there is a connotation of the loud noise produced by the hammer (like the association with thunder in other cultures) as a symbol of sublime forces that drive away darkness and evil. In Japanese symbolism, it is a symbol of wealth and good fortune, and in Christianity, it is a symbol of Jesus' *Via Dolorosa*. The wooden hammer symbolizes authority, mastery, focused power, male power. In Japanese symbolism, it is called "the creative hammer," the creative combination of male power and female power. In addition, it symbolizes good fortune.

Harp

The meaning of the harp resembles that of the ladder – stairs leading to the next world. In this sense, it is also linked to the white horse (that gallops to the next world or to other worlds). It serves as a bridge between the ones above and the ones below. There is also a close tie between the harp and the swan. The tension of the harp's strings that are yearned for by love and spiritual realms is an allegory of the tension in which the person lives on earth every moment of his life, enduring the anticipation of life in the next world. In the Hebrew tradition, the harp symbolizes King David. In the Celtic culture, it symbolizes Dagda, the god of fire, who calls the seasons and causes them to change by means of his playing.

Honey

Honey symbolizes eternal life, initiation, a change of personality or rebirth (following an initiation ceremony), wisdom and intelligence, purity of speech and articulateness. Taking into account the process of honey production, which is a mysterious and sophisticated process that is performed by the bee, which, in many cultures, is symbolic of the soul, it is possible to understand how it became the symbol of self-improvement. In India, honey is the symbol of the superego and is compared to fire. Honey nourishes the lotus of knowledge. In the European tradition, honey is the symbol of wisdom. Properties of fortifying the body, potency, virility and fertility were attributed to honey. It was also reputed to be an aphrodisiac. It served as an offering to the supreme divinities and the spirits of fertility. In astrology, honey is linked to the moon, and is therefore linked to blooming and growth. In the Chinese tradition, honey mixed with oil is a symbol of false friendship. In Christianity, it symbolizes the sweetness of the divine word. In the ancient Greek culture, honey is considered to be the food of the gods, a symbol of wisdom, of purity of speech and of poetic talent. Bees reputedly filled the mouths of Homer, Sappho, Pindar and Plato with honey.

Honey is understandably a symbol of the greatest sweetness, abundance, prosperity and comfort, which "descend" upon the person as a result of God's goodness. Thus, the Promised Land is "a land flowing with milk and honey," and even manna tasted like "wafers in honey." Honey is prohibited for use in sacrifice, according to the Torah, as opposed to other cultures in which honey is considered to be a desirable offering and was sometimes even forbidden for consumption because of its important role as an offering to the gods or the spirits. In the Mithraic culture, honey was used as an offering to Mithra, and it was customary to pour it onto the mouths and hands of people undergoing initiation. In the Sumerian culture, honey was considered to be the food of the gods. The superiority of honey as food derives from several characteristics – the unique production process itself, the fact that this process was carried out by bees, which have a deep positive symbolism, man's inability to produce it for himself (without the action of the bee), its beauty and its color, which links it to the sun and to gold (the supreme star and the supreme metal), its sweet taste, and its healthful properties. The production of something so perfect in form and taste by means of a mysterious process in the body of the bee contributed to the aura of mystery that surrounded honey and the fact that it was seen as a gift of the gods.

Hourglass

The hourglass symbolizes time and temporariness, the rapid passage of life, time that runs out, death. The two parts of the hourglass symbolize the cyclical nature of life and death. Its two parts, like the drum of the same shape, also symbolize the relationship between the upper world and the lower world. The sand that falls down symbolizes the attraction of the base, physical nature. It sometimes appears together with the "Reaper," death. In Christian art, the image that symbolizes temperance (according to its meaning in Tarot cards) frequently holds an hourglass. Additional symbolism of the hourglass relates to opposites – when a certain quality invokes the quality that is opposite to it, like death and life and vice versa, good and evil, and so on.

House

The house symbolizes the center of the world, the protective aspect of the Big Mother, protection. It is thought to be a mystical symbol of the female aspect of the universe. The culture and prayer house of a tribal group, its hut or teepee, symbolizes the cosmic center, while the house itself is a symbol of tradition.

A residence symbolizes the human body and human thought – human life. In psychoanalysis, some people consider a house that appears in dreams to be a symbol of the different layers of the mind. The external aspect of the house symbolizes the external appearance of the person – the personality he externalizes or the facade he displays. The floors of the house are linked to the symbols of breadth and length.

The roof and the highest ceiling are linked to the head and to the mind, or to the intellect, and therefore also to the conscious exercise of self-control. The basement is linked unconsciously to the instincts. In alchemy, the kitchen, in which the food is cooked, sometimes symbolizes the place or the moment of change in consciousness (just as the ingredients are cleaned, processed and cooked together to create a perfect dish). The adjoining rooms sometimes symbolize the ventricles of the heart, the chambers of the mind, the subconscious.

The stairs are the thread that links the different planes of the mind, but their exact meaning depends on how they are perceived – as ascending or descending. The house also symbolizes the ingathering stage in the initiation process, and the descent to the dominions of darkness prior to rebirth.

Ink
In the Islamic culture, ink symbolizes the reflection of all existing potential. According to Muhammed: "The ink of scholars is like the blood of martyrs."

Key
The key symbolizes the mystery or riddle that has to be solved, or a mission that must be accomplished, and the means with which to do so. It also symbolizes all the forces of opening and locking, of binding and liberating. Occasionally it symbolizes the threshold of the subconscious. It symbolizes release, knowledge and initiation, and is linked to the symbolism of Janus (the god of fate and time), who binds and liberaties, "the inventor of locks," and the god of initiation. The symbol that comprises two keys and is sometimes placed on the heart is linked to Janus. Janus stores the power to open and to lock in the keys, and the key of the door permits entry into the world of the gods. In alchemistic symbolism, too, the key symbolizes the power to open and close, as well as to dismantle, to coagulate, and to freeze. In the Greco-Roman culture, the key is attributed to Hecate as the guardian of Hell, as well as to Persephone

and Cybele. In Japanese symbolism, the three keys symbolize love, wealth, and happiness.

The combination of the symbols of the dove and the key symbolizes the spirit that opens the gates of Heaven. In popular legends, the three keys are used for the same number of secret rooms full of treasure, and represent initiation and knowledge. The first key – the silver one – represents what can be revealed by psychological understanding. The second key – the gold one – represents philosophical wisdom. The third key – the diamond one – grants the power to act. Finding a key symbolizes the stage prior to finding the treasure, and it symbolizes finding the key to the requested knowledge.

Knife

The knife as a symbol is the antithesis of the sword as a symbol. The knife is linked to death and revenge, but also to offering sacrifices. The knife's short blade, by analogy, represents the superiority of its holder's instinctive powers, while the long blade of the sword or saber symbolizes the spiritual "height" or spiritual stature of the swordsman.

The action of cutting with a knife symbolizes separation, detachment, division and cleaving, but also liberation and redemption and freeing the bonds. In Buddhism, too, the symbol of cutting with a knife has a similar meaning to the latter one. This action represents the liberation and detachment from the bonds of ignorance and pride. In Christian symbolism, the knife symbolizes martyrdom and Abraham.

Labyrinth, maze

The labyrinth is an architectural form, even though it also appears as a graphic symbol that ostensibly lacks a purpose. As an architectural form, it is so complicated that it is almost impossible to get out of it. It causes confusion in the mind of the observer or the person in it.

Ancient writings mention five large labyrinths: the Egyptian labyrinth, the two large labyrinths in Crete, the Greek labyrinth on the island of Lemnos, and the Etruscan labyrinth in Calosium. Diagrams and symbols of labyrinths are common almost throughout the world, but appear mainly in Europe and Asia. The labyrinth also appears in prehistoric paintings, mostly in an elliptical or circular shape, as opposed to the later labyrinths, which were generally square. This labyrinth is linked to the spiral shape, and is sometimes symbolic of the movement of the celestial bodies in the sky.

One of the mythological purposes of the maze, according to widespread legends and beliefs, was to house terrible monsters such as the Minotaur in the Cretan maze in such a way that they could not escape. This idea expresses the need for the existence of the facet of evil in the world (since symbolically, it was possible to get rid of these monsters) – but it exists so that the spiritual initiate can reach it (that is, struggle with the symbolic evil that exists in the world and in the human soul), and subdue it and find his way back into the world.

The deep symbolism of the labyrinth was that of losing one's spirit in the labyrinth of terrestrial life. The descent into the material world is like entering the labyrinth, and finding the way out again, to the world outside of the illusion of material existence, is not easy. Because of this, the labyrinth has a symbolism of initiation – an idea of reaching the center. From the center, which is the symbol of the human heart, namely, the essence of the microcosm, after the person has learned himself, the long and difficult journey of going out beyond the existential limits of the world of matter and illusion begins. For this reason, it is a symbol of the mysteries of life, of life's journey, and of the illusions that exist in it, which are symbolized by the paths inside the labyrinth that do not lead anywhere.

In the story of the most famous labyrinth, the Cretan labyrinth built by King Minos in order to house the Minotaur, the hero, Theseus, found his way out with the help of Minos' daughter, Ariadne, and the twine she gave him. By tying the twine to himself, he found his way out. Tying the twine given to him by Ariadne, who had fallen in love with him at first sight, offers a possibility of getting out of the symbolic maze – love.

However, not all labyrinths involved a battle with a monster. Most of them were empty and the objective was to reach the center, which was empty. The person who reached the center of the labyrinth after a long and arduous struggle and then looked around, discovered one being only – himself.

Ladder

The initiates of the Mithraic mysteries (the Mesopotamian high priestess) would climb up a holy seven-rung ladder, each of whose rungs was made of a different metal and symbolized a different planetary numeral and a different deity. Ancient religions often employed the sign of "a ladder to the sky," as in the story of Jacob and the ladder. The Egyptian ladders of Horus and Seth represented angels who assisted the Pharaoh in his climb up to the sky. In Egyptian tombs, amulets in the form of ladders ascending to the sky were found. Muhammed and Buddha also climbed up to the celestial realms and returned by using ladders that ascended to the sky. Climbing up a ladder to the sky and coming back again was a characteristic of Shamanic initiation in Central Asia, China, and areas of the Black Sea. In the Christian world, some people interpreted the symbol of the ladder as a spiritual ascent up the stairs of morality.

Lamp

The lamp, because of its action, possesses symbolism that is linked to light and stems from it. It has characteristics that resemble those of the symbol of the candle. As such, it symbolizes life, divine light, immortality and guidance. Another meaning that is unique to it more as a purveyor of light, is the fact that it symbolizes wisdom, intellect and spirit. Just as today, a light-bulb in cartoons appears above the head of a character who has just had an idea, so the lamp symbolizes intellectual wisdom, but also memory, mostly metaphysical (a memory of the world beyond the world of illusion). As a symbol of enlightenment or a flash of insight that creates a different perception of reality, the lamp appears as Aladdin's lamp, a legend that has parallels in other folk-tales as well. It is possible to find the symbol of the lamp as a symbol of good deeds, according to the notion that good deeds illuminate their doers and the world. Another symbolism of the lamp is light that is not independent. It depends on certain parameters in order to burn. It is the temporary nature of man (who burns until the wick of life is consumed), and individual life as opposed to cosmic existence – temporary and transient existence as opposed to the eternal truth. In Tarot, the lamp appears in the hand of the hermit in the "Hermit" card, illuminating the dark corners of consciousness by means of solitude and introspection.

The lamps of the ancients were shaped in accordance with their function: secular, religious or funerary, in order to match them to the nature of the gods to whom they were dedicated. Some people see the ancient oil lamp, shaped like a mandala or an almond, as a vaginal symbol, with the place for the wick associated with the clitoris. Lamps with twelve wicks symbolized the twelve signs of the Zodiac, and the altar lamps in sun or fire rituals were meant to be a symbol of the sun. In Christianity, "the seven lamps" are the seven gifts of the spirit. Altar lamps indicate the presence of the divinity. In Hinduism, the oil of the lamp is the ocean that expresses devotion, the wick is the earth and knowledge, and the flame is love.

Lance, spear

The lance and the spear are male, phallic symbols. They symbolize the axis of the world, life-giving force, fertility and heroism in battle, as well as the wizard's wand, the symbol of warriors and hunters. In the Celtic tradition, the lance together with the sling create the "long arm" of Lug or Lamfhada. In Chinese symbolism, the lance is the symbol of several secondary gods. In the ancient Greco-Roman culture, the lance and the shield of the adolescent boy on the threshold of adult life, which is called Epheboy, symbolize initiation and the passage from youth to adulthood, acquiring the courage and heroism of the adult. The lance and the spear are symbols of Athene/Minerva and Ares/Mars.

Lock
The lock represents a challenge, a search, standing before a spiritual revelation that requires active effort, and resembles the symbolism of the key, but in a passive way. It has feminine meanings, and may symbolize the female genitals with the connotation of virginity. In the Chinese tradition, the lock symbolizes longevity and good health.

Loom
The loom is linked to the symbolism of spinning and weaving, which symbolizes fate, the spinning of fate, and time.

It is linked to most of the lunar goddesses and the spinner of fate, and is the symbol of Penelope and Arachne.

Lyre, lute
In Greek mythology, the lyre is a symbol of creating harmony, reconciliation, resolving conflicts, and creating resignation and conciliation between the forces of nature, through self-knowledge and familiarity with arbitration techniques. As such, it appears as the lyre of Orpheus, the good shepherd, whose playing bewitched the wild beasts so that they did not harm the flock. As the good shepherd, Orpheus would use his sounds to bewitch the wild animals as a sign of self-knowledge and expertise in resolving conflicts. This symbolism reached Christianity via the early Christians, who borrowed the symbol of Orpheus with the lyre and turned it into a symbol of Jesus. As the good shepherd, Jesus drew his believers to the holy scriptures by his playing, which chased away the wild beasts and ensured safe passage for his flock.

In the Chinese culture, too, the lyre is a symbol of harmony between powerful parties who are supposed to use their power for collaborative purposes – harmony between rulers and ministers.

In addition, it appears in the context of the harmony of togetherness, as a symbol of companionship and friendship, and as a symbol of conjugal happiness. The lyre is one of the four symbols of the scholar, along with literature, painting, and chess.

Mask

The mask represents a change of identity, the blurring of identity, transformation, disguise, becoming the equivalent of something, protection, non-being. In ancient cultures, masks were sometimes worn so that the wearer could assume the properties of the image of the mask, and become the equivalent of a particular thing. It was sometimes also worn in order to create non-individualization, blur personality traits and assume others, lose one's identity in a new identity, and on the other hand, assume an identity and define a clear identity via the characteristic and defined features of the mask. The mask is also linked to the symbolism of shame and concealment, since the wearer remains the same entity, but the fact of wearing the mask may symbolize his rejection of his given entity and his search for another self-definition because he does not accept his given "character traits." The unique face of the person symbolizes his character, what he externalizes, and his states of mind that are imprinted on his features. Wearing a mask may indicate the blurring of his unique identity and exchanging it for some defined, unchanging and static identity.

Sometimes, the purpose of a mask is to "conceal" the transformation that is taking place beneath it. The mystic character of the mask stems from that fact that it enables the person as he is to become whatever he wants to be. This mystical character prompted the use of the mask in a broad range of religious ceremonies in various cultures. In various Oceanic cultures, the mask has an unusual use in initiation ceremonies, in the transition from youth to adulthood. In manhood ceremonies, the young male initiates cover their faces with a mud or clay mask, close their eyes, and behave as if they do not hear the instructions and the orders issued to them by the elders. However, the next day, the boys wash their faces and bodies, and their initiation ceremony is complete. This example shows the link between the mask and the process of apparent transformation that occurs below the mask and is revealed as "the new face" of an adult. The mask can also appear as something that covers up emptiness, an empty threat – the scary mask that stems from fear itself or from weakness. It is said that Shiva created a monster with a lion's head and a lean monster's body, and when it demanded prey, he ordered it to eat its own body. It did so, until only a mask remained.

Masks were also used for representing different entities. In the Mayan culture, masks that were used in sacred rituals represented the supernatural power of the gods, while masks that were used in ordinary pageants symbolized the inner personality, which is mostly concealed by the external appearance. Masks of animals symbolize the wisdom of the animals, their instinctive properties that man can learn from, or man's bestial nature, with which he has to come to terms. The Aborigine "soul of the bush" mask grants its wearer the identity of the plant, animal or bird it represents. In African tribes, the mask itself may have its own uniqueness and mystical power. In Greece, the mask symbolized the power that is linked to the death of the Gorgon, or the tragic or comic nature of a character in a play. The tragic mask is attributed to the muse Melpomene and the comic mask to the muse Thalia.

Milk

Milk symbolizes nutrition, softness, goodness and motherhood. The milk of the mother goddess is considered to be the food of the gods, celestial nourishment. As the newborn's food, milk was often used in initiation rites to symbolize rebirth. In ceremonial use, it is thought to be the liquid of life, frequently in conjunction with honey. Milk and honey are thought to be divine foods and givers of life, as well as symbols of abundance and prosperity. A mixture of milk and water symbolizes the spirit and matter, respectively. Milk, water and honey were considered to be a tribute to the Muses. In Buddhism, milk symbolizes the nutrition of the Buddha Dharma. According to Hinduism, there is a tree in paradise that yields milk. In the Zarathustrian faith, milk is holy as a product of the cow. In ancient Greece, the initiate would enter Mother Earth's womb, be reborn, and be nourished with milk from her breasts. In Christianity, milk symbolizes the logos and the church. It was customary to give the baptized infant milk and honey. In Christian art, a bowl of milk symbolizes the nourishing power of Jesus and the church. In the Jewish tradition and the kabbala, some people view milk as a symbol of kindness, of the beginning of the life cycle, and of nutrition, as opposed to meat, which symbolizes law and the end of the life cycle. This cosmogenic contrast explains the essence of the prohibition of mixing milk and meat.

Mirror

The symbolism of the mirror derives directly from the structure and function of the object. Since the mirror is multifaceted, the symbolism attributed to it is also varied, but common symbols can be found in it. The mirror is a symbol of truth, since it reflects precisely what is standing opposite it – not just personal truth, but also cosmic truth. It is thought to be a symbol of the clear and shining surface of the celestial truth. Since self-contemplation and self-examination are natural paths to enlightenment and to the development of the person's self-understanding, they symbolize self-realization, wisdom and intellect, and the understanding of the world via self-understanding, since the person is a microcosm that reflects the macrocosm. "Mirror of the universe" is the reflection of the supernatural and celestial wisdom, sublime wisdom that is reflected in the sun, the moon and the stars. The mirror is a symbol of the imagination and the consciousness because of its ability to reflect the reality of the visible world. It is linked to thought, since thought is a tool for self-contemplation, just as it is also a tool for contemplating the universe.

The mirror is linked to the myth of Narcissus. The universe is thought to be a narcissist who contemplates the reflection of his image in the consciousness of human beings. The mirror is linked to water because of the latter's reflective property. The appearance of the image in the mirror, like its disappearance, too, the division between the "populated" mirror and the "unpopulated" mirror – contributed to making the mirror a symbol with a lunar meaning, since the properties of disappearance and appearance are attributed to the moon. For this reason, it also has feminine symbolism. Like the moon, which reflects the light of the sun, so the mirror, with its passive and reflective characteristics, reflects the figure standing opposite it.

Since ancient times, the mirror has been related to ambivalently. It is a useful and banal tool on the one hand, and on the other, it possesses the unique function of reflecting and duplicating. It is a surface that duplicates images, and to a certain extent contains and absorbs them, and this is what caused the mirror to be used for sorcery and spells. In many folk-tales, magical powers are attributed to the mirror. The occultist, John Dee, became famous in the fourteenth century when he made contact with spirits through mirrors made of black glass. Many witchcraft techniques make various uses of the mirror for attracting spirits and influencing the image that was reflected in the mirror. This comes from the belief that the mirror absorbs or stores something of the image that is reflected in it.

Among the ancients, the mirror was a symbol of the multifarious nature of the soul, of its mobility and its ability to adapt itself to the objects that visit it or attract its attention. The prevailing belief stated that when the mirror was hung in a temple or on a grave, facing downward, it built an "axis of light," a path of elevation for the soul. Over time, the mirror acquired the mythical property of a door through which the soul could free itself during the passage to the other side, an idea that appears in Louis Carroll's book, *Alice through the Looking Glass.*

This helps explain the well-known custom of covering mirrors or turning them back to front during certain events or in certain circumstances, especially following the demise of one of the members of the household. It is considered to be a symbol of the memory, and the gateway to the realms of the world. The reflection of the mirror is also a symbol of the realization of the temporary, transient world.

In Buddhism, the mirror symbolizes the soul in a state of purity, the truth that is reflected and the enlightened mind. It is a symbol of the realization of form and the reflection of the body, of honesty and purity. As reflected light, it describes the samsara. It is one of the eight valuables of Chinese Buddhism. In Chinese symbolism, the mirror symbolizes honesty. A square mirror symbolizes the earth and a round mirror symbolizes heaven. The central idea of the mirror is the axis and the balance between two forces. It is thought to support conjugal happiness and to possess protective properties against satanic influences. In Hinduism, the mirror is a reminder that all images and forms are nothing but reflections, creations of the karmic state, inventions of the mind. In Taoism, the mirror symbolizes self-fulfillment. When the person contemplates his own nature, the evil disappears and is erased by contemplating the awfulness of his reflection – "when evil identifies itself, it destroys itself." The mirror also symbolizes the sage's mind, tranquillity and serenity: "The mind of the sage, since it is calm, becomes the mirror of the universe" (Chuang Chu). In Japan, the "kagami" – the mirror of accusation – reflects truth and reveals lies. The mirror also reveals the celestial sun. Some kind of divinity enters the sacred mirror during a ceremonial event in order to reveal itself from within. The mirror, as a symbol of truth, is one of the three treasures, along with the sword and the jewel. It symbolizes the sun queen, Amaterasu.

In the Mexican culture, the mirror is attributed to Tezkatlipoka, the "shining" or "smoking" mirror, which is both solar and lunar like the sun god of the summer and the moon god of the evening. In Hittite art, the mirror symbolizes the divinity as female together with a bunch of grapes as male. In Christianity, an immaculately clean mirror symbolizes the Virgin Mary, who is also called "the mirror of justice." In Islam, "God is the mirror in which you see yourself as if you were his mirror" (Ibn Arabi), "The universe is God's mirror... man is the mirror of the universe" (Ibn al-Nassafi).

Oar
The oar is a symbol that is attributed to all the river gods. It symbolizes power, ability and knowledge. It is a symbol of creative thought, and of the

word, the source of all actions. Because of its activity and its vitality, it symbolizes the staff or the spear that mixes the waters of the ancient ocean. Another ancient symbolism is that of the pole that guides the ship of the dead as it passes through the water to the bank on the other side. In this context, the oar, the staff and the mast, are linked to the symbolism of the golden bough. In ancient Egypt, the oar symbolized authority, government and action. In ancient ceremonies that were held in order to locate a suitable site for a temple, the king would tour the site holding an oar in his hands. Virgil mentions this ceremony in connection with the rebuilding of Troy.

Oil

In the past, as today, oil played an important role in a broad range of religious ceremonies. It symbolizes sanctification and dedication, devotion, spiritual enlightenment, mercy, fertility and abundance. Anointing with oil means the sparking of new spiritual life, sanctity and the granting of divine grace or sublime wisdom.

In the Hebrew tradition, oil was used for anointing kings, and olive oil was used in the candelabra in the Temple.

Oven

The oven is thought to be a symbol of the mother, as well as of the transformational female power, the womb and birth. In alchemists' terminology, the oven is called "atanur," most likely from the original Semitic word, which meant "fire."

The alchemistic "atanur" is the "body" of the mind or the soul of the person in which the process of the great work is being done – the change of the basic form of the matter – a process that symbolizes the person's development of self-management that is still under the influence of matter. The person's spirit represents the fire burning in the atanur. As such, the oven symbolizes the pure growth (because of the purifying fire) of spirituality.

Peace pipe

The Native American peace pipe symbolizes reconciliation, forgiveness, humility, sacrifice and purification. The symbolic act of passing the pipe from person to person symbolizes peace among them, which is authorized by the smoke that rises to the sky and "bases" the unity and peace. The pipe symbolizes the merging of man with wholeness and the union with the fire of the Great Spirit. The bowl of the round pipe symbolizes the universe, the heart, and the smoke rising to the sky. The stem of the pipe symbolizes the spine and the channel of the vital spirit.

Pen

The pen symbolizes intellect, study and the recording of the meaning of the writings of fate, the pen of the superior force. It is thought to be a phallic symbol. In Moslem symbolism, the pen symbolizes the universal intellect, which records fate on a tablet of *prima materia* – the primordial and undifferentiated matter upon which the pen creates forms and objectives. The pen and the book are the active and creative action together with the static creative material, and it is considered to be the first thing that was created from light. In ancient Egypt, the pen together with the staff or pole symbolizes the awakening of the soul. The pen is attributed to Thut or Logius. In Christian symbolism, it symbolizes study, the evangel (the "good news"), and serves as the symbol of Thomas Aquinas.

Roof

The roof symbolizes shelter, protection, the protective female aspect.

Room

The room symbolizes private thoughts and the individual. The windows reflect the individual's view of the outside world and the possibility of understanding this world and even beyond it, and symbolize communication. For this reason, a windowless room symbolizes a lack of communication. The doors of the room symbolize a passage to other realms. A completely closed door symbolizes virginity, and is used in the initiation ceremonies of many cultures as a sign and a mark of reaching sexual maturity. In this context, we can make a connection between the symbol of the sealed room and that of the "vase with a lid," one of the eight symbols in Chinese Buddhism that express good fortune and a symbol of perfection, of the idea of "no exit," and of victory of the mind over the birth and death that are found in the windows and doors of the room.

Rope

Like cords and cables, rope binds and limits on the one hand, but offers the possibility of lengthening and spreading, freedom and liberation; on the other hand, it can give access to the sky and is linked to the medicine man, the shaman, who "produces" the rope that is used for reaching the other worlds from his own umbilical cord. In the pre-Buddhist religion of Tibet, rope connected heaven and earth, and the gods used it to come down and become assimilated among human beings. After the rope was detached, only souls were able to use it to ascend to heaven.

The detachment of the rope turned man into a mortal. In Hinduism, gnosis – the knowledge of secrets – is the invisible rope of spiritual elevation. The Indian rope tricks symbolize magical elevation into the sky, elevation above terrestrial conditions and states, and the tricks themselves are thought to be a lower or degenerated form of the invisible rope of spiritual elevation.

In the Sumerian and Semitic cultures, the Akkadian "rope of the world" represents the water that surrounds the world and links the upper and lower worlds. The Babylonian water god is sometimes called "the rope of the universe." In Sumerian iconography, the rope that passes through a winged door indicates the rope that links the god and man, the mystical link. In the ancient Greek culture, the rope and the vase symbolize Nemesis, the goddess of revenge. In Christian symbolism, the rope symbolizes Jesus' *Via Dolorosa* and his betrayal.

In Egyptian hieroglyphics, the rope with the loop symbolizes the name of the person. Since the knot is a symbol of the individual's existence, there are several hieroglyphs to which names of people are attributed in the form of a knot, a belt, a crown, and so on. The cartouche has an identical meaning. The silver in Veda has a profound meaning – it symbolizes the sanctified inner path that links the person's external consciousness (his intellect) to his spiritual essence (the "center" or "the silver palace"). The silver cord is also thought to be a cord that joins the spirit to the body when it leaves the body during sleep at night or during astral travel.

Sail

The sail represents the spirit and breath of the wind, the air and the winds, and is linked to the element of air. In medieval Christian iconography, sails sometimes appear as a symbol of the Holy Spirit. Moreover, they symbolize fertility, pregnancy, and increasing strength, but conversely, they are also linked to shrouds.

In Egyptian hieroglyphics, sails are a sign of the wind, the breath of creativity, and the power to act.

Scale

The scale is a common and clear-cut symbol of justice, equality and equilibrium.

It also symbolizes harmony and frugality. In Christianity, the scale is the symbol of the angel Michael. It symbolizes the sign of the Zodiac, Libra. In the ancient Greek culture, it symbolizes law, order and truth.

Scalpel, chisel

In sacred architecture, the chisel or scalpel is the active, male principle in the relations with the passive, female principle. Together with the hammer and similar to it, it symbolizes will power, discrimination and discernment. It makes the decisions about the shape of ancient matter, the *prima materia*, by means of the sharp, formative male instrument. Moreover, the chisel also symbolizes education, knowledge, intuition and the cancellation and expunction of mistakes.

Scissors

Scissors are an ambivalent symbol, a symbol of life and death, creation and destruction. On the one hand, they symbolize crossing and unity – two working as one. On the other, they are a symbol of cutting off, of detaching. They cut the thread of life when they are attributed to the mystical weavers who use them for cutting the person's thread of destiny.

Scroll

The scroll symbolizes learning and the revelation of life and knowledge that are spread out before man like a scroll. It also symbolizes the passage of time, the duration of life, the scroll of the law and the scroll of the Sutra texts. In Chinese symbolism, the scroll symbolizes longevity and scholarship. In the ancient Greek culture, the scroll symbolizes Esculapius as medical study. In ancient Egypt, the scroll is a symbol of knowledge and is linked to the papyrus as a symbol of Lower Egypt. In Christian symbolism, the scroll symbolizes the Book of Life. The Scroll of the Seventh Seal, which no man can read, has the same symbolism as the ledger of fate. It is linked to the prophets, especially to Isaiah and Jeremiah.

Scythe

The scythe symbolizes death, time, the reaping of life, a symbol of Saturn/Chronos and of the Reaper or Death who appears, scythe in hand. The scythe also symbolizes the harvest, which hints at death and rebirth, and symbolizes the Big Mother's forces of creation and destruction. In general, curved or circular tools are considered to be lunar and female, while the vertical and straight tools are thought to be solar and masculine. The vertical character or the extent of the "straightness" of the tool symbolizes penetration and strength, while the curve symbolizes passivity. For this reason, the shape of the scythe is a union of the male – vertical and cutting – and the female – curved and gathering.

Seal
The seal symbolizes authority, ownership, strength, individuality, wisdom, secrecy, oppression, virginity and conclusion.

Shoe
The shoe symbolizes sovereignty on the one hand and freedom on the other. It also symbolizes inferiority, meanness of spirit and humility. The shoe as a symbol of freedom and liberty came from former times when slaves went barefoot, so that the person who "wore shoes" was a free man.
"Take your shoes off" – removing shoes at the entrance to a holy place symbolizes leaving the ties to the material-terrestrial world outside. As a symbol of the nature of inferiority, the shoe symbolizes both humility and the degraded and loathed person. Shoes are also thought to be the symbol of the female genitals, and it is possible that they appear in this context in the story of Cinderella.

Spoon
In Indian ceremonies, the ritual spoon is a symbol of Brahma and Ajni.

Steering wheel, helm
The steering wheel, originally the helm of a ship, but also the steering wheel of a car, symbolizes control, direction, guidance and confidence. The helm is the symbol of Fortuna, the goddess of fate and abundance.

Sword, saber
The sword or the saber that cuts through the air generally represents the active male principle with the phallic connotation, while the scabbard represents the female principle and acceptance. The sword symbolizes protection, strength, power, courage, authority, regality, leadership, justice and physical destruction. From a metaphysical point of view, the sword symbolizes discrimination and the penetrating power of the intellect, spiritual decision, and the non-breach and non-desecration of the sacred. It is a widespread symbol of the truth, since it cuts and removes all the "extras" that have become attached to the single, clear truth.

In the perception of the Tarot cards, swords symbolize the power of the intellect. When the sword appears in the context of fire and flames, it has a purifying meaning. In many ancient cultures, it is considered to be a protection against the forces of darkness and evil, and is closely linked to the chivalric symbolism as a protector of the forces of light against the forces of darkness.

Supernatural qualities are attributed to the sword on the surface of the earth, below its surface, and even beneath the water, and it is linked to supernatural giants and beings such as the Lady of the Lake. Moreover, it is wielded by the cosmic hero, or the hero of the sun, the dragon-killer or conqueror of the forces of darkness.

The Scythians would hold an annual ritual during which several horses were sacrificed by the sword, which represented the god of war for them. The Romans believed that iron, because of its connection to Mars, could chase away all the forces of darkness.

As a symbol of discrimination and differentiation, the sword represents the higher forms of chivalry, while the javelin represents the more inferior forms. The sword cuts and separates body from soul, the highest from the lowest, and the whirling sword – the sword of fire – separates man from paradise. The two-edged sword, the sword with two sharp edges, symbolizes dual strength, life and death, forces that appear to be contradictions and antitheses but actually complement each other and are really one.

The Western type of sword – the straight-bladed sword – is a solar and male symbol because of its shape. The Eastern sword, which is curved, is a lunar and female symbol. Most weapons, in their spiritual symbolic meaning, are the antithesis of the monster. The sword, since it symbolizes physical destruction, is also a symbol of spiritual development. It contains profound duality. The symbolic sword itself is mainly made of the cold and earthly metal or iron, and shaped by the purifying and spiritual fire. The haft of the sword is made of wood, an ancient symbol of life, while the sword itself is used for cutting down that life.

The four swords of the ruler during the coronation ceremony are the sword of state, the blunt sword of mercy, the spiritual sword of justice and the sword of earthly justice.

In the symbolism of alchemy, the sword symbolizes purifying fire that kills and revives like the piercing wind. In Buddhism, the sword symbolizes the discernment that eradicates ignorance. As a sign of wisdom, Manjustri holds the sword of discernment in his right hand. The tip of the sword of wisdom radiates the light of Vajra, who destroys and expels the enemies of the Dharma. In Hinduism, the wooden sword of the Vedic symbolizes lightning and the bellicose nature of Asuras. It is the symbol of the warrior caste. In Taoism, the sword symbolizes wisdom and victory over ignorance. In Islam, the sword is a symbol of the holy war of the believers against the infidels, and of man's battle with his own evil. In the Celtic culture, the sword is linked to the underwater and supernatural forces. It is thought to be an active power of the will, together with the crystal as a passive power of the will. It symbolizes the heroic king Nuada. In the ancient Greek culture, the sword of Damocles represents danger during a period that is seemingly prosperous – a danger that constantly hovers over the person's head, a punishment. In Greek mythology, the golden sword, Crysor, is a symbol of the granting of supreme spirituality. In Scandinavian symbolism, the sword is attributed to Freir, and fought by itself. Surtre, the giant of the flame, carries a sword of flames.

In Chinese symbolism, the sword symbolizes insight and discernment. A wavy sword represents a dragon swimming in the water. In the Japanese culture, the sword symbolizes courage and power. It is one of the three treasures, along with the mirror as truth and the jewel as compassion. In Christian symbolism, the sword symbolizes the passion of Jesus, martyrdom. The whirling sword of fire at each of the gates or corners separates man from the Garden of Eden. In Christian symbolism, the sword is also the symbol of the angel Michael

Torch
The torch is identified with the sun. It symbolizes purity via enlightenment, truth, life, and the flames of the principle of life. Because the fire that burns in the torch is a male symbol and the wood it is made of is female, the torch represents the celestial male principle that emerges from the female wood. The flame represents the soul that is linked to the wood of the torch that represents matter. For this reason, it is a symbol of becoming pregnant, of spiritual fire, of enlightenment, of wisdom, of truth, of eternity, and also of God who illuminates the darkness and sees everything through it. The erect, burning torch represents life, while the extinguished or inverted torch represents death. Sometimes they symbolize the rising and setting sun, light and dark. Carrying torches at weddings and at fertility ceremonies indicates the power created by fire.

In the ancient Greek culture, the torch symbolizes life, Hercules' weapon against the Hydra, a symbol of Eros and Venus as the fire of love, a symbol of Demeter, Hecate, Persephone, and Hephaistos. In the Hebrew tradition, in the Kabbala, the torch is the torch of wisdom and the light of balance, equilibrium. In Christian symbolism, the torch symbolizes Jesus as the light of the world, but is also a symbol of his betrayal. In the ancient Roman culture, the torch is a funerary symbol (used in funeral ceremonies), illuminating the darkness of the dead person and carrying light into the next world, the symbol of Vulcan and Heracles. In the Slavic tradition, the torch symbolizes the rebirth of the sun.

Tower

The tower symbolizes ascent and readiness, similar to the symbolism of a ladder, and the symbolism of a round tower is similar to that of a column. When the tower houses a virgin, a princess, and so on, it symbolizes the "locked garden," which symbolizes virginity, and in this case, forced safeguarding of virginity and the oppression of female power (generally, the oppressor is a terrible mother/father, a person who is suffocatingly over-anxious, a witch, and so on).

The ivory tower symbolizes the inaccessible as well as the female principle and virginity. From the point of view of the sexual affiliation of the symbol, it is ambivalent because of the aspect of protection and providing shelter that is attributed to the female principle, as opposed to the phallic-male shape of the tower. In Christianity, the tower, because it is closed and surrounded by walls, is the symbol of the Virgin Mary.

In Egyptian hieroglyphics, the tower clearly symbolizes height and the act of carrying oneself above the ordinary level of life or society.

In the Middle Ages, towers were used as watchtowers, but also, because of the symbolism of height (physical height characterizes spiritual height/development), they resembled the symbol of the ladder – a link between earth and heaven. The Tower of Babel has a similar meaning, but it also represents hubris, the pride of man against God, which motivates man to want to "touch the sky," an action that is not performed out of submissiveness and the acknowledgment of his own smallness in the face of God. For this reason, he is immediately punished.

Since the notion of ascent/elevation or development is inherent in the symbol of the tower, the alchemists' oven with its tower shape that undergoes transformation and development concomitantly, symbolizes the change in the shape of matter that is characterized by the process of elevation.

An analogy can be made between the tower and man. Just as the tree is closer to the image of man than the horizontal shape of animals, so too the tower is the only constructed shape that is clearly characterized by its vertical nature. Its windows, usually quite big, are found on the highest stories, and symbolize man's eyes and mind. This analogy also takes us back to one of the most ancient towers that is widespread in symbolism – the Tower of Babel, which represents a wild initiative that leads to disaster and mental dysfunction (the loss of language), and ultimately to the separation between people. This is a symbol of the fact that the action of separation between human beings is a consequence of their deeds, and not an indiscriminate punishment meted out by the divine force. The action of building the tower, which symbolizes both a desire for developing and building while ignoring the laws of nature and a desire to go beyond one's station, expresses the human lust for power that brings destruction in its wake. Urban and achievement-oriented life that is characterized by the exploitation of nature and the desire to "exchange" the deeds of God for man-made structures, a symbol of separation as opposed to unity, is reflected in concrete and stone edifices that create separation between the people of the community. The competitive rat-race and the attempt to amass and to build more and more on the material level lead to the consequence displayed in the sixteenth enigma of Tarot, the Falling Tower (a tower struck by lightning), which symbolizes disaster.

We can see a dual tendency in the tower's symbolism. Its height hints at a possibility of identical depth from the point of view of the foundations that are sunk in the earth – a duality of movement upward and downward, in-depth. The higher it is, the deeper the foundations. Nietzche's words about descending while ascending are connected to this symbolism. The depth of the foundations as opposed to the height of the tower may symbolize two contrasting possibilities in man's spiritual development. The first is a positive one – feet planted firmly on the ground and a head that sails through the celestial heights. The second symbolizes an imbalance in man's condition, wherein he aspires to the heights while he is deeply rooted in a terrestrial mindset. This dual tendency symbolizes human life that vacillates between heaven and earth, between the material world and the spiritual world. The researcher Norval relates to the symbolism of the tower and to this notion and writes, "I find myself in the tower, whose foundations are sunk so deep in the earth and whose top is so high, rising into the sky like a turret, that my entire existence seems destined to consist of climbing up and down it."

In Tarot, the sixteenth mystery is the tower that is struck by lightning. On the card, we can see a tower, half of which is destroyed by the flash of lightning that strikes the top of the tower (that symbolizes the person's head). Bits that fall off the tower look as if they first strike the king and then the architect. This card, which is linked to Scorpio, symbolizes the dangerous consequences of exaggerated self-confidence, or the sin of pride, which is linked to the symbolism of the Tower of Babel. The fall of the tower stems from megalomania, from the wild pursuit of material and financial achievements, and from cerebral problems.

Treasure

Treasure in folk-tales usually symbolizes what is hidden, desired, or difficult to attain, lofty spiritual knowledge, intellectual, moral, mystical knowledge, enlightenment, and the revelation of the divine nature in man. A treasure of precious stones, gold and silver evokes great difficulties for the hero who goes out to get it.

The symbolism of treasure cannot be separated from the journey undertaken to get it, since the treasure is just the jewel in the crown of the journey. During the journey, the hero undergoes physical, mental and spiritual tests. He must first discover the direction in which he has to seek the treasure, sometimes by means of consultation with wizards, wise women, and the other figures that represent spiritual guidance.

They do not always give up their secrets voluntarily; sometimes the hero has to force them to do so, sometimes he has to seize them and catch them, and sometimes he has to tempt or bribe them. He does all this in order to receive advice or direction.

After he has received the initial direction, he continues along his tortuous and danger-fraught road.

The journey to the treasure is a symbol of initiation. On his way, the hero primarily needs celestial assistance, since the symbolic and spiritual aim of the search for the treasure cannot exist without the help of the celestial or supernatural powers.

When the hero reaches the location of the treasure, the big test awaits him, a test in which he is liable to lose his life, in which he has to prove that he is actually worthy of the treasure – sublime and lofty knowledge.

In this test, he may reveal the "more" that exists in the hero, and a moment before obtaining the treasure, after his long, difficult journey, he has to combat. The treasure, symbolized by precious stones (that are imbued with a profound mystical significance that symbolizes the center) or gold (that symbolizes the highest stage of purity of mind and perfection), is the final stage at which the hero is granted enlightenment, esoteric, spiritual knowledge, the revelation of his true nature, and self-knowledge as a microcosm, and from that the knowledge of the macrocosm.

The symbolism of treasure as mystical knowledge or as knowledge that leads to mental perfection is reflected in the treasure according to the Japanese tradition, where it is simultaneously the end and the means for achieving the goal – the sword, which symbolizes courage and strength.

Vinegar

A jug of vinegar is an Eastern symbol of life. In alchemy, vinegar that contains antimony is a symbol of conscience. In Christianity, vinegar is a symbol of Jesus' *Via Dolorosa*.

Parts of the body

Arm

The arm symbolizes active force, the shift from theory to practice. Raised arms symbolize a request, supplication, prayer, and also surrender. The two arms themselves symbolize wisdom and action. One raised arm is an indicator of testimony or oath. In Egyptian hieroglyphics, the symbol of the arm represents action in a general sense. Other symbols that derive from it show specific types of activity such as work, protection, control and so on. The hieroglyph that presents two raised arms is a symbol of prayer, calling for help and also self-protection. A widespread symbolic and heraldic motif is that of a weapon held aloft by an arm protruding from a cloud. This is the avenging hand of God, or a heavenly call for vengeance.

In the Kabbala, a right arm is linked to enumerating goodness, and the left arm to enumerating heroism. The multiple arms of the gods and goddesses in the Hindu and Buddhist iconography symbolize compassion-filled assistance and the various forces and motives of the cosmic nature, as well as the specific function of the divinity. In Christianity, the arm of god is the instrument of sovereign power, divine will. In the Trinity, the arm symbolizes the Father. It can also symbolize vengeance.

Beard

The beard symbolizes power, strength, potency, masculinity, authority and dominance. The beard of the gods of the heavens such as Jupiter/Zeus symbolizes the sun's rays that appear over the earth, or the fertilizing rain. Bearded goddesses, such as Astarte and Venus Melita, symbolize bisexuality, androgyny.

Blood

Blood symbolizes the principle of life, the soul, regenerative power, and the energy of the sun. In Chinese symbolism, blood and water are presented as complementing and representing the yin/yang principle.

In various cultures, walking over blood is considered to be a fertility symbol. In the Near East, brides would walk over the blood of a sacrificial ewe. Drinking blood generally symbolizes resentment, but also absorbing the power of the enemy in order to render him harmless after death.

From the chromatic or biological point of view, blood, the source of the color red, symbolizes the end of the event that begins with the light of the sun and the golden color, the intermediary stage that is represented by the color green and plant life. Because of the close tie between the color red and blood, some of the meanings of the color red are attributed to blood. Blood symbolizes the life force that contains passion, expressiveness, and vitality. Blood itself has a profound sacrificial significance. That is why, in ancient times, the tributes of wine, milk and honey that were offered to the gods frequently represented blood, the most precious offering of all. Blood offerings were obtained mainly from sheep, bulls, pigs or chickens during the Classic periods, and from human beings among the Africans, the original natives of the American continent, and also the inhabitants of Europe in prehistoric times. The Arabic saying, "Blood has been spilled, the danger has passed," explains the central idea of making a sacrifice – the blood "reconciles" the forces and erases the severe prohibitions that are liable to exist if it were not for the sacrifice.

Bones
Bones symbolize the principle of indestructible life, vitality, the redemption of the dead and their resurrection, but also humanity and change.

Breasts
Breasts symbolize motherhood, nourishment, love, protection, and the nutritive facet of the Big Mother. Many-breasted goddesses symbolize nourishment, abundance and fertility. The bare breast symbolizes humiliation, grief, remorse and repentance. One breast is the symbol of the Amazons, the female warriors who amputated one of their breasts so that it would not interfere with their use of the bow.

Breathing
On the one hand, breathing symbolizes vitality and life, the soul, inhaling divinity, assimilating spiritual powers, and the power of the spirit. On the other, it also symbolizes transience, termination and the finite. Breathing is the symbol of the interaction of the person with everything outside of him, and the internalization of impressions or "life." Therefore, breathing difficulties can symbolize a problem of internalizing principles of the spirit and/or principles of the universe. The rate of inhalation and exhalation symbolizes the changing rate of life and death, repeated manifestation and assimilation in the universe. Some people view breathing as inhaling the sun's rays and light, as the alchemists said when relating to the heavenly bodies, specifically the sun: "We inhale this astral

gold unceasingly." "The correct rate" of yoga breathing is linked to "the correct voice" that the ancient Egyptians were obliged to use when they read the holy writings. In Christianity, exhaling on a person or a thing is a symbol of the effect of the Holy Spirit and the expulsion of evil spirits.

Ear

Because of its shape, the ear is linked to the spiral, the spiral shell, and also to the sun. Just as the shell is linked to birth, so the ear has a certain symbolism in this direction. Karma, the son of the sun god Suria, was born from his mother's ear. The ear is linked to the breath of life, as an object that symbolizes hearing the "word" of creation.

In Egyptian symbolism, the right ear receives the "air of life," and the left ear receives the "air of death." In Christian symbolism, the Holy Spirit is occasionally described as a dove entering the ear of the Virgin Mary. The ears of gods, kings and mammals or reptiles that are thought to bring rain are linked to the spiral. Pointed ears are linked to the god Pan, to satyrs and to demons. Donkey's ears symbolize Midas, the king with the golden touch, and as such symbolize stupidity.

Eye

The eye is one of the organs of the body that is reflected in a very broad range of symbols. The eye symbolizes the omniscience, the divinity that observes everything, the ability for intuitive vision. The eye is the symbol of all the sun gods and of their force that is life-giving and fertilized by the sun. Plato calls the eye "the most sunlike instrument," and says: "There is an eye to the soul... and only through it is the truth seen." Plotinus said that the eye would not be able to see the sun if, metaphorically, it were not the sun itself. Since the sun is the source of light, and light is symbolic of wisdom and the spirit, the process of seeing that is performed by the eye represents a spiritual action and symbolizes understanding and insight. The eye is closely linked to the symbols of light. It represents enlightenment, light, knowledge, wisdom, protection, stability and adherence to a goal, but also the limited nature of visible things.

Two eyes are physical normality and spiritual equality, while the third eye symbolizes the superhuman or divine powers. One eye is an ambivalent symbol. On the one hand, it is a symbol of the sub-human (since two eyes are the symbol of human normality), of evil, as with the cyclops or other one-eyed monsters that possess destructive forces. On the other hand, when it is located on the forehead, above the natural place of the eyes, it is a symbol of enlightenment – a single eye of enlightenment or the third eye, the eye of the god or the eye of eternity. Heterotopic eyes (that is, eyes that appear somewhere other than in their natural place) are thought to be equal to the spiritual form of physical sight – in other words, clairvoyance (extrasensory perception). They appear as a symbol on other parts of the body: hands, wings, arms, etc., and different parts of the head in supernatural beings: angels, deities, and so on. The organ or limb on which the eye appears is important, since it becomes a part of the symbolism of the heterotopic eye. For instance, when the eye appears on the hand, it symbolizes a clairvoyant action. "The eye of the heart" is spiritual perception, enlightenment, rational intuition.

The thousand eyes or the ten thousand eyes of the gods of the sky are the stars, the eyes of the night that symbolize omniscience, alertness and readiness that never sleep, infallibility. On the other hand, numerous eyes also indicate demonic beings such as the devil. The eye may also symbolize the androgyne as a unity of the female oval shape with the male circle. "The eye of the heart" is spiritual perception, enlightenment, rational intuition. A triangle with an eye at its center is "the all-seeing eye" that is omniscient and omnipresent.

In the Western hemisphere, the right eye symbolizes the sun, the eye of the day and the future, and the left eye symbolizes the moon, the eye of the night and the past. In the East, the symbolism is the opposite. The "eye," when a part of sacred architecture, is the opening to the sky in the center of the dome in the roof of a temple, cathedral or ceremonial hut. It symbolizes the solar door that permits access to the celestial domains.

In the ancient Egyptian culture, "the celestial eye," a clear symbol in hieroglyphics that is called vodeza, symbolizes "he who nourishes the sacred fire or man's wisdom," Osiris. The ancient Egyptians defined the eye, the arched circle with the pupil in the center, as "the sun in the mouth." The eye of Horus represents enlightenment, the eye of wisdom. The eye and eyebrow of Horus symbolize power and strength. The eye of Horus is also linked to the phases of the moon and symbolizes the offerings to the gods in the temple. Two winged eyes are two sections in the sky, the north and the south, the sun and the moon, celestial space. The right eye symbolizes the sun, Ra and Osiris; the left eye symbolizes the moon and Isis.

In the ancient Greek culture, the eye symbolizes Apollo as "scouting the heavens," the sun, which is also the eye of Zeus/Jupiter. In Hinduism, the third eye of Shiva is the pearl in the center of the forehead and represents spiritual awareness, celestial wisdom. The eye of Varuna is the sun. In Persian symbolism, Yima, evil and good, holds the solar eye and the secret of eternal life. In Islam, "the eye of the heart" is the spiritual center, the seat of absolute intellect and enlightenment. In Japanese symbolism, the right eye of Izanagi begat the moon. According to the Native American culture, "the eye of the heart sees everything"; it is the eye of the Great Spirit, which is omniscient. In Buddhism, the eye symbolizes wisdom and light. Buddha's third eye, "the burning pearl," is spiritual awareness and sublime wisdom.

In the Sumerian and Semitic cultures, the eye symbolizes, "the lord of the sacred eye," and it is a symbol of wisdom, omniscience, and magnanimity. The Phoenician Chronos had four eyes, two open and two shut – a symbol of eternal alertness. In the Celtic culture, the evil eye is a symbol of evil intentions and jealousy, and is the antithesis of "the good heart" of compassion and generosity. In Chinese and Japanese symbolism, the left eye symbolizes the sun and the right eye symbolizes the moon. In Christian symbolism, the eye symbolizes all-seeing God, power, light and omniscience. As the apostle Matthew said, "the light of the body is the eye." The seven eyes of the apocalypse are the seven winds of God. The eye of God in a triangle symbolizes the divinity. An eye in a triangle surrounded by a shining circle symbolizes the eternal holiness of the divinity.

Jung sees the eye as the mother's breast, with the pupil being the "child" of the eye. The peacock's feather, because of the eyes in it, is sometimes used as a symbol of the eye.

Face
The face symbolizes the externalized personality. Since ancient times, various cultures have devised theories for examining the face. These theories were called "face reading," and by examining the external facial features, their color, the structure of the face and its texture, the person's character was deduced, as were his personality structure and calling or karmic state. The many-faced Hindu gods symbolize the different aspects of the universe and the powers of the various elements. This goes for the four or five faces of Shiva or Brahma.

Finger
In many cultures, pointing a finger is considered to be casting a spell on the one hand and expressing an insult on the other. Fingers that are lifted or spread in greeting symbolize spiritual powers. Two fingers that are lifted symbolize learning or judgment. When the first and fourth fingers (not counting the thumb) are raised – a sign called *cornuto* – they symbolize protection against the evil eye, but are considered an insult if they are directed toward a particular person.

↔ SYMBOLS ↔

In Christian symbolism, raising three fingers in greeting symbolizes the Holy Trinity. In the ancient Egyptian culture, two fingers raised in greeting symbolize salvation and power and represent the two fingers of Horus extended to help Osiris climb the ladder from this world to the next world. The first finger is divine justice and the second finger is the spirit, the go-between. The infant Horus is depicted with his finger in his mouth. In the ancient Greek culture, a finger at the mouth symbolizes silence or absorption in thoughts, and it symbolizes Nemesis.

Foot, leg

The foot symbolizes freedom of movement, willing service, humility, the low and the inferior, and the ability to endure life in this world. In Egyptian hieroglyphics, the shape of the foot is the symbol of orthostation, elevation, bearing and orientation. The symbolic meaning of this may stem from man walking upright on his two feet, which differentiates him from most of the animals. The foot is also compared to status, to a basis, since the feet are used to hold up the body. Jung sees the foot as confirming man's link with terrestrial reality and with the earth, and sees it as basically a phallic symbol. The foot carries the entire body in a stable manner, and in certain cultures, is even compared to the rays of the sun, as can be seen in the symbol of the swastika .

In the Kabbala, the feet symbolize stability, strength and majesty. The right foot is linked to the sphere of eternity and the left to the sphere of majesty. In various cultures, gods with one foot symbolize the phallic or the axial, but also the lunar. The fire gods, such as Hephaistos, are sometimes depicted with one leg in order to symbolize the fickle nature of fire. Some people consider the symbolism of a lack of the leg in human beings or gods in folk-tales and mythology to be a symbol of a certain defect – a moral defect, for instance. Others employ the same examples to show that nature or divinity compensated for the lack of a leg (Hephaistos, Viveland the blacksmith and so on) with other unique abilities. Kissing or washing the feet symbolizes the self-demeaning or the humiliation of the kisser or washer, and the worship of the person whose feet he is kissing or washing. In Chinese symbolism, the foot symbolized the measure of time or a period of time. Stamping the foot symbolizes anger and frustration.

According to reflexology, the entire body, both internal and external organs, the balance of the elements in it, and even various mental states are reflected in the sole of the person's foot.

↔ SYMBOLS ↔

Hand

The hand has been one of the most clear-cut symbols in many cultures since ancient times, and the ways of interpreting it are numerous. The hand symbolizes the shift from potential to realization. It symbolizes power, strength, greeting, supervision, justice, and action. The hand represses and pushes away problems and evil. The divine hand is divine strength. The large hand ("with large hand and outstretched arm") symbolizes divinity, tremendous supernatural power. Aristotle said that the hand is "the tool of tools." The right hand is considered to be "the hand of strength." It is raised in greeting and a sign of the life force, the "giving hand." The left hand is the "receiving hand," the passive aspect of power, acceptance, and is sometimes linked to the left side and deceit. A three-fingered hand or a hand with some kind of defect symbolizes the phases of the moon. A hand protruding from a cloud symbolizes divine force as well as majesty. The *hamsa* is a symbol of protection and an amulet against the evil eye, and the *hamsa* with an eye in its center also symbolizes protection against the evil eye as well as clairvoyant abilities and supernatural power.

The positions of the hand also possess a unique symbolism: Hand on chest symbolizes submission, the attitude of slave or servant, and apology. Clasped hands are a symbol of unity, friendship, a covenant and a mystical marriage. Folded hands symbolize repose, calmness, immobility and also inactivity. Hands covering eyes symbolize shame and fear, unwillingness to see what is happening. The laying of hands symbolizes the transmission of the power and goodness of healing. Hands on neck symbolize the state of victim. An open hand is the symbol of abundance, liberty and justice. A tight-fisted hand symbolizes a threat, violence and miserliness. An outstretched hand symbolizes a greeting, protection and reception. Two hands together indicate supplication, a request, a peace greeting, submission, inferiority and a covenant. When they are placed one inside the other with palms facing upward, they are a symbol of meditation and acceptance. When the palms face downward, they symbolize greeting and divine goodness. A raised hand symbolizes adoration, worship, prayer, redemption, fear and wonder, but also the current of power. Two raised hands symbolize weakness, surrender, a request, supplication and dependence, but also prayer. A hand resting on the head represents thought, concern. Hand-washing symbolizes innocence, cleanliness, purity, shrugging off guilt and proof of innocence. Hand-wringing is a symbol of lamentation and mourning.

In Buddhism, the hand of Buddha symbolizes protection. The raised hand symbolizes limitless giving. In the Buddhist iconography, Buddha's right hand touches the earth to indicate his sovereignty over it and calls the earth to testify

– it is the active pole. Buddha's left hand, which holds the begging bowl or faces downward, indicates submission and acceptance – it is the passive pole. In Hinduism and Buddhism, there is a symbolic language that consists of symbolic hand signals called modra, which is thought to be the Hindi expression of the divine forces. According to this complex language, a raised right hand symbolizes courage, and when the palm faces downward, it symbolizes giving. Both hands together, palms upward or placed on the lap, symbolize meditation and acceptance. Both hands together, in front of the heart, symbolize the union of wisdom and method. A palm with an eye in the center symbolizes the helping hand of humility and wisdom. In the Celtic culture, Lug's long arm symbolizes the rays of the sun. In Chinese symbolism, hands together symbolize friendship, covenant. Concealing the hands symbolizes defensiveness and respect. The right hand is yang, power, and it is the opposite of the left hand, which symbolizes honor, except in times of war in which the right hand becomes the military hand of honor because it is the hand that clasps the sword. The left hand is yin, weak, the side of honor because strength leads to violence and destruction.

In Christianity, the hand symbolizes the power and strength of God. In Christian art, a hand that protrudes from a cloud symbolizes the presence and strength of God the Father. Sometimes, it releases the white dove that symbolizes the Holy Spirit. Raised hands with palms outwards are a symbol of greeting and divine goodness. A raised, three-fingered hand symbolizes the Holy Trinity. The fingers are also symbolic when they are all raised: the first finger symbolizes the Father, the second Symbolizes the Holy Spirit, the third symbolizes Jesus, and the fourth symbolizes the double nature of Jesus. A hand grasping a bag of silver symbolizes Judas Iskariot.

In the ancient Egyptian culture, "the hand of Egypt," there are two triangles joined to each other with the apex of the upper triangle pointing downward and touching the apex of the upward-pointing lower triangle. They symbolize the unity of fire and water, male and female.

In the Hebrew culture, when the forefinger and middle finger form one pair, and the ring finger and pinkie form another, and there is a space between the two pairs, it symbolizes the priestly blessing. "The strong hand" is the hand of God. The right hand is attributed to enumerating goodness and the left hand to enumerating heroism.

In Hinduism, Shiva's raised hand symbolizes peace and protection, and the down-turned hand points at the foot and indicates a statement. The drumbeats are the creative action, and the flame in the hand indicates the destruction of the world by fire (the inhaling, consuming power that wants to "eat" everything).

↔ SYMBOLS ↔

In Islam, the outstretched hand symbolizes greeting, adoration and hospitality. The hand of Fatima represents the hand of God, divine power, divine providence and generosity. The thumb symbolizes the prophet and the fingers are his four companions: the first is the heroine Fatima, the second is her husband, Ali, the third and the fourth are Hassan and Hussein, their sons. The fourth finger is also a symbol of spirituality and moral excellence, and the five fingers together symbolize the five basic examples and the five pillars of religions. In the Sumerian/Semitic cultures, the hand is the symbol of the Big Mother who exudes goodness and plenty and who protects. In the Tulteki culture (an ancient South American culture), the long arm of Huemak symbolizes the rays of the sun.

Hair

Hair symbolizes the life force, strength, energy, the stuff of life that emanates from the head, the power of thought, and the person's spiritual assets. Hairs are generally linked to the element of fire and the development of primordial powers. For this reason, long hair was sometimes a symbol of ambitiousness and the will to succeed. Beautiful abundant hair in both men and women symbolizes spiritual development in many cultures, while hair loss symbolizes failure and poverty. Conversely, voluntarily shaving the hair symbolizes making a sacrifice.

While in some cultures, the monks shave off their hair, in the Hebrew culture it was forbidden for priests to apply a razor to their hair. The hair of the head symbolizes the high powers of inspiration, while body hair symbolizes the more inferior powers of mind and body. Loose and flying hair symbolizes freedom. Hair that is tied back symbolizes marriage and submission. Hair that stands up on end symbolizes powers of magic and witchcraft, sublime abilities but also fear. Hair that covers the face may represent a veil. Stealing hair or snipping off a curl or a braid symbolizes submission, domination and robbing the male principle of its solar power. Furthermore, it symbolizes castration, as in the story of Samson and Delilah. In certain parts of the world, mainly in various countries in Africa in which black magic is widespread to this day, there are people who are in the habit of creeping up behind someone and cutting off some hair, a curl or a braid. They then use the piece of hair for making a spell to obtain the powers that were granted the owner of the hair. Hair is an important component in witchcraft. In various cultures, hair symbolizes fertility and fecundity, and sparse underarm or pubic hair is considered to indicate low fertility.

Secondary symbolic importance is ascribed to hair color. Black or brown hair represents earth energy, dark terrestrial energy. Golden hair is linked to the sun's rays and generally to the symbolism of the sun. Red or coppery hair is mainly thought to represent Venusian or demonic characteristics. In face reading according to the Kabbala, on the other hand, hair is the yardstick of the person's desire to draw energy, the desire to receive, with the negative and positive this involves. According to this tradition, red hair is the highest degree of desire to receive, after which comes brown or black hair, then yellow hair, and finally white hair – the lowest degree of desire to receive.

Disheveled hair and tearing out hair symbolize mourning and lamentation, but in Hinduism, Shiva's unkempt hair symbolizes the hermit, the ascetic, while Kali's black hair symbolizes time. In Hinduism, hair symbolizes channels of universal energy. In the Sumerian culture, hair, beards and side-locks were used to dispel evil spirits. Buddha's systematically curled hair symbolizes control over the life force, tranquillity and calmness. In Christianity, long, loose hair symbolizes repentance, and long hair in men symbolizes the strength of Samson. In Greek mythology, Medusa's serpentine tresses symbolize the evil aspect of female power. In the ancient Egyptian culture, the children of the nobles were depicted as wearing thick braids on the right side of their heads. In the Hebrew culture, long hair was the symbol of the priests and some of the prophets. The *sotah* (a woman who was suspected of cheating on her husband) had to come and drink cursed water with disheveled hair as a demeaning act. Some people see this as the source of the head covering and for married ultra-Orthodox women shaving their heads and wearing head coverings. Both in Judaism and in Islam, the hair on a woman's head is considered to be seductive and provocative, and for this reason, it has to be hidden.

Head

The head, together with the heart, is thought to fulfill a leading function in the body, since it is the seat of the life force and the soul with its powers. It represents wisdom, knowledge, control and, of course, intellect. The head is the organ of wisdom and stupidity at the same time, as well as the organ of respect and derision. The wreath of victory and glory is placed on the head, but so are the ashes of mourning and lamentation. In the Hebrew tradition, the significance of the head comes from its Hebrew name (*rosh*), from which the words "main" (*rashi*) and "first" (*rishon*) are derived. According to Plato, "The human head is a picture of the world." The head joins the symbolism of the number 1 as a symbol of unity, being one. A similar meaning is seen in Egyptian hieroglyphics. The eagle's head was used as a ṣolar symbol and a symbol of the central point of origin – that is, of the cosmic flame and the spiritual fire of the universe. In principle, the head represents the spiritual principle as opposed to the physical principle, which is represented by the rest of the body.

Winged heads symbolize the life force, the soul and supernatural wisdom. Bowing the head symbolizes the lowering of the life force as a result of obeying or submitting to someone else. The head that is wrapped in a veil is hidden and symbolizes hidden knowledge, secrecy. The veil is also thought to protect the inner life force inside the head. This is also true of head-coverings such as hats, skullcaps and so on.

Double-headed gods, such as Janus, symbolize the beginning and the end, the past and the future, yesterday and today, the solar and the lunar, the rising and the declining power of the sun, an obvious choice as opposed to a crossroads, a calling, the beginning of every enterprise or journey, leaving and returning, and the strength of opening and closing doors (in the mental and metaphysical senses). This is the reason why the key is a symbol of Janus. Janus' two heads also symbolize the longest day of the year, in Cancer, which is called "the door of man," and symbolizes the waning strength and the setting of the sun (from now on, its appearance in the sky will be progressively shorter) and is called *Fanua inferni*, and the shortest day of the year, in Capricorn, which is called "the door of the gods" and symbolizes the increasing strength and the rising of the sun, the *Fanua coeli*. The two heads also symbolize law and discernment, cause and effect, looking inward and looking outward.

When the head of a man and the head of a woman are joined, or "the king and the queen," they are an androgynous figure, the unity of opposites, and are also a symbol of spiritual power and physical power. The two heads of Dioscuri, one looking up and one looking down, symbolize the different appearance of the sun in the upper hemisphere and in the lower hemisphere, and also day and night. Three-headed gods symbolize the three realities – past, present and future, the three phases of the moon, and the three phases of the sun – rising, noon and setting. Among the gods presented as three-headed are Hecate and Serapis. Many-headed astral deities are "all-seeing," or can describe a number of cycles or seasons. The head of a monster or a beast grasping a ring in its mouth or between its jaws is a guardian of the way. (Later on, this symbol was translated into bronze or metal door-knockers.) Heads as springs or streams describe the power of speech and also symbolize freshening.

In the Celtic culture, the head is the solar organ, and symbolizes divinity, wisdom and strength from another world. A head with a phallus symbolizes fecundity, but is also a funerary symbol. There is a traditional Celtic link between the head and the phallus. The Celtic god Sernunus is sometimes depicted as three-headed. In the Slavic tradition, the three-headed Slavic god watches the sky, the land and the sea, paradise, earth and hell, and the past, present and future. In the Sumerian and Semitic cultures, Marduk is depicted as two-headed, looking right and left, and means the same as Janus. In Hinduism, Brahma's four heads are the source of the four Vedas. In Christian symbolism, Jesus is the head of the church.

Heart

In the vertical diagram of the human body, there are three main points: the brain, the heart, and the genitals. However, the central point is the heart. There is extensive symbolism concerning the heart as the center. It symbolizes the center of life, of the universe – both physical and spiritual, the divine presence of the center, the center of wisdom and emotion, "the wisdom of the heart," as opposed to the intellectual and calculated wisdom of the head. Both the heart and the head symbolize wisdom, but the heart also symbolizes compassion, understanding, kindness, "the secret place," and, of course, love.

The heart pumps and contains the blood and gives life. It is symbolized by the sun as the center of life. The sun that shines and the heart that burns share the symbolism of the center as a macrocosm (the sun) and a microcosm (the human heart). Another symbol that represents the heart is the inverted triangle. According to the Kabbala, the heart is linked to the *Tiferet* sphere, which constitutes the center of all the spheres, and the link to it helps the person link up to the middle line, the golden path, the straight path. In this sense, the heart directs and guides.

The importance of the value of love in the mystical doctrines of unity may explain why the symbolism of love is linked so tightly to the symbolism of the earth, since "to love" is thought to be an experience that propels the lover toward a certain center. The heart represents love as the center of enlightenment and happiness, and this is the origin of the symbols of the heart adorned with flames, with a crown, with a cross or with a fleur-de-lys.

In the ancient Egyptian culture, the heart was the only organ that was left in the body during the embalming and mummification processes, because it was thought to be a center that the body could not do without in the eternal world, since all the centers are symbols of eternity. In the Aztec culture, too, the heart symbolizes the person's center. It also symbolizes religion, love and the principle of unifying life. The sacrifice of the heart symbolizes the letting of the life-blood, the seed of life, in order to sprout and bloom. The pierced heart symbolizes remorse. In alchemistic symbolism, the heart is considered to symbolize the sun within the person, just as gold is the symbol of the sun on the earth. In Buddhism, the heart symbolizes the elemental nature of Buddha. The heart of the diamond symbolizes purity and the imperturbable person. In Chinese Buddhism, the heart is one of Buddha's eight valuable organs. In the Celtic culture, "the good heart" symbolizes generosity and compassion, and it is the antidote to the evil eye.

In Christianity, the heart symbolizes love, understanding, faith, joy and sorrow. The burning heart symbolizes religious zeal, fervor and devotion. A heart in the hand symbolizes love and a straight path. A heart pierced with an arrow symbolizes deep remorse.

In the Hebrew tradition, the heart is the center of life and of the senses, the emotions and the intellect. A collection of emotional and intellectual properties is attributed to the heart. Man was given a heart in order to know God. The heart is the place for worshipping God. The heart symbolizes the center. In Hinduism, the heart is the divine center, a place in which Brahma resides. The symbol of the heart is the lotus. "The eye of the heart" is Shiva's third eye. In Islam, the heart is the center of existence, and the "eye of the heart" is the spiritual center. It symbolizes absolute intellect, enlightenment. In Taoism, the heart is the seat of understanding. The wise person has seven openings in his heart, all of which are wide open.

Heel
The heel symbolizes the person's vulnerable part, the weak point of a blatantly invulnerable person. This is seen in Krishna's heel and Achilles' heel. However, it is also a part of the body that rushes around and crushes the serpent and evil.

Intestines, guts
The intestines or guts are thought to be the seat of the emotions. Because of their shape, they are linked to the snake and the labyrinth. In various cultures, animal intestines were used for predicting the future. In the Chinese symbolism, intestines symbolize compassion, affection, and the mystical knot (loop). In ancient Egypt, they expressed the idea of circulation.

Kidneys
In Chinese symbolism, the kidneys symbolize the element of water, the emotions and the sacred fish. In the Hebrew tradition, the kidney symbolizes the thought center and the conscience. The fettered kidney and kidney pains are

.guilt, pangs of conscience. God examines the kidneys and sees the interior of the person, his thoughts and his conscience.

Knees
The knees symbolize generative power, vitality, strength and obstinacy. Kneeling symbolizes submission or humility in the face of a superior or lofty force, submission and even inferiority. Placing on the knees (lap) symbolizes parenthood, adoption, maternal concern.

Lingam (penis)
The lingam are tall, phallic-shaped columns that are found in India. They represent Shiva's lingam, just as the Egyptian obelisk symbolizes Jeb's penis. Shiva's kingdom spreads out around each gigantic lingam to a radius of 30 yards. In this kingdom, miracles may occur and sinners may be redeemed. In temples, we find smaller lingam, the size of a human penis, that represent the breaking of the virginity of brides on their wedding night. They were apparently actually used for this purpose. The first son to be born was thought to be a gift that came from the power of the god, because of the tradition of breaking the bride's virginity. This tradition did not only exist in South East Asia, but also in the Near East and in Rome. Sons that were born after this ceremony were dedicated to the worship of the god. Generally, the lingam or the phallus was painted red and anointed with holy oil. The Greeks called it chrism. Of course, the anointing of the lingam with oil during those ceremonies had a practical meaning, but afterwards, the process became a symbol in and of itself.

The lingam or linga symbolizes the male sex organ, creativity, the male principle, along with the yoni as the female principle. The symbol does not relate only to physical power, but rather to the cosmic power of creation and the renewal of life. It is also a symbol of spiritual potency among yogis. In China, the lingam is called koi, and it is a long piece of jade that culminates in a triangle. The seven stars of the Big Dipper are often engraved on it.

Liver
In Judaism, the liver represents the organ that is responsible for anger. In ancient cultures, the liver was used to predict the future. Clay, stone or metal models of livers with the areas for predicting the future and the meanings of the various regions of the liver indicated, were found in Assyria, Babel and Phoenicia. The Bible describes a Babylonian king who availed himself of liver-reading, among other soothsaying techniques. Tribes in central Africa still

believe that the liver is the seat of the mind or the soul, and that eating raw liver expands and amplifies the mind or the soul of the person eating it.

Marrow

Marrow symbolizes the life force, vitality and strength, and possesses a symbolism that is similar to that of blood. The existence of marrow and the fullness of marrow symbolize vitality and youth, while a lack of marrow symbolizes aging. In Hebrew symbolism, marrow symbolizes an internal part, the moisture of life.

Mouth

The mouth symbolizes the detaching, tearing, predatory aspect of the Big Mother. It also symbolizes the entry into the underworld or into the whale's belly. A wide-open mouth symbolizes judgment, the power of speech, and the utterance of powerful words.

In the Aztec iconography, a huge, open mouth is the hungry and all-consuming land. The doctrine of Buddha is called "the golden mouth."

In the Hebrew tradition and in the Kabbala, the mouth is the organ of the lowest sphere, *Malkhut* [kingdom], so the person who wishes to have a spiritual life in it must guard his mouth from evil.

In the Bible, the perceptions of the mouth and fire are linked since both of them "devour" and "consume." Fire is said to "consume," like the mouth does. Both the ability to use fire and the ability to speak are considered to be the two main characteristics of human beings, differentiating them from animals. Like fire, the symbolism of the mouth also has two main characteristics – creation (by speaking) and destruction (by the action of the mouth on food, and by the words that come out of the mouth).

Jesus also warned of utterances that come out of the mouth and stressed that what comes out of the mouth is far more important than what goes into the mouth. The mouth is considered to be the meeting point of the inner world and the external world. The person's inner world is expressed to the world outside of him by means of the mouth, and the external world finds its way into the person's stomach in the same manner.

In Egyptian hieroglyphics, the glyph that represents a mouth symbolizes the power of speech and the creative word. Another closely related sign presents a mouth containing a solar disk. The disk, which represents the sun, is linked, but not identical, to the symbol of the eye. The mouth of the river symbolizes the door or the gate to the entrance to another reality and to the ocean of unity.

There is an analogy between the mouth and the female sex organ, which can be seen both in the description of the mouth and the vagina having lips, and in various patriarchal societies in which the woman had to hide her mouth. This is also expressed in the Hebrew saying, "Hearing a woman's voice is indecent."

Nail
The nail is considered to symbolize the cosmic axis. It is linked to the symbolism of fate and survival ("hold on by one's fingernails"). In Christianity, the nails symbolize Jesus' *Via Dolorosa* to save the world.

Saliva
Saliva symbolizes the personality, healing powers, the seal of fidelity, a remedy against the evil eye, and, when spat, scorn. In many traditions, there are stories about healing with saliva. Jesus mixed saliva with earth and spread it on the eyes of the blind man, thereby restoring his sight. Muhammed also used his saliva for healing. On an ancient Semitic clay tablet, there are instructions for the preparation of a potion for curing blindness, comprising saliva and mother's milk. Until the 19th century, folk-healers in Italy used the same ingredients for mixing medicines for blindness.

In Chinese Tantrism and Taoism, female saliva was thought to be one of the three marvelous yin medications, along with mother's milk and menstrual blood. In witchcraft, mainly in medieval Europe, saliva was used extensively, and there was a prevalent belief that saliva could exorcise demons and evil spirits, especially if it issued from a person who had been fasting. The custom of spitting into a river or a stream while crossing it originates from the same belief. Another widespread belief states that spitting over one's shoulder can alter the course of bad luck, and spitting through a ring is thought to induce prophetic visions in the spitter. Spitting in an infant's face is thought to protect him from harmful spells and witchcraft. Those are just a few of the popular beliefs regarding saliva.

Scalp
The scalp symbolizes material success. Its symbolism is similar to that of the head regarding the meaning of containing the person's strength. The scalp is perceived to represent the person's strength, which explains the widespread Native American tradition of scalping enemies.

Skeleton
The skeleton is widely used in symbols as a personification of death. This

symbolism is a result of the fact that it is the main part of the body that remains after death and disintegration – the outlines of the living body, dry and devoid of vitality. For this reason, the skeleton symbolizes the mortals and the fact of their mortality, death and the rapid passage through time and life.

Together with the scythe and the hourglass, the skeleton symbolizes the "Reaper," the Angel of Death that harvests life. It also symbolizes the moon, the shadows and the gods of death, and is linked mainly to Chronos/Saturn and to the god of death and the underworld of the ancient Mayan culture.

In alchemy, the skeleton symbolizes the stage of decay and is depicted by the color black.

Skin (human and animal)

The skin symbolizes the mantle, the exterior and also the human casing as part of the symbolism of the "thickness" of the human body as opposed to the (divine) light.

In the Hebrew tradition, the first man, prior to being caught in his sin, was described as wearing skin, and afterwards as cased in skin that divided him from the world and from receiving the divine light directly. Skin symbolizes matter and is linked to the idea of birth and rebirth. One of the Egyptian hieroglyphs clearly shows three skins joined together, and its meaning is "to be born." The glyph appears as a combination of words such as "to beget" or "to cause," "to raise," "child", "to form." The amulet placed by the Egyptians on the newborn was made of three animal skins joined to a solar ball. The number of skins – three – relates to the nature of the essential triangle of the human creature – body, mind and spirit – while the ball symbolizes the unity with wholeness.

The well-known ceremony called "the passage through the skin" is performed by priests and pharaohs in order to renew themselves and their powers. The symbolism of the skin also contains the belief that a person can acquire the powers of a particular animal by wearing its skin, a process that was part of many different ceremonies throughout the world. By wearing the animal skin, the person – usually the shaman – makes contact with the spirit of the animal and with its instinctive knowledge. The skins were worn during initiation ceremonies, where they symbolized the stages of initiation and rebirth. The white and black skins of animals or of birds that were worn in ceremonies of this type symbolize man's dual nature, as well as the realized and the unrealized. Sloughing the skin, like snakes do, symbolizes the transformation: casting off "the old person" and turning him into "the new person," the renewal of youth, the attainment of a higher level, immortality. In pre-Columbian Mexico, the human sacrificial victims were wrapped in animal skins as part of the sacrificial ceremony.

Skull

The skull is a symbol of man's mortality and of life's transience. This meaning may derive from the skull's being what is left of the person after the disintegration of his body. Since it guards and protects the brain, it symbolizes a vessel of life and thought, and is therefore the symbol of the life force that is stored in the head. On the other hand, it also symbolizes the pursuit of the suffering of this world. It symbolizes death, the moon, the shadows, the dying sun, the gods of the dead and time. A skull and crossbones symbolizes death, and a flag bearing this sign is the symbol of pirates. In alchemy, the skull, along with the grave and the raven, is a symbol of the darkness and the decay in the first stage of "dust to dust," and symbolizes death to the world. However, since it is the part that survives after death, it is considered to be a reminder of life and of metamorphosis.

In Buddhism, in the Tantric texts, a skull full of blood symbolizes the denial of life. It symbolizes Yama, the god of the dead, and Tara in her dark aspect.

In Christian symbolism, the skull symbolizes the pursuit of the suffering of this world, but also the contemplation of death, and for this reason it is the symbol of the monks. The skull with the cross symbolizes eternal life after the death of Jesus.

In the Greco-Roman cultures, the skull is attributed to Chronos/Saturn as a symbol of time.

In Hinduism, a skull full of blood symbolizes denial of life, and is attributed to Kali/Durga. The skull appears together with Yama, the god of the dead, and with Shiva and Kali, the "destroyers."

In the Mayan culture, the skull appears along with the skeleton as a symbol of the god of the dead and the nether world.

Spinal column

The spinal column symbolizes the axis of the world, which is why symbols of the axis of the world are sometimes used to describe the spinal column as mountains, columns, trees, horns, legs, and so on.

The spinal column represents support, power of endurance and the person's ability or inability to stand up for himself. In Hinduism, the spinal column is the passage to the awakening power of the kundalini that sleeps coiled up like a snake at the base of the spinal column. Among the Japanese Inu, there is a prevailing belief that the spinal column of the first person was created from the pliant branch of a willow tree.

Spleen

The spleen symbolizes anger, melancholy, sick humor or a lack of humor. In Chinese symbolism, spleen is one of the eight treasures and is linked to the earth.

Stomach, paunch

Different symbolism is attributed to the stomach in the West and the East. In the West, it symbolized a tremendous appetite, while in the East, it symbolized the seat of life. The stomach symbolizes the cosmic night, the fetal state of creation, death and rebirth, the end of time, the acquisition of esoteric or sacred knowledge.

In alchemistic symbolism, the darkness of the stomach is the transformation laboratory. Since all the processes that occur in this laboratory are completely natural, the stomach laboratory is considered to be the antithesis of the brain. The large paunch of the Chinese god of wealth and of the Indian god Ganesha symbolizes gluttony but also prosperity. In Japan, the stomach is considered the center of the body, the seat of life, and for this reason, *hara kiri* is performed on it, in order to strike and damage the center of life.

Teeth

The teeth are the most primal weapons of attack, and for that reason symbolize attack and defense. Baring the teeth symbolizes enmity and defense. Grinding the teeth symbolizes repressed anger, reluctance to cooperate, dissent and resentment. In Chinese symbolism, the teeth symbolize war. In several ancient initiation rites, it was customary to extract one of the initiate's teeth, who would then immediately swallow it as a symbol of death and rebirth, since the tooth is the hardest part of the body, and continues to exist for a long time after the physical body has disintegrated. The Gnostic perception views the teeth as a wall with battlements, the person's inner fortress from the material or energetic point of view, just as the eyes or the gaze are the defenses of the spirit. This view explains the symbolism of the fear of losing or breaking teeth, which in various cultures symbolized fear of failure in life.

Thigh

The thigh frequently serves as a phallic symbol. For this reason, it symbolizes creative force, re-creation and strength. In ancient Egypt, the bull's or hippopotamus' thigh is "the phallic leg of Seth." In Greek mythology, Dionysos appeared out of the thigh of Zeus. In Islam, Fatima gave birth to her sons from her thigh, thereby preserving her virginity forever.

The skull and crossed thighbones symbolize the two essential sources of power, the head and the hips of the person after his death. Magical powers are attributed to them, attracting the life force, and for this reason, they are a symbol of death.

Thumb

The thumb symbolizes power and transfer of power. The up-turned thumb represents supportive and beneficial power, good fortune and goodwill, while the down-turned thumb represents the opposite. The erect thumb (and finger) is considered to be phallic.

Tongue

The tongue symbolizes the voice of the divinity, the manifestation of an extremely powerful voice, and preaching. It also has a phallic symbolism and is linked to the snake. Fleshy tongues often indicate demons in Eastern art and medieval Christian art. The devil is sometimes depicted poking out a fleshy tongue. In the East, sticking out a tongue symbolizes going from the dark to the light, and can also be a kind of peace blessing.

In the Hebrew tradition, the tongue has a profound meaning. It is considered to be an organ from the *Malkhut* [kingdom] sphere, like the mouth, the sphere of the manifestation of the material world, and is found in the head, which is linked to the higher spheres. It is the physical manifestation of the power of thought in the world of action, and for that reason can grant life or death to the speaker who uses it. The importance of holding one's tongue is the basic principle in the moral code.

In the ancient Egyptian culture, the god Bes has a long tongue. In Greek art, the tongue is considered first and foremost to be a divine symbol, and then as the Gorgons' instrument of instilling terror. In Buddhism, Buddha's long tongue recited sutras and disseminated the knowledge pertaining to them. In China, the tongue is linked to the supernatural power. In Hinduism, Agni's tongue is the priestly voice that touches the sky. Kali is mostly depicted with her tongue sticking out. In the Sumerian culture, monstrous Babylonian beasts usually have long tongues.

Uterus, womb

The uterus is one of the most significant female symbols. It symbolizes the Big Mother, Mother Earth, the womb of the earth. The uterus also symbolizes what has not yet actualized, the totality of all the possibilities. It is a symbol of abundance and fecundity.

The well is often used as a symbol of the uterus, as are the other water symbols and everything that surrounds something, such as the city walls. As a symbol of the womb of the earth, it is linked to the symbolism of the cave. Dying gods are born in a cave and emerge from the womb of the earth. In alchemistic symbolism, the uterus symbolizes a mine, with the fetus symbolizing the ore, or a quarry – minerals are born in the womb of the earth, and man's job is to help nature and expedite the birth.

Yoni (vagina)

The Sanskrit term, *jagad yoni*, was sometimes erroneously translated as "the womb of the world," but it symbolizes the external part of the female reproductive organs, which were perceived by the ancients as the seat of the woman's sexual power. The Tantric theories perceived this organ as the source of the creative energies. This approach, in contrast to the Western approach, did not describe female sexuality as "passive," but rather viewed the female orgasm as the energetic principle of the universe. In the established mythology of this sexual symbol, the island of paradise, "Jumbo", was shaped like a yoni, that is, like a vagina. It was the location of the life-giving rose-apple tree and "the seat of the diamond," which evidently represented the cosmic clitoris, as a result of concentrating on the creative powers of the female goddess. The symbol of the yoni was transmitted to the Western world under the guise of names such as mandorla – almond, vesica piscis – "the pelvis of the fish." Its original meaning was not completely forgotten – it is mostly described as a "gate." In a curious twist, the followers of the Christian saint, "St. George the Dragon Slayer," adopted the yoni as their holy symbol, and reinterpreted it as a spearhead. The believers in the male god Indra gave the symbol another new meaning. Initially, the god's entire body was marked with yoni symbols in order to indicate that he was the man who had overpowered the fertile force of the goddess. In later depictions of him, the direction of the yoni symbols was changed to symbolize eyes, and Indra became the "scout," or the "one with a thousand eyes."

Symbols of landscape and nature

Abyss

The abyss symbolizes descent, the lowest place. However, the descent into the abyss also contains the potential of climbing out of it, and this joins the two meanings of the abyss into a single one, since getting out of the abyss after being inside it grants the person who was in it profound understanding.

The abyss of water is the ancient source of the universe, the Big Mother, the underworld. In Gnostic symbolism, the abyss is considered to be a lofty entity. In the Bible, the abyss appears as the primordial waters, the sea of Genesis. The Assyrian and Ugaritic word for "abyss" means sea in general and is also the name of the goddess of the sea, who, in the days of Genesis, fought the god of the sky. The Babylonian god of creation, Mardok, vanquished her, killed her, cleaved her body and made an upper and a lower sea out of it. Traces of this myth can also be found in the Bible.

The two different aspects of the abyss (depth and darkness) are interlinked, and this generated a mystical attraction to the concept in many cultures. Many of the ancient peoples identified fissures in the surface of the earth or in the depths of the sea with the concept of the abyss. As far as the Celts were concerned, the abysses lay inside the mountains. In Ireland, Japan and the South Sea Islands, the abyss lay in the depths of the sea and the lakes. Among the Mediterranean peoples, the abyss lay beyond the horizon. For the Aborigines in Australia, the abyss was the Milky Way.

The abyss is mostly identified with "the land of the dead," with the nether world, and is therefore sometimes linked to the Big Mother. The link between the world of the dead and the abyss is reflected in many legends in which palaces or creatures emerge from inside the abysses of the lake or the sea. After the death of King Arthur, his sword, Excalibur, which was cast into the lake according to his instructions, was caught before it sank by a hand that emerged from the water. In the book of Ezekiel, Chapter 31, there is a parallel between the abyss and hell and the nether land, in a prophecy concerning the destruction of the Egyptian Pharaoh as a result of his pride and megalomania.

From the psychological point of view, the abyss symbolizes the descent into the dark depths of the mind (like the person's descent into the underworld in Greek mythology). This can also be seen as powerful depression that buffets the mind, or a visit to the "dark" regions of the mind, which contains tremendous strengthening potential for the person who overcomes the depression and snaps out of it. In this sense, the abyss serves as a highly significant "place of initiation" for the fearless person who descends into it in order to explore the dark mysteries of the mind, and emerges from it strengthened and endowed with profound understanding. It is if he has been reborn after his sojourn in the belly of the earth. Being in the mental abyss is also compared to the situation in which the person is hidden from the eyes of God and is deprived of God's grace, generally in order to make him acquire some degree of understanding or to test his faith. This is the sense in which the word "abyss" is used in the story of Jonah, who spent three days and three nights in the belly of the fish (Jonah 3:3-9).

Air

Air, like fire, is an active and male element, in contrast to water and earth, which are passive and female. It symbolizes communication, the senses, thinking, perception, intuition, and flight. It is considered to be the primal element, since many material forms and activities are dependent on it and require its intervention both for their existence and for metamorphosis. It symbolizes freedom, liberation, spirituality, rising up and elevation. Air operates on fire, the element that is linked to creation, and on water, the element that is linked to emotions, and is thought to be the element that activates and elevates these elements and properties. Moreover, it is linked to the sense of smell and to memory. Some people see fire as the first of all the elements, but air can also occupy this place. Compressing air and various manipulations of the element create heat or fire, from which all forms of life derive.

Air is linked to the breath of life and to speech, to the gale that is linked to the idea of creation in many mythologies, to space as a means of motion and to the notion of the beginning of the process of life. Also linked to it are light, lightness and floating (rising above the terrestrial element). Air is linked to the dynamic of dematerialization – turning matter into spirit. The human spirit and human thought are also linked to the element of air. The symbol of the element of air is a circle with a dot in its center.

Cave

The cave symbolizes inward withdrawal, introspection, retreating and withdrawal for the sake of going out and developing. It was used in this context in initiation rites and in many folk-tales. In addition to it being a place for personality analysis, it is a symbol of the meeting-place of the divine and the human. This can be seen in one example out of many – the story of Simeon Ben Yohai and his son Eliezer, who received many of their spiritual messages in the cave in which they lived for seven years (and 12 additional months after that).

The cave symbolizes the human heart in that it is linked to the symbolism of the center, and is analogous to the mental processes people undergo. It is linked to the symbolism of the uterus, since it is located in the depths of the earth. It therefore symbolizes birth and rebirth in the mental and spiritual layers.

We should remember that in ancient times, caves were used both for burial and for "second birth" rituals. Because of the properties of the earth, and since birth and the womb are linked to it, the cave has female characteristics.

Cloud

The cloud has two main symbolic meanings. The first comes from the context of fogginess, as a symbol of the world that links the material, formal world with the amorphous world. The second is the symbolism of fertility, since the cloud brings rain. As a fertility symbol, it does not only symbolize physical fertility, but (since it is linked to the symbolism of the sky and the air) also spiritual fecundity. A black cloud, or a dark cloud over the person's head, generally symbolizes a "curse" or some kind of negative feeling that hovers over the person. According to Jewish mysticism, there is an evil spirit (a negative energetic force) that is called a "big cloud," and it is the evil spirit of sadness.

Crescent moon

The crescent moon is a symbol of the Big Mother, of the lunar Queen of Heaven, of the Heavenly Virgin, and it symbolizes all the moon goddesses. It is a blatantly female symbol that represents the female principle, the passive, and the things connected with water and the sea. Since it is a formation of the moon, it is a symbol of the phenomenal world (this world) and the world of changes. The changing phases of the moon symbolize the changes that occur in this world. The crescent moon is the ship that sails in the dark night skies.

A solar disk together with a crescent moon, or a solar disk between cow's horns (cow's or bull's horns symbolize the crescent moon because of their shape), symbolize unity, two in one, a link between the deity of the moon and the deity of the sun, and the holy marriage of the heavenly couple.

In the ancient Egyptian culture, the crescent moon symbolizes Isis, the Queen of Heaven, and Hator as a cow with the solar disk between her horns. In Hinduism, the crescent moon symbolizes the newborn, rapid and enthusiastic growth, and the cup filled with the potion of eternal life. When it appears in

Shiva's hair, it symbolizes the bull Nandi. In the Celtic culture, the crescent moon, or two back-to-back crescent moons symbolize eternal life. In Christianity, the crescent moon symbolizes the Virgin Mary as the Queen of Heaven. In medieval symbolism and in the Western world, the crescent moon has an additional symbolic meaning, especially when a star appears next to it. As such it is the symbolic image of the Garden of Eden. The crescent moon is the symbol of Byzantium, of Islam and of the Turkish nation. In Islam, the crescent moon with the star symbolizes divinity and sovereignty. In the Maori culture, the crescent moon symbolized light in the darkness. In the Sumerian culture, it is the symbol of the moon god Sin.

Dawn
The dawn symbolizes hope, enlightenment, a new beginning, new possibilities, a delicate light that comes after the darkness of the night and hints at the arrival of brightness and understanding. In Christianity, dawn symbolizes the resurrection of Jesus, bringing light to the world. In Buddhism, the light of dawn symbolizes the clean and pure light of emptiness, space.

Day
The day is linked to the male, active aspect, to the overt and the bright, to what is on the surface, and to the conscious. It symbolizes brightness, activity, work, legality, organization, awakening and life, since in many beliefs, night sleep is thought to be a time when the soul leaves the body. In the Jewish tradition, for instance, the day begins with the "I thank" prayer in which the person gives thanks that his soul has returned to his body after giving an accounting to the Lord while he was asleep. In the Kabbala, daylight symbolizes receiving in order to give as well as the seven lower spheres.

Desert
The desert has an ambivalent symbolism that stems from the fact that it is an empty and waterless landscape. On the one hand, it symbolizes emptiness, loneliness, abandonment and emotional emptiness, since it lacks the element of water. For the same reason, however, it is a symbol of a place in which lofty prophecies and information are received, since it is the most abstract landscape, and the emotional element does not hinder the recipient of the prophecy or messages. He is therefore free to link up to information that goes beyond the mental level.

↔ SYMBOLS ↔

Dew

Dew symbolizes the light of dawn, a blessing (mainly spiritual, but also physical) and spiritual refreshment. Since it comes from the sky, it has a holy nature, and since it is one of the symbols of the rising dawn, it also symbolizes soft and blessed spiritual awakening.

Ebb and flow

Ebb and flow symbolize the principle of reciprocity, the balance between externalization and internalization, and the departure from and entry into cosmic levels. They also symbolize opportunity. Ebb and flow are linked to the soul's departure from the world during death. There was a belief that the soul departed during the ebb.

Field

The field symbolizes Mother Earth, the one who nourishes and the great provider. In various cultures, it is expanded into the symbolism of the accepting woman who waits for the man's seed in order to yield her harvest. According to Hinduism, "The woman is the field, the man is the seed." An almost identical saying exists in Islam: "Women are the field."

Fire

Fire is linked to the perception of creation, life and vital force, health, movement, and also superiority and control. It symbolizes the property that creates the person's libido, ego and ambition to progress, as well as the properties of fire itself. For this reason, this element requires self-knowledge in order to direct and control the flame so that it will create and not destroy. Fire is an important symbol of transformation and participates in many transformational processes. In ancient cultures, fire was linked to the sun and served as its terrestrial manifestation. It is linked to the symbolism of lightning and gold. It is thought to be a purifying element, but also a destructive one. In this context, it is also thought to have the power to purify and expel negative forces.

In the Chinese tradition, the element of fire represents the spark (which guards the fire of the hearth) and abundance, heat, light, realization, glory, success and wealth. It is linked to the summer, to the color red, to the bitter taste, and to the south. The graphic symbol of the element of fire is an empty circle.

↔ **SYMBOLS** ↔

Forest

The symbolism of the forest is very widespread and appears in many folktales. It is linked to female symbolism and to the Big Mother and serves as a common symbol of the subconscious. Because of that, it symbolizes a place to which people retreat in order to experience enlightenment, rebirth and initiation. The forest is a symbol of a place that is free and liberated from the limitations of the laws and obligations that exist in "orderly" and clear-cut urban life. It is wide open, like the unknown, and as such contains dangers as well as wonderful opportunities for development. It is possible to get lost in it, as it is in the unknown, but also to find the true self and the meta-self, the profound spirituality that is free from the laws of the material world.

Today, the forest is the symbol that is the diametric opposite of everything represented by city life – pressure, volatility, restlessness, aspiration for orderly material comfort, and fear of anything undefined. Entering the forest symbolizes the courage required by the person who is developing spiritually in order to discover the existential truth. In the Druid tradition, in accordance with the female symbolism of the forest, the forest is the bride of the sun. Through the person's link-up with the forest, a connection between the lower beings in their free and terrestrial state and the upper beings occurs, a connection that is possible in a place where the laws of man neither prevail nor limit. The forest contains the secrets of nature and ancient knowledge, and there is a prevalent belief that the trees of the forest communicate with one another and with the rest of the members of the natural realm. They are aware of what is going on in the world and inform the person who is linked to them of these secrets and this knowledge. The forest represents a spiritual world into which the spiritually courageous person must penetrate in order to discover meaning. The Aborigines in Australia viewed it as a place for initiation, as the kingdom of the shadows, and as a passage. In the Sumerian and Semitic cultures, the forest was the residence of the spirits, and the Indians consider the person who resides in the forest to be a person who has relinquished material bonds and illusions and has "died" as far as that world is concerned, but in reality lives a life of total spiritual fullness.

Garden

A garden symbolizes the Garden of Eden, the blessed fields, the "good land," and belongs to the symbolism of the center. Accordingly, many gardens are built with a fountain in the middle, similar to the springs gushing from the Tree of Life that is in the center of the Garden of Eden. The garden is also a symbol of the soul and the qualities that are nurtured in it, as well as a symbol of a restrained and pleasant nature. It is possible to see the garden (in contrast to the symbol of the forest) as symbolizing the conscious state – since the garden is the place in which nature is "domesticated," chosen, organized, ordered and bordered, as opposed to the forest with its free, unorganized growth, which symbolizes the subconscious.

The garden is considered to be a female symbol because of its characteristics as an enclosed space, and particularly when it is locked. Locked or fenced-in gardens are a female symbol, a symbol of the protective principle. They also represent virginity.

In Christian symbolism, the locked garden is a symbol of the Virgin Mary. According to the Hermetic tradition, the "good garden," whose actions bring about renewed blooming, is the logos. In the Inca culture, the "garden of the sun" is the image of the world. According to Islam, the four gardens of paradise are those of the soul, the heart, the spirit and the "essence" (vitality), and symbolize the mystical journey of the soul. In Taoism, miniature gardens are the terrestrial imitation of paradise.

Ice

Ice symbolizes not only rigidity and coldness but also instability – because it melts (symbolism that is expressed in the popular saying, "written in ice"). With reference to people, it symbolizes a cold heart, a heart of ice, coolness and a lack of love. Melting the ice is softening the hard heart. With reference to the heart, which symbolizes the emotions and emotional openness, ice is symbolic of the barriers between people. The expressions that describe this notion in everyday language are "break the ice" and "thaw out the atmosphere." This symbolism also stems from water having an accepted symbolism of communication, and ice is a change in the state of water to a state in which it no longer has its special properties of symbolizes communication, movement and dynamism. Water is the symbol of the communication between the official and the unofficial, the medium of passage between different cycles that are also linked to the idea of fertility and material prosperity. Ice symbolizes the change in their state by means of the cold, freezing – which also has a symbolic meaning of freezing and halting the dynamism and the movement. The ice actually thwarts the properties of the water from which it is created. Water is symbolic of the world of emotions and the subconscious, and for this reason, some people see ice as a symbol of the rigid dividing line between the conscious and the subconscious, and again as a symbol of frozen emotions.

Island

On the one hand, the island symbolizes loneliness and solitude, far from human surroundings. On the other, it symbolizes a refuge and a haven from the chaos of the sea. Jung applies this symbolism to the world of the mind and sees the island as a haven from the seas of the subconscious – symbolized by the sea – and therefore as a synthesis between awareness and will.

Lake

The lake symbolizes the moist, female principle. In Egyptian hieroglyphics, the schematic sign that depicts a lake expresses mystery and the occult. In the temple of the god Amon at Karnak, there was an artificial lake that symbolized the "lower waters" of primeval matter. On certain dates during the year, groups of priestesses would cross the lake in boats, in imitation of the "nocturnal passage" of the sun. According to the belief, the sun passed through an underground lake during the night in order to return and reappear in the morning. The Irish and the Britons believed that the land of the dead lay at the bottom of a lake or ocean.

According to the symbolism of stature, everything that is low in stature is also low in spirituality, and has negative and destructive properties. Since the symbol of the lake is closely related to the symbolism of depths or abysses, it links up to the negative aspects that are expressed in the numerous legends and folk-tales in which water monsters reside on the floor of the lake. On the other hand, since it is a female symbol, it also constitutes the residence of marvelous feminine beings such as "the lady of the lakes." Because it is a smooth surface that reflects everything around and above it, the lake is linked to the symbolism of the mirror, and for this reason possesses a symbolism of introspection, awareness and discovery. In Chinese philosophy, the lake is the seventh house among the eight trigrams of the Pakua. It symbolizes wisdom and openness to new ideas, creation, creativity and children, assimilation and passivity and also the physical aspect of the sensory organs: taste, touch, smell, sight and hearing. Its direction is west, and it is linked to the fall and to the color white.

Mist

Mist symbolizes uncertainty and the non-absolute, confusion, a lack of clarity, a state of going astray and erring, and difficulty in distinguishing and recognizing the correct path. Mist symbolizes a combination of the elements of air and water and the blurring of the outlines of each aspect in every stage of the developmental process. "The mist of fire" is the stage in cosmic life that follows the state of chaos and unites the three previous elements to form earth: fire, air and water. This symbolism of mist was used in mystical religions as a motive in initiation rites. The soul has to pass through the darkness, confusion and lack of clarity of the mist to the bright and clear light of enlightenment. The passage through the mist is the stage of "positive" uncertainty that follows chaos. It is impossible to relate to the previous reality in the same "old" way because of the mistiness. However, because it is unstable, moving and transient, the mist will definitely dissipate at a certain point and new "earth," a new and more enlightened spiritual reality, will be revealed. The mist operates as a delaying, but not a blocking, factor. The delay it creates induces introspection, since the outside is neither clear nor understood. The introspection and its results have a direct relation to the dissipation of the mist. The clarification of the element of water can be an act of man, while the clarification of the element of air is an act of the "upper" beings that fall in line with the actions of the "lower beings."

Mountain

The symbolism of the mountain stems from its characteristics – its height, its verticality (steepness), its mass and its shape. The mountain's height has made it into a symbol of the inner elevation of the spirit, which is attained mainly by the effort that characterizes the tortuous climb up to the peak, symbolism that attends the pilgrimages to holy mountains. Because of its height, the mountain symbolizes a link between the upper and the lower beings, between heaven and earth. The mountain peak touches the sky and is surrounded by clouds, so it is a symbol of a place where one can channel with the gods, or a place to which the Spirit of God or spiritual enlightenment of the person descends. This occurs in many legends and stories about spiritual enlightenment and revelation. The verticality of the mountain has made it one of the symbols of the "axis of the world," and it is identified anatomically with the spinal column. Because of its massive dimensions, the mountain constitutes a symbol, especially in China, of greatness and magnanimity. In China, these mountain characteristics are ascribed to the emperor.

In the Pakua, the mountain is the eighth trigram, and expresses knowledge and observation. It represents intelligence, attention, repose, and inner knowledge.

It is linked to the direction of north-east, to the colors turquoise, dark blue and green, and is thought to characterize the elderly sages who retreat to mountain solitude.

The shape of the mountain, when standing at the peak and looking down, is reminiscent of the shape of the cosmic tree, inverted, whose roots face upward, and whose broad and extensive top faces downward.

Mountains with multiple peaks correspond mainly to the number 2, to the duality and symbolism of Gemini.

Mud

Mud symbolizes the accepting earth, earth that is fertilized by water, the source and potential for fecundity and growth. It is the union of the totally accepting principle (earth) and water, which symbolizes movement and metamorphosis. Since it is the union of the two female elements, and unites the accepting and the fertilizing, mud is thought to be the cradle of the natural processes and the source of the development of the life forms. Earth constitutes the basis for development and provides the required stability, and water constitutes the movement and metamorphosis that accompany the primal development. Mud also symbolizes the unconscious person who needs "fertilization" and "processing" in order to bear fruit.

Night

The night is linked to the female, passive, subconscious aspect. It is a symbol of potential, of a seed from which things emerge and are created. Like water, it is also a symbol of fertility. The night symbolizes the lack of knowledge prior to revelation, cognizance, the rising dawn. Confusion and the lack of knowledge are necessary for the sake of true revelation. In symbolism, the night is linked to death and the color black. It is also identified with the unenlightened state of material life, from which the person can emerge by dint of his spirituality. Alternatively, if he remains weak, he can let the darkness rule him and stay inside him. In the Kabbala, the night symbolizes light that receives for itself, that is, the three first spheres, while the day symbolizes light that receives in order to give (the seven lower spheres).

Ocean, sea

The two essential characteristics of the ocean, besides its enormous size, are its incessant motion and the amorphous quality of its waters. For that reason, it symbolizes the dynamic forces and the interim states between the stable (solid) and the formless (air or gas). The ocean symbolizes merging, a lack of individuality, and universal life as opposed to uniqueness. It is considered to be the source of the renewal of life. It symbolizes the sum of all the existing possibilities on one existential surface, the unconscious, the primal and the chaotic, both in the positive and negative senses. This means that it is the begetter of many mythological monsters that emerge from its waters (like from the waters of the unconscious in human beings). It is identified with the collective and personal subconscious, and its stormy or quiet movement symbolizes these states in the individual and collective mind.

It is the symbol of the primordial waters, chaos, amorphism, material existence, changing and incessant movement, and the potential for everything that exists, and it is also the symbol of the Big Mother. Furthermore, it symbolizes the sea of life that has to be crossed. In Hinduism, the cosmic ocean symbolizes Vishnu sleeping on a slithering serpent on the waters of the ocean.

In Islam, the ocean symbolizes eternal divine wisdom.

The two seas – the one sweet and fresh, the second salty and bitter – symbolize the upper waters and the lower waters, heaven and earth, which were originally one, and also two types of wisdom: the sweet and fresh, which symbolizes esoteric wisdom, and the salty, which symbolizes external wisdom.

In the Sumerian and Semitic cultures, too, the ocean, the primordial waters, are linked to eternal wisdom. All forms of life originated from the sweet waters – Apsu, and from the salty waters – Thihamat, which symbolized the power of the water, the blind powers of chaos and the female principle.

Rain

Rain is linked to the symbolism of water, the liquid that joins formlessness and the solid, formed matter. The rain falling on the ground is a symbol of divine blessing. It is a symbol of abundance, fertility and fertilization – both in the physical sense and in the spiritual sense, because it falls from above onto the earth, onto matter, onto man. For that reason, it is also a symbol of spiritual revelation and divine influence. As a divine blessing, it is mainly appreciated for its vitality because man depends on it for life. Moreover, it is a symbol of both physical and spiritual purification. It is also linked to the symbolism of the sun's rays and of light.

Rainbow

The rainbow possesses very strong, positive symbolism and this has been the case since ancient times. It is a symbol of the encounter between earth and sky, of the covenant between the upper beings and the lower ones, and of peace and tranquillity after the deluge – which is a symbol of trouble and hardship. The rainbow is a symbol of the states of consciousness that differ from one another in the same way as the colors of the rainbow differ from one another. It is also an accepted symbol of unity –the different colors that represent the plurality and the difference in the material world united into one entity. It symbolizes the bridge between the world and the Garden of Eden.

In Native American cultures, as well as in Africa and France, it is linked to the celestial serpent that quenches its thirst in the sea. The Native Americans view the rainbow as a ladder to the sky. "The rainbow warriors," according to the ancient Native American prophecy, will save the world from the destruction wrought by human beings, who destroy every good part of it with their material and physical aspirations and their contemptuous attitude toward Mother Earth and her children – the animals, the plants, and the people.

The notion of the rainbow also contains the notion of the unity of the different, since the rainbow is composed of all the colors of the spectrum, united into one harmonious entity. For this reason, it possesses a symbolism of absolute peace and acceptance. In Buddhism, the rainbow symbolizes the highest state that can be attained in Samsara, which precedes the clear light of Nirvana. In Christianity, it symbolizes God's forgiveness of man. In the Greco-Roman cultures, it symbolizes a sign engraved by Zeus for human beings so that he would be remembered.

River

The river symbolizes the creative power of both water and time. As the creative power of water, it constitutes a fertility symbol. When linked to time, it symbolizes the passage of life, so it is linked to loss and to the flow of physical life.

In initiation ceremonies and rites of passage from one conscious state to another, the passage from one bank to the other occurs frequently, such as when crossing the river of life or death. Some people see mystical symbolism in the name "Ivri" ("Hebrew" – from the Hebrew verb *avar*) that was given to Abraham, who passed from one state of consciousness to another (that is, passed over the river).

Rock

The rock symbolizes stability, permanence, safety, rigidity, reliability, coolness and hardness. "The living rock" is the person's primordial self. Double rocks are the celestial gate to another dimension. In Christianity, water issuing from a rock symbolizes the waters of baptism and salvation that flow from the church. The symbol of Peter is called a rock. Jesus was compared to a rock, a source of the water of life. The rock also symbolizes power, shelter and stability.

In the Mithraic culture, Mithra was born from a rock. In the Bible, extracting living water from an arid rock by talking to it was a sign of God's power, and since Moses did not heed God's command to talk to the rock and instead struck it with his staff, he was punished by being forbidden to enter the Promised Land. Extracting water from the rock by talking to it was a test of faith in God's power to perform miracles. A similar story exists in Greek mythology: When the city of Athens began, two gods, Apollo and Athena, wanted to be the patron gods of the city. In a "miracles" contest they held, Apollo extracted salt water from a rock.

In Chinese symbolism, the rock symbolizes permanence, strength, solidity, stability and honesty. Like the stone, the rock is thought to be the residence of a god in many cultures. According to the Kafkaz tradition, "In the beginning, the world was covered with water. The Great Creator lived inside a rock."

Sand

Sand symbolizes instability, impermanence and plurality. In Islam, sand symbolizes purity since it is used for ritual washing and purification when water is not available.

Seasons

The seasons symbolize order, normality (no deviation from the path of nature), the cyclicality of nature, and the four stages of human life. The seasons are represented by animals – the spring is represented by the sheep, the summer by the dragon, the fall by the hare and the winter by the salamander. The Greeks presented the seasons in the form of four women: the spring is represented by a woman wearing a chaplet of flowers and standing next to a blooming flower. The summer is depicted as a woman wearing a crown of ears of corn, holding a sheaf in one hand and a scythe in the other. The fall is represented by a woman carrying bunches of grapes and a basket full of fruit. The winter is depicted as a bare-headed woman standing next to bare trees. The signs of the Zodiac are linked to the different seasons. Aries, Taurus and Gemini are linked to the spring. Cancer, Leo and Virgo are linked to the summer. Libra, Scorpio and Sagittarius are linked to the fall, and Capricorn, Aquarius and Pisces are linked to the winter.

In the Chinese tradition, the seasons are symbolized by flowers – the spring is symbolized by cherry, peach and almond blossoms; the summer by the lotus and the peony; the fall by the red maple and the chrysanthemum; and the winter by plum blossoms, bamboo and pine. In psychological symbolism, which influences and is influenced by the general symbolism of the seasons, the spring is a symbol of the beginning, of blooming, of renewal, of new life and of a new chapter in life. For this reason, the beginning of the spring is the first sign in astrology – Aries – as well as in the Bible, where the month of spring, Nisan, symbolizes a new beginning. This is true in many other cultures. The summer symbolizes reaping and harvesting, the end, wilting, rest after the active spring, heat and dryness. The fall symbolizes an interim period of inner withdrawal, contemplation, sloughing off the old, transformation. The winter symbolizes cold, freezing, stopping, sleeping and death, but in relatively warm regions, it is a symbol of powerful fertility because of the rain it brings.

Shadow

The shadow symbolizes the negative principle as opposed to the positive principle of the sun. It is used in various ceremonies, and various cultures consider it to possess a mystical uniqueness that represents the mind or the person. A similar meaning is attributed to the shadow in various acts of witchcraft; the way in which the person's shadow falls is important, because according to this, various conclusions are drawn. Jung uses the "shadow" as a name for the primitive and instinctive side of man.

Sky

The sky is a symbol of infinity, sublimity, heights, and heaven in its spiritual and religious meaning. It is a symbol of universal order, the blessed realms, the residence of the righteous and of the gods of the sky and sun. The gods of the sky are generally the ones who possess all knowledge and have inclusive control of the universe. They symbolize cosmic rhythm and are thought to be the law-keepers of the universe and the ones who impose order. In matriarchal societies, the sky deities are mostly female.

Sometimes the deity of the sky is asexual. In the Chinese tradition, the sky is the sixth trigram of the Pakua called Chien. It is the most male (yang) trigram of all, symbolizing power, confidence and enlightenment, the father, an open door to helpful friends, supportive friends, philanthropy, unconditional giving, and a wish to receive in order to give.

The trigram of the sky belongs to the element of metal (greatness), and to the north-west, and indicates what is going on outside the walls of the house, such as journeys, or an external power that is coming to help the person, such as loyal work mates, teachers, or faith.

↔ SYMBOLS ↔

Smoke

Smoke is the antithesis of mud, since mud combines the elements of earth and water, while smoke reacts to the elements of fire and air.

There are popular traditions that attribute a beneficial power to smoke and the ability to expel the evil that befalls man, beast or plant. Among the Bedouins, healing with smoke is a common tradition. "Clean" smoke from a suitable branch is used for curing sight ailments, drawing out phlegm in order to cleanse the body, and so on.

In the Bible, smoke symbolizes divine wrath and the disappearance of enemies and the wicked. However, the pillar of smoke signifies divine guidance and direction. In Christianity, smoke symbolizes the brevity of life and the vanity of fame, pride and anger. A pillar of smoke rising from a chimney or from an opening in the temple roof symbolizes the *axis mundi* (the axis of the world), the escape route from time and space to the eternal and the boundless. It also symbolizes prayer ascending to heaven and an invitation to a spiritual or divine entity to participate in a ceremony or to pay heed to prayers. It may also symbolize the ascent of the soul to heaven, purified by fire.

The pillar of smoke is a symbol that is linked to the symbolism of the contrast between valley and mountain, that is, the relationship between heaven and earth, indicating the path that passes through fire to salvation. According to the alchemist Jaber, smoke symbolizes the soul leaving the body.

Snow

Snow symbolizes not only physical coldness, but spiritual and mental coldness as well. The melting of the snow symbolizes the thawing of a cold heart. In Europe, the snowflake, on the other hand, symbolizes purity, whiteness, humility, and hope. In Christianity, it symbolizes the Virgin Mary. In the Bible, it symbolizes purity, innocence from sin and crime.

Soil, earth

Earth symbolizes the Big Mother, Mother Earth, the nourishing element that receives fecundity, the material and the consumed. Mother Earth is a universal archetype for fertility, creativity and existence. It is a female symbol in most cultures, symbolizing the source of man's physical body and the element that nourishes (and activates) the person's physical and material layer. In the sky-earth symbolism, the earth is the symbol of matter and the sky is the symbol of the spirit.

In the Native American culture, earth is the mother. The earth lodge is the cosmic center. The circular surface of the floor symbolizes earth, the footstool-shaped roof symbolizes the sky, and the four pillars symbolize the stars and the four winds/spirits of the sky.

In the Celtic culture, soil symbolizes the corruptible body, along with salt, as a symbol of the immortal spirit. The Celts were in the habit of placing a handful of soil in the dead person's chest. In Chinese symbolism, the earth symbolizes the female principle, the yin principle, which is symbolizes by the square, the yellow-brown color, sweet taste and the leopard. It is thought to be the base, the center, the heart of the action of all the elements and an intermediary between all the elements in order to balance them with one another. It is linked to the end of the four seasons.

In the symbolism of the planet Earth, the northern hemisphere is thought to represent light and reacts to the positive principle of yang, while the southern hemisphere is linked to darkness and reacts to yin.

The symbol of the element of earth is a circle divided into four segments by a cross with four equal arms, vertical and horizontal, placed in its center.

Spring

The spring symbolizes the waters of life and the source. It occurs in many folk-tales and mythologies as a factor that sparks or renews life and grants youth or eternal life. This is linked to the phenomenon of the spring that flows from the earth or through stones and rocks as a vital force that comes from the depths and flows upward. In contrast to rivers and seas, it is not wild and stormy, and does not share their inherent dangers, but despite its moderate and sometimes sparse flow, it overcomes whatever stands in its way.

In the Hebrew tradition, the "overcoming spring" symbolizes the scholar whose intellectual powers derive from his creative inner being, as opposed to the "plastered cistern," whose powers of study come from what he manages to store in his memory. This symbolism is also linked to the four rivers of the Garden of Eden that originate from the foot of the Tree of Life, from the primal source, and this explains the mystical contexts of receiving knowledge, wisdom, renewed life, spiritual refreshment and immortality from the enchanted spring.

Jung sees the image of the soul in the spring as a source of inner life and spiritual energy. Springs, or currents of water that flow from a mouth, symbolize the power of speech and of the word, as well as guidance and being refreshed. Springs of light symbolize water and light that flow from the same source.

A sealed spring is the symbol and description of virginity, according to the Song of Songs.

Star

Since the stars are nocturnal, their symbolism is linked to that of the night and to the notion of the light that shines in the darkness, guiding and aiding. Since it is light that sparkles in the dark, the star symbolizes the eyes of the night, the spirit, and the forces of the spirit that strive against the forces of darkness. For this reason, it also symbolizes hope. It also appears as a symbol of tidings from the gods. Jung mentions the Mithraic saying, "I am a star that walks with you and shines from the depths." The star symbolizes the divine presence, supremacy, the astral, the highest achievement. This symbolism is expressed in the popular sayings, "touch the stars" and "reach for the stars."

The stars are linked to the idea of multiplication, as they appear in the Bible in God's conversation with Abraham. Beyond the idea of multiplication, the idea of "going outside" beyond the control of the stars, according to which Abram and Sarai were supposed to be barren, also appears in this verse. The saying, "It's written in the stars," is linked to the astrological influence of the stars that derives from God. The stars are therefore linked with order and with destiny.

The stars are attributed to all the queens and goddesses of heaven, who generally wear crowns made of stars. The star is the symbol of Ishtar and Venus, as the Dawn and Evening Star. The North Star symbolizes the gates of heaven at night. It is a symbol of continuity and appears as such in Hindi marriage ceremonies. After the death of the Egyptian Pharaoh, he was identified with the North Star. In the Aztec culture, the Dawn Star symbolizes the male, rising, spiritual power of the sun, and the Evening Star symbolizes the female, descending, terrestrial power of the moon.

In the Chinese culture, a star or stars with the sun and the moon symbolize the spiritual wisdom of the rulers. In Christianity, the star symbolizes divine guidance and grace. The birth of Jesus was marked by the appearance of a special star. The Virgin Mary, as the Queen of Heaven, wears a crown made of a star. In Islam, the star symbolizes divinity, supremacy, and it appears together with the crescent moon. In the ancient Greek culture, Venus is both the Dawn Star and the Evening Star. In ancient Egypt, Isis, as the Queen of Heaven, wore a crown made of a star. In the Maori culture, the star symbolized guidance along the path to the triumph of good over evil. In the Mithraic culture, the stars symbolized the all-seeing eyes of Mithra. In the Oceanic culture, the stars are the children of Mother Sun and Father Moon. In the Sumerian and Semitic cultures, Ishtar is the Dawn and Evening Star, and she and Astarte are mostly described as queen of the heavens with crowns made of stars.

↔ **SYMBOLS** ↔

Storm

Despite its destructive properties, the storm was actually a positive symbol in ancient cultures. That was because it symbolized the natural forces that represent the power of the god/s as manifested in the material world in full view of everyone. Its positive meaning, as a symbol of the creative force that brings the rain clouds and the fertilizing rain, stems from the occurrence of rain during or after the storm. Thunder is the voice of the storm god, while lightning brings fertility and enlightenment.

Stream

The stream symbolizes the flow of the celestial power, just as rays flow from the sun or water flows from springs, falls, and so on.

Streams that burst forth and flow from a vase or from the body of some deity represent the flow of the waters of celestial magnanimity and grace, fecundity and life. The stream is a symbol of the nature of the self in Buddhism.

Thunder and lightning

In ancient times, thunder and lightning were linked to the gods of the sky. Thunder was thought to be the voice of the god of the sky, and lightning was his weapon, which destroyed the serpent and spiritual foes. Since they are linked to the gods of the sky, thunder and lightning also symbolize celestial wrath. Because of the "bombastic" and generally sudden occurrence of thunder and lightning, and because they are a symbol of strength, they also became the magicians' symbol – a symbol that is "applied" in practice over hundreds of years in sleight-of-hand performances. Thunder and lightning are the "terrestrial" imitation of the wizard and the magician. However, they also served as the symbol of Monrach.

Thunder is linked to the lunar changes. Its roar is compared to the bull's bellow, and it brings the fertilizing rain. Since it brings the rain, thunder is linked to fecundity, along with the water that comes down from the sky and fertilizes the earth. Rain that arrives with thunder is considered to have powerful fertile attributes, and for this reason is extremely nourishing. The symbols of thunder, which are attributed to all of the gods of the sky, are the hammer, the drum, the lightning-ax, the bull's bellow and the oak tree. The rolling thunder is also symbolized by the dragon, the spiral and the burning pearl. The gods of thunder usually have red hair.

Lightning is considered to be celestial fire as an active, terrible and dynamic force. The lightning of the gods were thought to symbolize the supreme creative power. Lightning is also linked to sunrise and enlightenment. Because of these two characteristics, lightning is linked to the first sign of the Zodiac, Aries, and symbolic of the principle of the spring and the first stage of each cycle. Lightning also symbolizes the holy union between the god of the sky and the receptive goddess of the earth. It is attributed to all of the blacksmith gods, such as Thor, Vulcan, and Hephaistos. Lightning is thought to be the symbol of sovereignty. Winged lightning expresses the idea of power and speed. In many religions, the supreme god is thought to be hidden from human eyes, and lightning is thought to be a revelation of his tremendous power in one rapid flash, of the logos that pierces the darkness. Lightning also symbolizes the action of the upper beings on the lower beings. In the Native American culture, the thunderbird is the universal spirit, the creator, the tremendous powers of nature, the dynamic power of the sky, and is also linked to the destructive powers of war. The dog, the snake and the pig are thunder animals and rain-bringing animals.

In Tibetan Buddhism, the Vajra, the Tibetan symbol of both lightning and the diamond, is also linked to the axis of the world. The Chinese Ju-Yi and the Japanese Noy are also lightning or the diamond, the "hard one" that represents the celestial power of the Buddhist doctrine. It also symbolizes sublime truth and enlightenment. "The Dharma's thunder wheel" is the dissemination of the study of freedom to all living things. In Chinese symbolism, the god of thunder, Lei-Kung, is depicted as a terrifying blue-bodied man with wings and claws. His symbols are the drum, the wooden hammer and the chisel. In Hinduism, the Vajra is the lightning of Indra and Krishna. Lightning is also thought to be the look from the third eye of Shiva, the destroyer of all physical forms. He symbolizes celestial power, cosmic wisdom and enlightenment, but like the characteristics of lightning itself, he kills and creates at one and the same time, and therefore symbolizes the forces of both creation and destruction.

The gods of thunder in Japan symbolize the celestial thunder and the "lower" thunder, the volcano bubbling beneath the earth's surface. The god of rolling thunder is Kami-Nari, and the gods of thunder are linked to the ladder as a tool that connects heaven and earth. Bolts of lightning surround the head of the god of compassion, Ayizen-Miu, and are grasped in his hands. He uses his bolts of lightning in order to subdue evil passions and lusts. In the ancient Greco-Roman cultures, the bolts of lightning of Zeus/Jupiter symbolize opportunity, fate and divine providence – the forces that shape the future. As the god of the sky, he sends lightning that may be his weapon, but may also be the personification of the god himself.

Lightning is also thought to be the "heavenly ax" of the Cyclopses. The

Bronts represented thunder and the Args represented lightning. In the Scandinavian and Teutonic cultures, Thor is the god of thunder and Donar is the god of the storm. In the Sumerian and Semitic cultures, Adad, the god of the storm, rides on the back of a bull and grasps bolts of lightning. Marduk also holds bolts of lightning. In the Babylonian beliefs, thunder is linked to the bull.

Twilight

The twilight of the morning or the evening is a symbol of uncertainty, ambivalence, dichotomy, a transition area between one state and another, which represents the dividing line that simultaneously unites and separates a pair of opposites. Twilight also symbolizes the light of the setting sun, with all the symbolism that attends the idea of sunset. Half-light is characterized by a lack of definition and ambivalence, and for this reason is lined to the symbolism of expanse and space of the Hanged Man or any other object hanging between earth and sky. Twilight is also a symbol of a threshold because it is a transition area between states.

Evening twilight is linked to the West, and symbolizes the place of death, since the place and time of sunset indicate the end of one cycle (Pisces in the Zodiac) and the beginning of another. According to legend, King Arthur was critically wounded in the West, where he was healed by the fairy Morgana, whose name comes from the word *morgen* – morning. According to an Indian legend, Indra swore to the demon Namusi that he would not tear him to pieces either during the day or at night – and he killed him at morning twilight. In the Jewish tradition, twilight time is the mystical time of between the suns. From the Halachic point of view, this time requires special attention, since it is the departure of one day and the beginning of a new day. Some people mark this time with the appearance of two stars.

Valley

In landscape symbolism, the valley, which, because of its lowness is viewed as being situated at sea level, represents the natural region for the development of the entire Creation and for all material advancement in the physical world. Its fecundity contrasts with the nature of the desert (symbol of a place of purification), with that of the ocean and of the mountain (which represents a life of observation, solitude and intellectual enlightenment). The valley is symbolic of life itself and is thought to be the place of the shepherd and the priest. In addition to being a symbol of life and fertility, it also symbolizes the working of the soil and the protected female aspect. In Chinese symbolism, the valley is the yin, the gloomy, shady state, as opposed to the sunny mountain, which is yang. As stated previously, it contrasts with the mountain since it indicates a place of material development, while the mountain indicates a place of spiritual development. The two together symbolize the low as opposed to the high.

Vegetation

There are three common symbolic interpretations of vegetation, the first two of which are linked. The first one is death and resurrection, which comes from the fact that vegetation is a clear symbol of the yearly cycle of the seasons, in accordance with the winter and the spring, or with the winter and the summer in warm regions. The second one is that of abundance, fertility, life – and this explains the many ceremonies regarding vegetation, whose goal is to encourage the cosmic forces to continue the cycle of renewal and abundance. From this symbolism, the manner in which vegetation grows and thrives symbolizes the celestial goodness that is granted to or withheld from the agricultural community.

The third symbolism stems from the fact that vegetation is a life form that lacks mobility. Because of this, it symbolizes unconscious life, immobility and the inability to move, inactivity and a low level of reincarnation or of life force (only inanimate objects have a lower level than this).

Water

By its very nature, water is one of the most common symbols of man's emotional layer. Like water, the emotions are in a constant process of change – change that can uplift the person or bring him down (as a spiritual creature), especially when the water – the emotions – is in a state of stagnation and becomes a murky swamp. Water is a symbol of fertility and fecundity since it gives life and is necessary for every living being. It symbolizes movement and flow. It is considered to be the first form of matter, since it is the source of all the potential in the world. It is a female element and is linked to the Big Mother, to the *prima materia*, to birth and to the universal womb. It symbolizes the subconscious as well as the "oblivion" that occurs in the material world (that helps the person live in a world of illusion and forget the "real" world that preceded the material world and is superior to it). It is a symbol of vitality, since it symbolizes the movement of the blood, new life, cleansing and purification (from previous lives as well). It appears in various purification and baptism rituals.

In Chinese symbolism, the element of water symbolizes sensitivity, depth, concentration, introversion, memory and flexibility, as well as fear, danger and defensiveness. Water is linked to the winter, to black and blue, to the salty taste, to the north. The hidden, delicate topics of money and sex belong to it. The symbol of the element of water is a circle divided in two by a horizontal line.

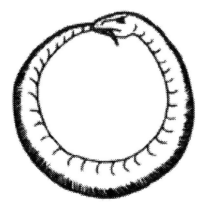